Soldiers of the Faith

SOLDIERS OF THE FAITH

Crusaders and Moslems at War

Ronald C. Finucane

J.M. Dent & Sons Ltd
London & Melbourne

for Muriel and Matthew

ALSO BY RONALD C. FINUCANE

Miracles & Pilgrims : Popular Beliefs in Medieval England
Appearances of the Dead : A Cultural History of Ghosts

First published 1983
© R.C. Finucane 1983

This book is set in 11/13 Linotron Garamond by
Text Processing Ltd., Clonmel, Co. Tipperary
Printed in Great Britain by
Richard Clay (The Chaucer Press) Ltd. Bungay, for
J.M. Dent & Sons Ltd
Aldine House, 33 Welbeck Street, London W1M 8LX

British Library Cataloguing in Publication Data

Finucane, Ronald C.
  Soldiers of the faith : Crusaders and Moslems
  at war.
  1 Crusades
  I. Title
  909.07   D157

ISBN 0-460-12040-9

Contents

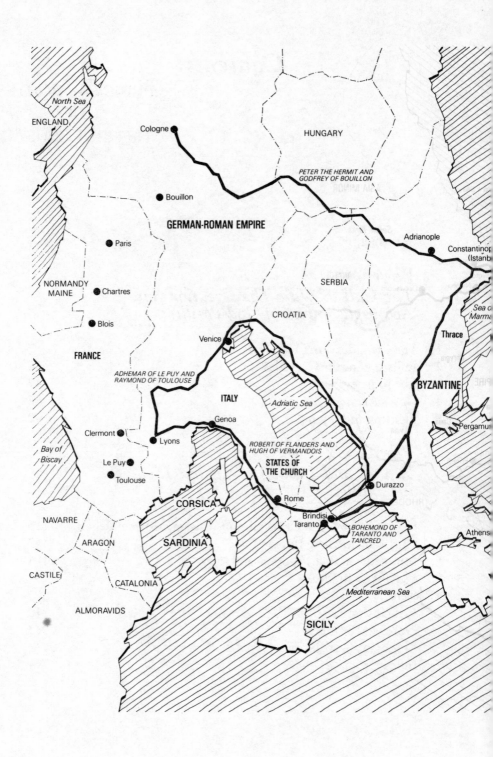

North Sea

ENGLAND

Cologne

Bouillon

GERMAN-ROMAN EMPIRE

HUNGARY

*PETER THE HERMIT AND
GODFREY OF BOUILLON*

Paris

Adrianople

Constantinop
(Istanb

SERBIA

NORMANDY
MAINE

Chartres

CROATIA

Blois

Thrace

Venice

FRANCE

Sea o
Marma

*ADHEMAR OF LE PUY AND
RAYMOND OF TOULOUSE*

ITALY

Adriatic Sea

BYZANTINE

Genoa

Clermont

Lyons

*ROBERT OF FLANDERS AND
HUGH OF VERMANDOIS*

Pergamu

Bay of
Biscay

Le Puy

STATES OF
THE CHURCH

Toulouse

Durazzo

CORSICA

Rome

NAVARRE

Brindisi
Taranto

*BOHEMOND OF
TARANTO AND
TANCRED*

Athens

ARAGON

SARDINIA

CASTILE

CATALONIA

ALMORAVIDS

Mediterranean Sea

SICILY

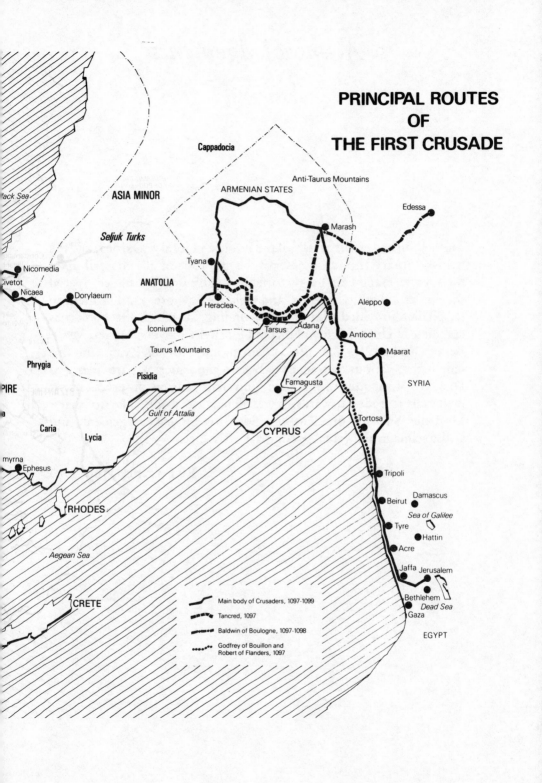

PRINCIPAL ROUTES
OF
THE FIRST CRUSADE

Cappadocia

Anti-Taurus Mountains

ASIA MINOR

ARMENIAN STATES

Edessa

Black Sea

Seljuk Turks

Marash

Nicomedia

Tyana

ivetot

ANATOLIA

Nicaea

Dorylaeum

Aleppo

Heraclea

Iconium

Tarsus

Adana

Antioch

Taurus Mountains

Maarat

Phrygia

Pisidia

SYRIA

Famagusta

Gulf of Attalia

Caria

CYPRUS

Lycia

Tortosa

a

myrna

Ephesus

Tripoli

RHODES

Damascus

Beirut

Sea of Galilee

Aegean Sea

Tyre

Hattin

Acre

Jaffa Jerusalem

CRETE

Bethlehem

Dead Sea

Gaza

EGYPT

——	Main body of Crusaders, 1097-1099
▬▬▬	Tancred, 1097
•••••	Baldwin of Boulogne, 1097-1098
••••••	Godfrey of Bouillon and Robert of Flanders, 1097

Acknowledgements

The helpful and efficient staff of the Bodleian Library (Oxford) and the British Library (London) deserve the gratitude of all who call upon their services, and I am happy to acknowledge their assistance. Special thanks are due to friends and relatives whose kind American hospitality provided pleasant surroundings in which the book was completed. These include Philip and Hortense Meyers, Mr and Mrs J. Beaver, Mr and Mrs C. Smith, and my mother, Mrs O. Ryan. I am also indebted to various colleagues in Britain and America, particularly to Dr Gavin Langmuir of Stanford University, for his observations on medieval attitudes towards Jews. Finally, I would like to thank Mr Peter Shellard of Dent and Sons for his encouragement, and C. Engelmann for valuable editorial assistance.

RCF Oxford, July 1983

Introduction

At the sound of sword hammering on lance young
children's hair turns white.
This is war, and the man who shuns the
whirlpool to save his life shall grind
his teeth in penitence.
(al-Abiwardi)

In 1286, the great hall of the famous crusading order, the Hospitallers, echoed with song and pageantry about medieval Europe's legendary heroes: there were recitations about King Arthur and the men of the Round Table, and tableaux recreating the romanticism of Lancelot and Tristran. The Frankish nobles and knights who gathered in that hall, in the Christian city of Acre in the Holy Land, would have sensed an affinity with these chivalrous archetypes, for the crusaders had themselves performed many famous deeds in battling the cunning Moslem enemy. By 1291, however, Acre was no longer a Christian city: 'When the Franks had come out...' according to a Moslem chronicler, 'the Sultan set the women and children apart and decapitated all the men, of whom there was a great number.' Priests as well as knights were mercilessly slaughtered; the last defenders of Acre themselves passed into chivalrous legend. This contrast between the make-believe gaiety of 1286 and the cruel massacres of 1291 at Acre emphasizes the weakness of that great Christian adventure, the crusades: ideal and reality seldom meshed smoothly; internal bickering harassed the Christians of *Outremer*, blinding them to the dangers that surrounded them, while the motives of western Europeans who went to the Holy Land were not always of the most honourable intent.

Amazingly enough, however, hordes of western Christians did manage to capture many cities of the Levant, including Jerusalem, and to hold them for nearly two centuries. By examining the hardships of life en route to the Holy Land, conditions in crusader camps, conflicts among crusaders, disputes between western and eastern Christians, the harrowing tales of atrocities and cowardice, the bravery of men and women who dedicated their lives to an ideal, the religious zeal that gripped even the fiercest warriors, I hope to show what it was like to

1

participate in these crusading armies. Other areas considered include the financing of the crusades, recruiting methods, and the fate of wives and families left at home. Though much of the material is anecdotal, such as the speeches of Moslem leaders imagined and 'recorded' by western Christian writers, or legendary accounts of miraculous successes in battle, all of it, nevertheless, is part of the story. It represents what contemporaries wished to believe about the holy conflict.

The second part of this survey deals with ideological aspects of the conflict. Mohammad (d. 632) was the founder of one of the world's great religions, but in a way the story began long before he started to receive messages from the Archangel Gabriel on a hill outside Mecca. It began with Abraham and continued with Jesus, for Mohammad had absorbed much of the Judaism and Christianity of his day, to the extent that many parts of the Koran might seem to a modern Jew or Christian to be mere variations on the Old or New Testaments. Islam (submission to God), a monotheistic religion accompanied by the simplest of rites, united and inspired believers with a zeal for *jihad,* or holy war. It will be shown that Moslems believed themselves to be fighting for the One God of the True Faith, no less than Christians. All too often, surveys of the crusades intended for the informed general reader disregard Islamic commitment and faith; it is hoped that this neglect will be avoided in the present study. A brief account of the effects of the crusades upon women and Jews, and the decline of the medieval crusading spirit, concludes the work.

Medievalists will discover in this study an extensive debt to the great historians of the crusades such as Mayer, Alphandery, Runciman, Rousset, Erdmann and others, as well as to more recent writers and translators, such as Peters, Brundage and Riley-Smith (Mayer's masterly bibliography and later additions in *Historische Zeitschrift* might suggest that almost every medievalist has, at one time or another, written about some aspect of the crusades). In addition, there are extensive collections of documents and editions of chronicles of the crusading movement available to historians, as well as the many translations into English accessible to the general reader. Some of these, with other basic works and more recent articles, have been noted in the Sources.

Finally, there is continuing discussion among historians about precisely what constituted a 'crusade'. In this book, crusade is used in the limited, traditional sense: (apart from introductory material in the first chapter) crusades launched against non-Moslems, or in places other than the Near East, will not be examined. The whole crusading enterprise is important not only because of what was achieved under incredibly adverse conditions, but also because it reveals a great deal about the social changes and religious aspirations of western European medieval society. I hope that this study will fill the gap between scholarly monographs and popular expositions, while contributing to an understanding both of contemporary Christianity and of Moslem reactions to Christianity. By examining some of the tenets of medieval Islam, modern Christians will perhaps better appreciate the problems that still separate the believers in two of the world's great religions.

PART ONE

The Call to War:
The Creation and Accomplishments
of God's Militia

1
The Crusades: An Overview

Wake—it is time to be a martyr at Kabul
(Rebel folksong, Afghanistan 1982)

'He who fights so the word of God may prevail is on the path of God.'
The sentiments embodied in this saying attributed to Mohammad do
much to explain the amazing success of Islam, which, through the zeal
for *jihad* or holy war, extended from the borders of France to those of
India by the early eighth century. Religious enthusiasm also lies behind
the equally amazing accomplishments of the Christian warriors of the
First Crusade. In both Moslem expansion and Christian conquest,
however, luck was just as important as zeal. The Moslems were able to
profit from the weaknesses of early seventh-century Christendom just
as the crusaders, when they entered Jerusalem in bloody triumphs four
and a half centuries later, were able to attribute their victory in part to
dissension and weakness among the Moslems.

Because of assassinations and rivalry which could be traced back to
the period following Mohammad's death, by the tenth century the
Moslem world had fallen into two major (and several minor) rival
camps. One of these, the Shi'ite faction, was supported by the
successors of Ali, Mohammad's cousin and son-in-law. By the later
tenth century, they had gained control in Egypt as the Fatimids; a
fanatical offshoot, the Assassins, would spill the blood both of
Christians and other rival Moslem groups. The other faction, the
Sunnites, originally supported the succession of Abu Bakr, one of
Mohammad's closest allies. On both sides the picture is further
confused by the establishment of semi-independent emirates and
caliphates of varying political and religious allegiances. Moslem Spain,
for example, began to go its own way as early as the eighth century.
Not only was there internal rivalry, but also, from the tenth and early
eleventh centuries, the Moslem world was shaken by progressive
incursions of the Seljuk Turks. These people, having become Sunnites,
brought to the Near East a vitality and fervour that were reminiscent of

7

the earliest stages in the rise of Islam. They were proud, warlike, zealous and—more to the point—very successful: in the 1050s, they captured Baghdad; by the 1070s, Asia Minor (with the defeat of the Byzantines at Manzikert in 1071), Palestine and Damascus; and by the 1080s, Antioch and Edessa. After one of their strongest leaders, Sultan Malik Shah, died in 1092, Turkish unity was dissipated by the establishment of several rival emirates, particularly in Asia Minor and Syria. This was why, during the 1090s, even as crusader swarms were moving from western Europe, the Holy Land was the scene of internal conflict and rivalry; why the crusaders often found themselves, from practical considerations, willing to accept or ask for the assistance of one or other of the Moslem parties in the ever-shifting sands of near-eastern politics. The fact that Greek Constantinople was to many westerners suspect as a perfumed den of vice and treachery, only complicated matters.

Perhaps the fate of the city of Jerusalem, from its loss by one Christian power to its recovery by another, will illustrate these mutations of fortune. The city was under Byzantine control until 614, when the Sassanid Persians succeeded in taking it from the Greeks. Emperor Heraclius recovered the holy city by 629, but was unable to withstand a Moslem takeover in 638. With the rise of Seljuk power, Byzantine policy was to play off the rival Moslem groups against each other; hence, the (Shi'ite) Fatimid caliphate of Egypt was, by the early eleventh century, in control of Palestine and Jerusalem, and a buffer against the Seljuks. After the Byzantine defeat at Manzikert, however, Jerusalem passed to (Sunnite) Seljuk control in 1071 and then back to the Egyptians in 1076; several months later the Seljuks regained it. Finally, in the midst of these confusing military and political shifts, and with the Near East distracted by the incoming crusaders, the Fatimids recaptured the city in 1098; in July 1099 it fell to the Christians.

The crusaders, then, were aided not only by their own religious zeal, cupidity, curiosity and many other motives that pushed them eastwards, but also by the turmoil and rivalries among the Moslems themselves. Though this may help to explain how they succeeded in their extraordinary venture, an even more interesting problem involves timing: why, since Jerusalem had been continuously occupied by Moslems since the seventh century, did the Christian West only attempt recovery at the end of the eleventh century? What had changed in European society and thought? One way to approach this question is through an examination of earlier military relations between the

Moslem and Christian worlds, beginning, for convenience, with Spain. Visigothic Spain was attacked in 711 by Tarik and his converted Berbers in a campaign which, according to legend, was brought on when the daughter of Julian, a local lord, was abducted and impregnated by King Rodrigo of Toledo. In revenge, Julian is supposed to have invited the Moslems from North Africa to overthrow Rodrigo. Finding the job so easily accomplished, they went on to take over Spain itself, though there was resistance; by tradition the first important battle launched against the invaders by the Christians occurred in 718. Though they were eventually pushed into a narrow coastal lair behind the northern mountains, by the ninth century the Christians had begun their *Reconquista*. They had also provided themselves with a supernatural champion in St James, at Compostella, which would become one of Europe's premier pilgrimage centres, as Jerusalem was at the other end of the Mediterranean. By the middle of the eleventh century, determined Christian kings had extended their hegemony southwards, bringing many Moslem princelings under their control. This success at last united the Moors and persuaded them to invite more ruthless co-religionists from north Africa, who reversed many of the Christian conquests. This was the confusing milieu for El Cid's sometimes unchristian adventures. In any case, on the eve of the First Crusade, Spain had already witnessed more than three centuries of warfare with the Moslems.

It was from Spain, about 720, that the Moslems moved on into south-west France. Historians still debate the extent of this threat and its potentialities, though in the short term many cities and towns undoubtedly suffered its harmful effects. Charles Martel, the 'hammer', earned his epithet by turning back in 732 or 733 near Poitiers this Moslem advance, the start of a long tradition of Frankish resistance to the Saracens. By about 770, most of the enemy had been pushed from Gaul, though they continued to harass Charlemagne and his successors. The Frankish *Annals* report that around 799 Moslem insignia captured while defending the Balearics were sent to Charlemagne, and, in 801, at the fall of Barcelona, it is said that many Saracen prisoners were taken. Heroic deeds in the Spanish March or borderlands gave rise to one of the seminal works of medieval literature, the *Chanson de Roland*; though nominally-Christian Basques seem to have attacked the proud Roland, the ultimate enemy was the Moslem. Charlemagne's son, Pepin, King of Italy (d. 810), sent a fleet against Moslems pillaging Corsica in 806, but this did not stop their overrunning both Sardinia and Corsica in 810. Even before Charlemagne's death, the *Annals* compiler mentions the ravaging of Nice—a hint of unpleasant things to come, for later in the ninth century enterprising Moslems set up a bandits' nest some fifty miles along the coast from Nice, near Fréjus, from which they terrorized the neighbourhood, the Alpine passes and the north Italian seaports. There were other robbers' dens, but Fréjus was particularly troublesome. The stronghold was destroyed in the later tenth century when a league of aggrieved parties finally captured it.

It is not surprising that Moslem pirates should show an interest in Italian ports, since the peninsula and Sicily jutted out so invitingly into what the Moslems could call, with almost as much justification as the Romans, *Mare Nostrum*. Mohammad had been dead a mere twenty years, for example, when the first (recorded) attack on Sicily occurred. Things became serious during the ninth century, and, by 902, Sicily belonged to the Moslems. Southern Italian cities also suffered during the ninth century, and Naples often found it more expedient to ally itself with the Moslems than to fight them. Even the Eternal City itself was lusted after by the infidel, though they had to content themselves with a rampage through the suburbs, including St Peter's basilica. Pope Leo IV, in consequence, threw a wall around the saint's church and thereby laid the foundations—in the figurative sense only, considering the extensive resiting and rebuilding of later centuries—of the Vatican mini-city. Another casualty of ninth-century Moslem activities in Italy was Monte Cassino, the venerable home of Benedictine monasticism. At last the Italians began to organize resistance, and by the early tenth century managed to expel the Moslems from Italy proper. Pope John X himself took the field in 915, successfully adding spiritual to martial forces. From this point on, Italian cities turned to offensive tactics: Pisa and Genoa in particular began launching aggressive raids against Moslem ports and, by the early eleventh century, were attacking the enemy in north Africa itself. These two cities were interested in protecting their western Mediterranean trade. On the other side of the peninsula, Venice was equally concerned about maintaining commercial ties with rich Byzantium to the east.

The Byzantines were just as anxious about the Moslem threat; when Pope John X defeated the Moslems at the Garigliano in 915, it was with the help of Byzantine military power, whose encounters with the Moslems stretched back to the seventh century, with Emperor

Heraclius. In fact, Roman emperors were sending troops out to skewer Saracens long before Mohammad's birth. About AD 354, as Ammianus Marcellinus tramped around the Prefecture of the East, he took time to record some notes about the *Saraceni,* whom he introduced as people 'we never found desirable either as friends or as enemies'. They were rapacious vagabonds, half-naked folk clad in dyed cloaks 'as far as the loins', who used swift horses and camels to carry them far and wide in times of peace or disorder. They eschewed farming and had no fixed abodes. The men were not interested in permanent wives. Ammianus claimed to be amazed at the sexual appetites of both women and men. After noting that some were even ignorant of grain and wine, he writes them off with a terse *hactenus de natione perniciosa*: so much for this dangerous (or troublesome) tribe. They and their desert fellows would become far more dangerous after the Prophet united them in the seventh century. Three centuries after Ammianus scorned these trifling nomads, they had captured Jerusalem during the winter of 637-38, a mere half-dozen years after Mohammad's death, despite the efforts of Emperor Heraclius. By the eighth century, emperors (and an empress) were defending Constantinople itself, though the belligerent Saracens had approached the walls of the famous capital as early as the 670s. Sometimes at peace, sometimes at war, the two sides vied for generations for mastery of the Near East.

Among the more successful of mercenary troops hired by the Byzantines were the Varangian Guard of Scandinavians, who were established in service in Constantinople about AD 1000. After the conquest of England in 1066, many displaced or dispossessed Anglo-Saxon warriors joined them. One of the key figures and victims of that 1066 conflict, Harald Hardradi, had taken service with the Varangians for a short time in the 1030s. According to his *Saga,* on this tour he attacked the lands of the Saracens and captured eighty towns, some of which surrendered, the rest being taken by assault. Even as Harald was spilling Moslem blood, however, the Seljuk Turks were moving westward, thus creating a new, formidable enemy whose incursions would compel Emperor Alexius Comnenus to call upon the West for help and set the scene for the First Crusade.

Long before this, western Christians had acquired centuries of experience battling Moslems in Spain, France and Italy. This aggression had been encouraged by the Church in its articulation of a doctrine of holy war. Warfare presented early Christians with yet another problem through the continuous process of accommodating their ideals to the 'real' world. It was true that one could temper Christ's admonition to turn the other cheek with his call to respect the things of Caesar, including, presumably, Caesar's legions: about AD 200 Tertullian defended Christians against charges of subversion by pointing out that they, like other Romans, served in the army. But the dilemma remained and, a century later, a centurion named Marcellus was executed because he had thrown away his arms, choosing to serve Christ rather than the emperor. With the advent of Emperor Constantine and his toleration of and eventual conversion to Christianity in the fourth century, however, the pressures relaxed. By the early fifth century, that giant who helped to shape medieval thought, St Augustine, had formulated a doctrine of just war in Christian terms. Provided that a war were declared by legitimate authority, for a just cause, and fought with the· right intention, Christians should have no qualms about participating. In addition to this, even during Augustine's lifetime Europe was being transformed by incoming peoples whose leaders held prowess and *virtus* in battle of great importance and needed no excuses for rushing into battle. These Germanic tribes were eventually converted, thereby bringing to Christianity their own sublimation of the warlike virtues. With the rise of the Moslems, these new Europeans, and especially the Franks, stood out as defenders not only of their kingdoms, but also of Christianity itself. And yet, this was not holy war—though it may have been just—for the rewards of victory or valour were not yet envisaged as essentially spiritual. That impetus, most historians claim, came from the papacy after the middle of the ninth century when, for example, Leo IV and John VIII promised a variety of heavenly benefits (the nature of which is uncertain) for those who fought or died in battle against the infidel. In any case, a link was established between fighting the Moslems and other pagans, and the enjoyment of still vaguely-formulated spiritual benefits.

After sinking into the dissolution of the tenth century, when a contemporary scandal-monger claimed that the papacy had become a pornocracy, the strong secular rulers of a renewed Empire, now centred in Germany, helped to raise the status and, eventually, the powers of the popes. As part of a general eleventh-century revival, exemplified by spiritual awakenings in both monastic and secular circles, the papacy moved into a great period of reform and the concept of holy war also revived. Eleventh-century popes encouraged certain warlike projects either by bestowing holy banners upon the leaders of various expeditions (such as the conquest of England) or, in the case of Leo IX (d. 1054), by personally taking the field against their enemies as John X had done in 915. In the 1060s, Alexander II gave to Christians fighting Spanish Moslems not only his blessing, but also an alleviation of the penalties attaching to sin, though again the precise nature of his gift is still debated. With perhaps the most famous eleventh-century pope, Gregory VII, renowned for his fight with Emperor Henry IV and the melodramatic confrontation in the snows at Canossa in Italy, the penultimate stage in the application of concepts of holy war to an expedition to the Near East was reached. In 1074, Gregory VII asked the Burgundian Count William to send troops to help eastern Christians against the Saracens, and later in the same year he wrote that he would personally lead troops to the Near East, even to the Holy Sepulchre at Jerusalem. But these schemes were abandoned a year later, when the pope was plunged into a conflict with the emperor that absorbed all of his energies until his death in 1085. Even so, as Brundage concludes, a holy war specifically under papal leadership against the Moslems of the Near East had been formulated some twenty years before the Council of Clermont of 1095 and the calling of the First Crusade.

The Church helped to prepare the ground for such holy wars in yet another way, discussed by Carl Erdmann (though he was not the first to draw attention to it), through the application of a sacramental mystique to knighthood. By the early eleventh century, religious ceremonial sometimes accompanied bestowal of the sword. At the same time, knights were encouraged to observe the growing Peace and Truce of God movements. The Church, and papacy, thereby (in theory) turned this potentially dangerous lynchpin of feudalism into an ally, a knight of St Peter. Before the First Crusade, these free-ranging fighters, trained to battle but exposed (at least) to religious exhortation, formed a corps which the Church was on occasion able to direct against her enemies. In 1064, for instance, Pope Alexander II offered spiritual rewards to encourage French knights to attack the Moors at the town of Barbastro in north eastern Spain. Adventurous knights responded from northern France and Aquitaine and their fellows continued to respond to such campaigns in Spain until the end of the eleventh century. In a parallel development, during the eleventh century the cult of warrior-saints seems to have become more popular in western Europe.

Not only had they battled Moslems for centuries, but, long before 1095, western Christians had grown accustomed to the idea and practice of going to Jerusalem, to the Holy Sepulchre and other shrines of eastern Christendom. They had done so centuries before the death of Mohammad and continued to do so after Jerusalem became a Moslem city. Though political conditions in the Holy Land during the first and second centuries were extremely unsettled, nevertheless outsiders were drawn to the home of Christianity. The satirist Lucian described how, in the mid-second century, a Cynic philosopher from Greece (who died in AD 165) 'learned the wondrous lore of the Christians, by associating with their priests and scribes in Palestine'. There is evidence of pilgrimage to Jerusalem from the West during the third century and by the fourth century pilgrims were writing up their

1 The goal of crusaders and pilgrims, Jerusalem's walls withstood the Christian assault for a month in 1099. The conspicuous domed building at the centre of this nineteenth-century view is the Dome of the Rock, one of Islam's holiest places. (*The Holy Land*, David Roberts illus., vol. 1, London, 1842. Oxford, Bodley Mason EE 67.)

travel-journals and itineraries. A pilgrim from Bordeaux left the first extant record of such a journey in AD 333-34, while an even more famous guide was written by the Spanish nun or abbess, Etheria, who visited the Holy Land at the end of the fourth century and described, among other things, the religious services she witnessed in Jerusalem. After the Moslem occupation of the city, Christian pilgrims continued to visit the holiest place in their world and they were acknowledged by Islam to have the right to do so as people of the book (the Bible). In any case, their tolls and purchases were useful to local Moslem shopkeepers and guides. By the later tenth century, pilgrimage to Jerusalem was on the increase because of the growing sacramental custom of assigning the journey as a penance. The monks of Cluny also encouraged visits to major holy places, western as well as eastern, and built hostels for the poor along the main routes. In the eleventh century, pilgrimage, especially to Jerusalem, was looked upon by the laity as a ritual particularly appropriate to their own status in society and by which they could work out salvation for themselves without reference to the clergy. For them the Jerusalem pilgrimage was another means of redemption. Of course, the clergy still played their part: by the eleventh century, special pilgrim blessings were in order before departure, and pilgrims en route were supposed to be under the protection of the Church in their persons and in the property they left behind. Furthermore, it could be said that spiritual benefits were expected to accrue almost automatically, in addition to any supernatural assistance pilgrims obtained for themselves at the holy places. This is suggested in 1089, for example, when Pope Urban II offered the spiritual benefits of a Jerusalem pilgrimage to those assisting in an anti-Moslem project in Spain (at Tarragona). The hope of such benefits must have motivated many of the 7,000 pilgrims who moved *en masse* from Germany to Jerusalem in 1064-65.

Besides these spiritual and theoretical predispositions, eleventh-century men and women were also being 'prepared' for the first great crusading outburst of 1095-99 by changing conditions within their society and economy. Decades ago Henri Pirenne used words like 'optimism', 'native strength', 'fecundity' and 'revival' to describe eleventh-century Europe, while another equally famous medievalist (Marc Bloch) spoke of a new feudal age beginning about 1050. In general, this is still the fashion among most historians, who date the inception of the 'High Middle Ages'—the flowering of medieval society—to the eleventh century. Obviously the crusades cannot be understood without reference to this general awakening of western Europe, any more than they can be 'explained' only by the factors mentioned above. Perhaps the most important and correlated developments, in a strictly material sense, were the economic as well as the demographic expansion that affected all social levels. After the external invasions of western Europe had come to an end by about AD 1000, life was less precarious, food production rose, families increased in size, new arable fields were created in forest and waste land, and more and more merchants plied their trades in and between the growing towns. About 1080, the monks of St Aubin of Angers issued the following regulation, among others, for their peasants at Meron:

> If several men have loaded an ass with different kinds of merchandise, they shall owe toll for the ass, save if it is foreign or costly merchandise.
> For [these] other things, the toll shall be paid according to its value...

The good monks were not about to ignore possible profits from these small-time business ventures by their villeins. Something similar was happening to more and villagers throughout western Europe. An obvious motive was the desire for immediate personal gain from new and growing markets; another, especially for peasants, was the wish to escape the sometimes crushing obligations of manorial regimes. Many others would take up the generous offers of their lords—medieval land developers—and, especially in the twelfth century, pack up their families and rude furnishings and move off as colonists to take advantage of the lighter rents and work-loads. In the eleventh century, then, social and geographical mobility were distinct possibilities.

But larger families, especially among the middle-range nobility (of feudal Normandy for instance), created problems. As the medieval tradition of primogeniture spread, hunger for land and lordship drove many frustrated younger sons far from their home territories. Even where primogeniture was not the rule, many sought escape from the limitations of too many siblings and too little land by venturing into Spain, Italy and the Balkans. The enthusiastic knights of the First Crusade were aware of the practical opportunities, as well as spiritual advantages, awaiting them in the Holy Land. These conditions may also have complicated relations between neighbouring aristocratic families, who now would have to guard constantly against trespass (while, of course, encroaching against neighbours whenever possible). Often, the Church and peasantry suffered more than anyone else in these petty feudal wrangles. It was in the interests of both that the middling nobility should curb their appetites for contention, or at least satisfy them elsewhere. This was the background to another set of conditions, which led to the crusades—the part played by the Church not only in controlling the behaviour of the laity, but in imposing its own ideals upon ordinary men and women of high and low estate. This goes beyond the aspects mentioned above, such as the concept of Holy War and papal leadership, or the sacralizing of knighthood and encouragement of pilgrimage to Jerusalem.

By the eleventh century, in the general social revival, the Church, too, had entered on a new phase, marked most spectacularly by the so-called Investiture Controversy between imperial and papal, or secular and ecclesiastical, authorities. Besides the reforming movement within the papacy, eleventh-century spirituality was characterized by an increase in monastic experimentation as men sought out new methods of pursuing communal salvation and came to recognize and organize *communitas* in more subtle ways. One of the best-known foundations was the work of Robert, a Benedictine abbot who rejected the traditional monastic life about 1075, by founding a small settlement at Molesme. But after twenty years, even this was too secure for him, so once again he went in search of spiritual solitude, finally settling at Cîteaux. By the next century, the Cistercians were perhaps the most influential of all new-model monastic orders. In this new spiritual environment, eleventh century monks were beginning to envision Jerusalem as a spiritual goal to which the pilgrim-soul ascends. This revived interest in an ancient theme, expressed in hymns composed in the eleventh century, would fit in well with crusading aspirations and even help to formulate them.

On a less exalted level, the eleventh-century Church turned directly to the problems of the laity in sponsoring the Peace, and then Truce, of God. These were attempts to curb the feudal brigandage that affected clergy and laity alike. Great numbers of the laity were brought into immediate, emotional union with Church leaders and their ideas. These peace demonstrations often turned into outpourings of lay enthusiasm, equivalents of modern revivalist meetings, orchestrated by the secular and regular clergy through sermons, the use of relics, and processions. There may also be less sublime reasons for popular participation in such outbursts. The overcrowding that has been suggested for the mid-range nobility may have afflicted even peasant families in some regions, and the new socio-economic nexus of the town could have produced as much frustration as opportunity, removing the individual from the cocoon of kinship and patronage shared with his fellow-villagers. Among these anxious, overcrowded and insecurely employed groups, as Norman Cohn emphasized in a

17

classic study, messianic hopes may have been generated, the belief in the coming Millennium and return of Christ—which was to take place in Jerusalem. A quickening of spiritual life during the eleventh century is indicated in others ways as well. For example, Glaber claims that, just after the year 1000,

> there occurred, throughout the world, expecially in Italy and Gaul, a rebuilding of church basilicas. . . It was as if the whole earth, having cast off the old by shaking itself, were clothing itself everywhere in the white robe of the church.

By the eleventh century, the teachings of the Church were infusing the lay community, *ordo plebis,* with a new eschatological longing, a sharpened desire for salvation, that R. W. Southern calls a 'restlessness' of the soul. This restlessness was the fund drawn upon by the preachers of the First Crusade, men as diverse as the popular wanderer Peter the Hermit and Pope Urban II.

As the foregoing suggests, the crusading movement developed out of different sets of conditions laid down before and during the eleventh century. At least this seems to be the consensus today, when the political-colonial motives and immediate papal stimulus tend to be played down, while the socio-psychological background to the movement is emphasized. Urban II is no longer thought of as the 'founder' of the crusading surge, but as a catalyst acting upon preformed sentiments and social circumstances. Yet there is no doubt that his sermon of 1095 was crucial. Also, in the decades leading up to 1095, military conflicts with the Moslems accelerated and thereby intensified pre-existing attitudes. In Spain, for example, the army of King Alfonso VI suffered overwhelming defeat in 1086 at the hands of the north African Murabits (or Almoravids, the Veiled Ones). Christian knights from France and elsewhere in western Europe were encouraged to attempt to regain lost Spanish territory. 'My Cid plies his lance until it breaks and then takes his sword and slays Moors without number, blood dripping from his elbow down.' In Italy at about the same time—1087—several cities collaborated in launching attacks against a north African Moslem base; the successful foray was led by a papal legate. In southern Italy, the ambitious Roger and his brother Robert Guiscard—products of a large, ambitious Norman family—were active as early as mid-century. By 1072, the two had successfully blockaded, besieged and conquered Sicily's Moslem capital, Palermo. The job was completed by Roger in 1091, when the island, as well as Malta and southern Italy, came under Norman control, a southern pendant to the Norman conquest of England a generation earlier. Meanwhile Bohemond, a son of Robert, was attempting to further familial and personal aspirations in the Greek world by attacking the Balkans, which at that time were under the hegemony of the Byzantine Emperor, Alexius Comnenus. By the mid-1080s, however, Bohemond's successes had come to an end and the Greeks were able to turn him back. Ironically, he would become one of the leaders of the First Crusade once again confronting Alexius at Constantinople en route to the Holy Land. On that occasion, the emperor's teenage daughter, Anna, gazed on this uncouth Frank with a mixture of disgust and admiration:

> The sight of him inspired admiration, the mention of his name terror
> ... there was a hard, savage quality to his whole aspect... in him
> both courage and love were armed, both ready for combat.

Elsewhere Anna called Bohemond a liar, a cheat, a loud-mouthed barbarian. This ambivalent relationship between two cultures, exemplified by Bohemond and Anna, would continue to plague the entire crusading movement until the end of the Middle Ages.

But neither Bohemond nor any other crusade leader would have had the chance to harass the emperor on their way to fight Saracens without Urban II's famous call to arms in 1095. After the Byzantine defeat at Manzikert in 1071, the eastern Empire was in need of increased military assistance, and it is, therefore, not surprising to find an imperial embassy asking Urban II for help at the council of Piacenza, in northern Italy, in the spring of 1095; the pope agreed to assist Alexius. It is possible that the Byzantine envoys mentioned the 'rescue' of Jerusalem as part of the programme. Moving into France to honour his *alma mater*, Cluny, on the way the pope conferred with Adhèmar, Bishop of Le Puy, who would become his legate in the crusade. At Le Puy, Urban issued the call for a council to be held at Clermont and, after visiting Cluny, he entered Clermont by mid-November. Most of the prelates present were from southern France; many laymen attended as well. The business of the council involved various reform measures as well as the papal (as opposed to diocesan or regional) proclamation of the Truce of God. At the end of the council, Urban preached his famous sermon. It is well known that no fully reliable account of this sermon exists, and debate continues about the actual message as it can be reconstructed from the four major versions. One of the main questions is whether the pope specifically called for the liberation of Jerusalem, or merely for assistance for Alexius, or help for the oppressed Christians of the eastern Church, or even all three. Whatever Urban said in the fields on that 27th of November, the enthusiasm of his auditors certainly surpassed all expectations, as they stamped the ground and shouted 'God wills it', some in tears. In later months, Urban definitely included the freeing of the Lord's city from the Moslems as one of the goals of the armed pilgrimage.

Another controverted point is the indulgence that the pope is supposed to have granted to his listeners. Popes had been holding out such promises since the ninth century, but whether or not Urban's was a proper plenary indulgence, and the conditions under which it was operative, is actually a non-issue. As Hans Mayer says, 'Where even theologians found much obscure, there was little chance of popular opinion being well-informed.' The whole series of interrelated concepts—purgatory, remission of temporal penalties, remission of enjoined penance, the Treasury of Merits—was of long, slow and not always well-guided growth. Again, no matter what Urban actually said, the people who eventually heard his message (through wandering preachers and others at second and third hand) believed that they would receive great spiritual benefits, even immediate entry into heaven, by going to Jerusalem or even by taking a vow to do so in response to the Clermont message. The vow, by which the individual bound himself to visit the Holy Sepulchre, would become by the thirteenth century a redeemable promise useful to the Church as a source of income and political leverage. But, like Jephthah who killed his daughter because of a vow (Judges 11.30-31), most Christians took the oath very seriously indeed. Again, the exact form of the vow taken by the first crusaders, and in what particulars it differed from ordinary pilgrimage vows, is not clear. The 'taking of the cross', the placing of cloth crosses on one's garments, seems to have been the formal, outward symbol of the vow; by the later twelfth century, rites for blessing crusaders would be differentiated from the parent rite, the pilgrim-blessing. But in 1095, all was fluid, new, unformed; in 1095, there was as yet no such word as 'crusader', no such expression as 'the Holy Land'. Urban, by combining two motifs which would henceforth be the mark of the crusade, pilgrimage and holy war, sparked off the latent energies that would bring one of the greatest adventures of medieval history into being.

Some indication of the more important chronological developments of the crusades will provide a context for topics considered in later chapters. Urban's speeches and letters were iterated in more sermons by bishops and travelling preachers like Peter the Hermit, who operated in Germany and especially France. Though Urban had cautioned that only the fit should undertake the armed pilgrimage, and only after proper preparation, the crowds reached by Peter and his colleagues tended to be simpler folk, presumably easily moved to enthusiasm. They began the trek to the Holy Land in early 1096, months before the August date established by Urban for the official departure of the armies. This caused problems for Emperor Alexius, who had not had enough time to prepare the necessary markets for crusaders who would pass through his domains en route to Asia Minor. The mobs helped themselves as they traversed Hungary on their way to Byzantine territory. Their violent, xenophobic behaviour made Alexius only too glad to be rid of them; such a rabble at the gates of Constantinople was not a pleasant prospect. Arriving in Moslem territory at last, mutual antipathies split the 'peoples' crusade' into factions, which dispersed independently to attack Christian villages. In October, the Turks descended upon and slaughtered the crusaders, except for the more attractive girls and boys, taken as prisoners. A few thousand of the rabble were rescued by Alexius, but the majority were wiped out, after advancing less than 100 miles into the land of the infidel. Some contingents fared even worse. Other preachers and local adventurers had stirred the German masses who, by mid-1096, were indulging their hatreds and jealousies by massacring Rhineland Jews. These crusaders, led by Volkmar, Emicho and Gottschalk, then turned eastwards to carry on pillaging and killing in Hungary. For the most part they were scattered by the Hungarian king and people even before they entered Byzantine territory, let alone the Moslem lands.

Urban II had not called for undisciplined mobs, but for trained knights and feudal leaders. This was the class he hoped to attract in his sermons delivered in France and Italy, in his letters and envoys sent to Spain, England, even Scandinavia. By the autumn of 1096 these better-equipped, organized and disciplined armies were on the road to the Holy Land. Or rather, roads, for there were two main, plus other subsidiary, routes. The Hungarian route led from western Europe through modern Hungary, Yugoslavia (at Belgrade), Bulgaria (Sofia), then to Constantinople. The Italo-Greek route crossed the Adriatic from Italy to modern Durrës (Durazzo) in Albania, eastwards through northern Greece (Thessaloniki, Komotini), thence to Constantinople. At this time these areas, except Hungary, were within the Byzantine Empire. The main armies following these routes were led by about a half-dozen French noblemen, including Hugh of Vermandois, brother of King Philip I of France, Robert Duke of Normandy, brother of King William II of England, Norman lords from southern Italy like Bohemond and Tancred, as well as the Count of Toulouse and others. Despite better discipline, some of these contingents became embroiled in skirmishes as they passed through eastern Europe. Differences with Alexius over provisions, and oaths to return recovered territory to Byzantine control, even led to crusader attacks on Constantinople itself. Eventually, they crossed over the Bosporus and in 1097 began their march south through Asia Minor (Anatolia or Turkey) where the 'peoples' crusade' had ended miserably. By October 1097, they were at Antioch.

By then rivalries had split the crusader armies. Some of the leaders detached their contingents and went off on their own, like Baldwin of Boulogne, who travelled east to establish himself as ruler of the Armenian Christians at Edessa by March 1098. Meanwhile, the bulk of the crusader army besieged Antioch, captured in June 1098. Bohemond of Taranto (southern Italy) took over as Prince of Antioch, with the backing of Genoese merchant-shippers who gained concessions in the city. Raymond, Count of Toulouse and *soi-disant* leader of the crusade, after bickering with Bohemond about Antioch, finally gave in to pressure from the rank-and-file and pushed on in January 1099. Jerusalem was reached and taken in mid-July 1099; Godfrey, Duke of Lower Lorraine, became 'advocate' of the Holy Sepulchre, claiming to be unworthy of any higher honour in Christ's city. On his death in 1100, his less fastidious brother, Baldwin of Edessa, took the title King of Jerusalem. Thus, on the eve of the twelfth century, the crusaders had taken the Holy Land and had established the Kingdom of Jerusalem, Principality of Antioch, County of Edessa and (by 1109) County of Tripoli, held by Bertrand, son of Raymond, Count of Toulouse. These were the so-called Crusader States. The capture of Jerusalem renewed interest in the West and resulted in three crusades in 1101, which ended in victories for the Turks and worsening Western-Byzantine relations. In fact, by 1105, Bohemond of Antioch, fearing Byzantine pressure, convinced Pope Paschal II to preach a crusade against Byzantium itself. Nothing came of this, but it was an ominous foretaste of things to come. Meanwhile, King Baldwin of Jerusalem managed to extend crusader control by taking Acre in 1103 with Genoese help and Sidon in 1110 with Norwegian and Venetian assistance. But his attack on Tyre failed, and a raid into Egypt accomplished little. Yet by 1118 when he died, most of Palestine and much of Syria were under Christian control, the crusaders now assisted by the sometimes mutually antagonistic military orders, the Templars and Hospitallers.

Zengi, an ambitious Turkish leader, managed to reverse these Christian advances. He had moved into northern Syria by 1130, about which time the first generation of crusaders had nearly all died off. In 1143, after the death of King Fulk of Jerusalem (Fulk had been Count of Anjou, grandfather of England's famous King Henry II), Zengi exploited the inevitable squabbles among crusader leaders and, in 1144, captured Edessa. Hoping to reverse this, Pope Eugenius III was helped by Bernard of Clairvaux in the recruitment of men for what is called the Second Crusade. King Louis VII of France and King Conrad of Germany enlisted. What remained of Conrad's army, after a disastrous defeat in Turkey, joined with Louis' at Nicaea. By this time, although Zengi was dead, the Turks had made the recovery of Edessa impossible. The crusaders continued south, therefore, and, after various internal disputes, the newcomers foolishly decided to attack Damascus, which had maintained friendly relations with the Christians for political reasons. The attack failed, but it showed the Damascenes that the Franks were not to be trusted, a fact known only too well at Constantinople. The promise of the First Crusade was vanishing.

Zengi's son Nur ed-Din continued to encroach upon rival Moslem as well as Christian territories: he took Damascus by 1154 and five years later agreed to help the Byzantine Emperor, Manuel Comnenus, against both Moslem and Christian enemies. When Amalric, King of Jerusalem, decided to invade Egypt in the 1160s, Nur ed-Din answered the Egyptian plea for an alliance by sending his trusted henchmen Shirkuh and his nephew, a man in his mid-twenties called Saladin. These two, however, were just as interested in conquering Egypt as were the Franks, a situation which led to a complex series of attacks and alliances resulting in Saladin's control of Egypt by 1169. Nur ed-Din took advantage of the confusion to carry out attacks in Syria. Realizing the growing threat, representatives of the crusaders sailed west with letters to the leading powers of Europe. Even though Pope

Alexander III backed their appeal, western Christendom was too embroiled in mutual jealousies and internal problems to care. In the East, the crisis led the Franks into alliances not only with the Byzantine Empire but even with the Assassins. In 1174, both King Amalric and Nur ed-Din died: the death of the former led to dissension over who controlled Jerusalem; of the latter to the unification of the Moslems under Saladin, who took over Damascus in the same year. By 1187, Saladin was attacking Tiberias on the Sea of Galilee. The King of Jerusalem, Guy of Lusignan, allowed himself to be persuaded to attack Tiberias, though a scorching July was hardly the best month for such a campaign. Nevertheless, the crusaders set out from Acre across the territory of Galilee. By 3 July, the heat and lack of water forced them to stop at Hattin. Next day Saladin's men attacked: almost the entire Christian army were slaughtered, including nearly all the Templars and Hospitallers; those noblemen who were not killed (a few managed to escape) became Saladin's prisoners. The Moslem reconquest of the Holy Land followed in quick order, with Saladin taking Jerusalem in October 1187. He allowed Christian refugees to go to Tyre and Antioch, which were almost all that remained of the principal Christian conquests. After hearing the news of the fall of Jerusalem, Pope Gregory VIII sent out letters and encouraged preaching of what is known as the Third Crusade. Richard of Poitou (later Richard I) took the cross in late 1187, while his father King Henry II raised money for the enterprise through the 'Saladin Tithe' and the Archbishop of Canterbury went on a crusade-preaching mission, which took him even into the wilds of Wales. After Henry II's death, Richard I met Philip II of France at Vezelay to plan their mutual campaign. Although Frederick Barbarossa was already en route with a great army, after his death by drowning most of his men returned to Germany and imperial territories. Meanwhile, King Guy of Jerusalem, embroiled in conflict with his rival (Conrad of Montferrat at Tyre), attacked Moslem-held Acre. He was soon joined by others who continued desultory fighting through 1190. By early 1191, however, the crusaders at Acre had made little progress and were, in fact, approaching a state of exhaustion and starvation.

Philip and Richard left Vezelay on 4 July 1190, wintered in Sicily, then sailed for Acre. Philip arrived in April 1191, but Richard was delayed by the conquest of Cyprus and other adventures and did not reach the city until June 1191. By July, when Acre was at last captured, King Philip returned to France. As for Richard, since peace terms with

2 Tyre, as seen by the Scottish artist David Roberts in the 1830s. The city fell
to the crusaders in 1124, with Venetian help, and was conquered by the
Mamluks in May, 1291. Archbishop William of Tyre was a leading crusade
historian. (*The Holy Land*, vol. 2, London 1843. Oxford, Bodley Mason
EE 68)

Saladin could not be finalized, he slaughtered the captive garrison of
Acre and headed south in August. Many of the rank-and-file were
sorry to leave, having found the wine and women of Acre much to
their taste. This problem of dissolution in the languid atmosphere of
the Near East was nothing new; it had been faced by Roman army
commanders in the area a thousand years earlier. As Marcus Cornelius
Fronto described it about AD 150:

> The army. . . was demoralized by luxury and immorality and
> prolonged idleness. The soldiers at Antioch were wont to spend their
> time applauding actors and were more often found in the nearest
> tavern garden than in the ranks. . . Gambling was rife in camp, sleep
> night-long, or, if a watch was kept, it was over the wine cups.

While marching south from Acre, Richard succeeded in scattering
Saladin's army in a classic cavalry charge, which proved that the great
Moslem could at least be beaten, if not conquered. Richard also
stopped to refortify Jaffa, which gave the king a chance to send for
some of the crusaders who remained in or had slipped back to the
fleshpots of Acre. About this time, Richard proposed a marriage

alliance between first his sister, then his niece, and Saladin's brother. These negotiations came to nothing and, though some English historians of an older school were shocked into disbelief, such deals would seem to have been well within Richard's capabilities. The army moved towards Jerusalem but Richard realized that, though he might conquer the city, he could never retain it with his limited resources and men; therefore, some compromise with Saladin was necessary. In any case, his crusaders were finding more causes for dissatisfaction and internal bickering. Local successes, however, momentarily changed the king's mind and, in May 1192, he promised to continue the attempt to capture Jerusalem until at least Easter 1193. But by July 1192, he had given up for good and, after one final victory at Jaffa, he entered into an agreement entailing a five-year truce with Saladin that allowed access for Christian pilgrims to Jerusalem and Christian possession of various coastal towns. Richard, unable to enter Jerusalem as conqueror, refused to visit it as a pilgrim. He left for the West in October, 1192. Though no one could have known it, he had led medieval Europe's last major military campaign into Palestine.

Saladin died in 1193 leaving many offspring to battle among themselves for a share in their father's conquests. The Christians, too, were squabbling as usual, about control of Cyprus for instance. In the midst of this, the Germans, in an apparent attempt to efface the failure of Barbarossa's contingent in the third crusade, sent new forces to the Holy Land. There they promptly botched crusader-Moslem co-existence by blundering about in search of heathens to kill. Eventually, deprived of glory, the Teutonic invaders marched back home.

The next significant development, chronologically, was the infamous Fourth Crusade. This campaign had originally been encouraged by Pope Innocent III but control quickly passed from him. In 1203, the crusaders found themselves before Constantinople, led on by the Venetians and an exiled Byzantine pretender. By early 1204, when the pretender was killed, the crusaders attacked and savagely plundered the richest Christian city in the world. In the end, despite Innocent III's condemnation, the West gained much booty and many holy relics, while the East witnessed the establishment of a Latin Empire of Constantinople that lasted nearly sixty years. These were the fruits of decades—even centuries—of western cupidity, xenophobia and ignorance.

With few exceptions, the thirteenth century was dominated by disappointing attempts to rescue the Holy Land, though none were so devastating as the sack of Constantinople. The mass movement of French and German peasants and others, misleadingly (as Raedts has shown) called the 'Children's Crusade' of 1212, ended at Marseilles, Genoa and Pisa for most German participants, who returned sadder but wiser to their homes after the seas inexplicably failed to part for them. A few of the younger participants may have ended up in the slave-markets and harems of the Moslem world, and possibly a better life than the one they had so readily abandoned. Three years later Innocent III, having reluctantly accepted the Fourth Crusade as a *fait accompli*, again announced during the famous Fourth Lateran Council of 1215 that a new venture was to go forth. The result, the Fifth Crusade, was an attack upon Egypt (Damietta) in 1218, which was a total failure thanks to disease, bad weather, cunning Moslems and the incredibly stubborn Cardinal Pelagius, who mismanaged the entire affair on behalf of the papacy. Not even St Francis, who travelled all the way from Italy to convert the bemused Egyptian sultan, had much luck. By 1221, the fiasco mercifully ended in a truce.

Although the clumsiness of Pelagius and the fanaticism of Francis had no effect in Egypt, the cynical opportunism of Frederick II succeeded in Palestine. Emperor Frederick II's crusade is one of the more bizarre thirteenth-century campaigns. The man himself was believed to be superhuman—he was, after all, known as *Stupor mundi*, the wonder of the world, who reputedly used his leisure to experiment on humans and (as one of my students once expressed it) 'to collect wild animals and women'—and he was a very real threat to the papacy. He was under papal excommunication when he did eventually sail to the Holy Land, after marrying the heiress to the Kingdom of Jerusalem. Taking advantage of Moslem political rivalries, in 1229 he concluded a ten-year treaty by which Jerusalem and other cities were returned to Christian control. This peaceful settlement outraged western Christians as well as the Moslems of Syria, both complaining of treacherous dealings with unbelievers. The Emperor crowned himself King of Jerusalem, visited Christian and Moslem shrines with regal impartiality, then sailed off to his beloved, sunny Italian domains and to conflict with the papacy.

Frederick left a country steeped in rivalries in both the Moslem and crusader camps. This simplified matters for the middle-eastern successors of the Seljuks, the Khwarismian Turks. Invited westwards by the Egyptian rival of Syro-Palestinian Moslem princes, the

Khwarismians rampaged through Syria and into Frankish territory, capturing Jerusalem in 1244 and ending Christian hegemony there until modern times. A few months later, the Turks and their Egyptian allies defeated the Damascene Moslems and their allies, the crusaders, a disaster for the Frankish army. The West responded with another crusade. In 1245, Pope Innocent IV at the Council of Lyons (the primary purpose of which was the deposition of *Stupor mundi*) especially commissioned the King of France, Louis IX (later St Louis) to fulfil his crusading vow. Once again an attack on Egypt was thought to be a better strategy than a direct descent upon the Holy Land, and, by 1249, Louis' army seemed to be succeeding. As they moved towards Cairo, however, they were overwhelmed by the enemy. Thousands died, though the richer prisoners were spared for ransom; King Louis himself was taken into captivity. After attaining hs freedom, he went to Acre, where he remained from 1250 to 1254, trying to bolster the crusaders' cause. In the West, though European leaders did very little about this humiliating Christian defeat, one noticeable reaction occurred among the rural poor of France—the *Pastoureaux*—led by a charismatic demagogue named Jacob, who promised that the waters would part for his followers on their march to the Holy Land to aid their beloved king. When Jacob's rabble turned violently anti-clerical and anti-semitic, however, they were cut down or dispersed in France. As for King Louis, he never entirely put aside his dream of a successful crusade. Years later when the opportunity seemed to arise again, he set out once more to battle the infidel. All he found was death, from disease, in Tunis in 1270. All over Europe the dream of a conquered Holy Land was fading.

Even before Louis' death, the Near East witnessed a revolution that would bring about the loss of the last crusader possessions. During the 1250s, the pro-Christian Mongols were moving westwards, taking Baghdad, Aleppo and Damascus, but sparing Christians who often co-operated with them. The Egyptian sultan counter-attacked and, in 1260, the Mongol threat was quashed. In the process, a new Turkish ruler, the Mamluk sultan Baibars, consolidated Egypt, then moved into Palestine, where he took several coastal cities as well as castles of the military orders. By 1268, Antioch had fallen to the Moslems; in 1271, the magnificent fortress of Krak des Chevaliers was taken. Not even the brief crusade by England's Lord Edward (soon King Edward I) in 1271-72 halted the Mamluk advances. Only the death of Baibars in 1277 brought some relief to the Christians of *Outremer*. Through the next decade while the Mongols were repeatedly snubbed in their attempts to form an anti-Moslem alliance with the Christian West, crusader princes and Italian merchants continued their endless rivalries. The Egyptian sultan, exploiting these quarrels, was at last able to conquer Tripoli in 1289, an event which finally awakened the remnant of the crusader cities, and especially Acre, to the danger. There was no great response from the West. The badly organized help that did arrive, for instance in 1290, was a liability in any case. The end came in 1291. Acre was besieged and taken in the spring, and after the fall of the city the Moslems easily overran the handful of remaining Christian towns and forts. Christian refugees crowded into the safety of Cyprus or went farther west, into a Europe that was a strange new world for many of them, who had been born and nurtured in *Outremer*.

It is true, as most historians correctly stress, that this did not by any means end the crusading impulse. Even after the end of the Middle Ages popes would plan, princes would attempt, preachers would propagandize and scholars would draw up Grand Strategies for the reconquest of the Holy Land. But for all that, from now on the only Christians who would tread the famous sites or bathe in the Jordan were the pilgrims whom the Moslems allowed to visit the sacred places. Though the Moslems were finally ejected from Spain in the 1490s, on the eastern front later medieval military actions were either inspired by questionable motives, such as the sack of Alexandria in the 1360s, or were quite ineffective, for instance in the attempt to repulse the Ottoman Turks at Nicopolis in the 1390s. By the middle of the next century, these Turks were attacking Constantinople itself, which fell in 1453. Pope Pius II, the humanist pope, called a meeting in 1459 to plan a rescue of the Christian east. Few European leaders bothered to show up, a fact which disturbed and disappointed the pope. 'If we continue thus', he complained, 'it will be all over with us.' As far as the crusades were concerned, it was.

2
Enlisting for the Crusades

And when ye go forth to war in the land, it shall be no
crime in you to cut short your prayers, if ye fear lest the infidels
come upon you.

(Koran)

From 1095 to the end of the Middle Ages, the call to the Holy Land
resounded across Europe as preachers harangued crowds amidst the
green valleys and mountains of Wales, or from wooden platforms
erected in the golden fields of France, or in the echoing, dark naves of
Rhenish cathedrals. Enthusiastic priests, prelates and popes exercised
all the tricks of the orator's trade, cajoling, threatening, promising;
using allegory, hyperbole, anaphora; rousing with revenge-motifs,
entertaining with short stories called *exempla*. In the sometimes
hysterical atmosphere of these mass meetings, it is understandable that
preachers on occasion might be carried away with their own rhetoric:
'Your bed awaits you in Paradise, should you die in God's service', one
of them rashly promised; 'the angels are ready to carry off your souls
and present them to God.' Some of the Christian recruitment-
propaganda has a distinctly modern ring: 'But someone says, "The
Saracens don't harm me. Why then should I take the cross against
them?" But if he thought it through, he would realize that the Saracens
cause grave injury to every Christian.'

Preaching was the most effective way to reach the illiterate masses.
Although the clergy and nobles of Europe were used to receiving
letters begging aid for the Holy Land, for the most part the emotions
and hopes of the mass of potential recruits could only be stirred by
speaking tours. Perhaps the best-known example is the sermon which
ultimately resulted in the First Crusade. Pope Urban II was probably
as surprised as anyone by the response to his speech that November
day in 1095 outside Clermont. The propaganda was so effective that
Guibert of Nogent (d. *c.* 1125) claimed that the expedition 'was on
everyone's lips'. The Second Crusade is associated with one of western
Christendom's most famous figures, St Bernard of Clairvaux. When
the news of Edessa reached the west, Bernard avidly applied his famous

30

eloquence to the job of raising recruits. At Vezelay in 1146, he expounded the papal encyclical outside the town which straggles up the hill to its magnificent cathedral. As at Clermont, the response was overwhelming. So many demanded crosses to sew on their garments that Bernard offered his own cloak to be cut up into these crusader badges. From Vezelay the famed Cistercian went to eastern France, then to the Rhineland, preaching constantly. His charisma attracted followers, his magical words enthralled them, the miracles he performed convinced them. He also wrote letters to the places he could not visit; Leclercq has shown how Bernard's original sentiments were adapted by his secretariat for specific addressees. Bernard was the best-known, but certainly not the only, man to respond to the need to preach the crusade. About the same time, for example, out on the coast of Portugal, the Bishop of Oporto, preaching to a group of Englishmen, told them not to worry about killing mere Moslems: 'You will not be censured for murder or taxed with any crime' in taking Lisbon from the infidel.

Towards the end of the twelfth century, Saladin reconquered most of the crusader territories, including Jerusalem. The Archbishop of Tyre himself went to beg assistance from the leaders of western Europe, while Pope Gregory VIII and then Clement III engineered the Third Crusade. In England the Archbishop of Canterbury went on a preaching circuit, which took him far afield. Gerald of Wales left a full description of the prelate's tour of Wales, which began in early March 1188 and continued for six weeks. Generally speaking, he was well-received even though his sermons had to be translated into Welsh. Occasionally he ran into problems, like the sullen indifference of a group of young noblemen sitting on the rocks at Anglesey who chose to ignore his plea. But the amazing thing about the whole journey is the fact that less than six months after Saladin entered Jerusalem, the leading churchman of far-off England had crossed into one foreign world to ask men to fight in the deserts of another. And, according to Gerald, he enlisted some 3,000 eager warriors. The efforts of people like Archbishop Baldwin were augmented during the next century by the new orders of friars, especially the Franciscans and Dominicans. Since these wanderers specialized in preaching to, and mixing with, the secular world, their talents were often enlisted in the cause. Occasionally, however, even they failed to elicit either enthusiasm or financial contributions, like the Franciscan who claimed to prefer going to prison to preaching in Ireland again. In England they played a significant part in advertising the Lord Edward's crusade, and their efforts were usually seconded by English prelates. Some idea of their numbers is provided in a letter of 1292 from the Bishop of Lincoln, who noted that the Provincial Minister of the English Franciscans was then preaching a crusade, along with thirty-five Franciscan assistants.

It is difficult to recapture the sense of drama or urgency which enlivened crusade sermons, impossible really to re-create the emotional and physical excitement, which must have animated many audiences of so long ago. That some of the crowds behaved as if on the brink of hysteria, however, is suggested by the reputed miracles that took place in their midst. The intense emotional pressures generated by crowds of believers worked what seemed to be wonders. These phenomena were recorded during later crusading sermons as well, such as the previously-mentioned miracles at the gatherings addressed by St Bernard before the Second Crusade. Fulk of Neuilly, whipping up crusade enthusiasm on his preaching tour in France in the 1190s, was supposed to have wrought many wonders, while an early thirteenth-century crusade preacher in Germany said that miraculous crosses appeared in the skies just in time to astound his enraptured audiences. Crusade sermons could be such emotional events that, even in their aftermath, miracles might still be perceived. At the place in the fields where Archbishop Baldwin once preached in Wales, the local people raised a chapel to commemorate the event. 'Later on crowds of sick people thronged to this spot', Gerald of Wales claimed, 'from all parts of the country, and many miracles were performed there.'

Though we are able merely to glimpse the psychological tumult that must have gone on during these mass meetings, at least we are fortunate in having the texts of some of the sermons themselves. Two famous thirteenth-century crusade preachers were Jacques de Vitry and Odo of Châteauroux, both of whom accompanied crusades to Egypt. In one of his sermons aimed at the military orders, Jacques de Vitry (d. 1240) warned that it was necessary for the knight of Christ (*Christi miles*) to keep himself pure, free from sins of lust, vanity, anger, sloth and avarice. Jacques, often citing Bernard de Clairvaux, complains of the knight 'who thinks more about his horse than about Christ'. On the other hand, some knights overdid it: here, as in all things, they should follow the wise counsel of the clergy and the dictates of reason. For instance, he says, he saw knights in the Holy

Land (he was Bishop of Acre) who were so zealous in fasting and self-punishment that, worn out by this, they were easily overcome by Saracens. One such knight, Jacques claims, was knocked down twice and twice rescued by another knight, who finally complained, 'Lord Bread-and-Water, watch yourself, because if you fall again I'm not picking you up!' The sermon then switched to consideration of heavenly rewards. Those who died in battle—like some slaughtered Templars dangling from the walls of Ascalon—were martyrs, now floating blissfully in heaven. The preacher gave an example of an ordinary crusader who was mistaken for a tonsured Templar because he was bald and bearded; instead of denying that he was a Templar, he proudly went to execution and his celestial reward. The sermon ended with a call to the 'dearest brothers' not to be deterred from the good fight either by difficulties or too much pride, or distracted by the flattery and adulation of others. In another sermon to the Templars, Jacques de Vitry included edifying tales of a knight who urged his horse into the midst of the enemy, knowing that the animal would thus take him to Paradise; another Templar, carrying money from Tyre to Acre, escaped the Saracens by spurring his horse to a tremendous leap from a cliff into deep water below. The place, Jacques claimed, was still called 'Templar's Leap' (*saltus Templarii*). But such feats should not puff up the Order with excessive pride, a moral driven home with the tale of the fox who snatched some cheese from a too-proud raven by coaxing the vain bird to sing (a well-known folk motif in the Middle Ages).

In a sermon to those who had taken or were about to take the cross, Jacques de Vitry sets out the spiritual benefits (remission of sins) and tells a little story by way of exemplification. A visionary Cistercian saw the Blessed Virgin Mary, who said that she gave her child to whomever took the cross with contrite heart (*signum crucis corde contrito recipiebat*). In another sermon to a similar audience, he claims that 'you would not be able to pass over the worldly seas without the cross, nor reach the higher [i.e. spiritual] Jerusalem'. In attractive phrases which play upon the physical dangers of sea-crossings, Jacques says that man is to pass through 'the current of this mortal life with the staff of the cross', 'through the torrents of this world in the sign of the cross, transported to the celestial kingdom'; the cross aids those who 'perilously labour in the waters of this sea'. The cross—that is, the crusaders' cross—is the 'port in storms, safety in dangers'. Taking the cross can even save those who are *in articulo mortis*; furthermore, the dead also benefited when their living relatives took the vow to go on crusade.

Jacques de Vitry knew that his listeners were practical people, so he emphasized the spiritual advantages. 'If Noah worked for a century building the ark to escape physical [or temporal, *mortem temporalem*] death, how much more should you labour for a few years to evade eternal death, and to acquire eternal life?' Though God could free the Holy Land at once, he allowed its possession by the enemy so that good Christians had a means of gaining salvation. 'For many are saved through this holy pilgrimage' (*sanctam peregrinationem*) who would otherwise have remained in sin. Today, he remarked, many hustle about and hurry along quickly enough when there is cheap pork to buy at market, but are slow to take up the incomparably greater offer of a heavenly kingdom. Jacques summarized the many benefits offered: even in coming to his sermons, one's conscience was aroused; whoever heard the sermon earned twenty or forty days of indulgence, a great boon especially considering that those in purgatory would give a great treasure to be released from their torments for only one hour. It was also good to attend these sermons, since many decided to take the cross after seeing others do it. Jacques then told a little story of a man who overcame his wife's efforts to keep him away from a crusade sermon. 'The Devil, through a wife or worldly friends, frequently destroys good intentions.' But, he pointedly reminded his audience, 'You do not follow your wives' advice about going to the Devil; why do you wait for [their] counsel about going to God?' The sermon ended with a mention that almsgiving for the crusade was as meritorious as going to the Holy Land, and, finally, that being signed with the cross was almost as efficacious as a second baptism. Just as lords usually invested vassals with some small token of their rich gift, so the thread and cloth of the crusader's cross was an investiture representing God's much greater gift.

Though Jacques de Vitry was one of the masters of his art, the genre was well-articulated by his day. He borrowed freely from St Bernard, whose letters and sermons extolling the crusade were widely known and imitated. Indeed, many stock expressions, usually based on Old or New Testament passages, crop up again and again in crusade propaganda. The call to take up one's cross and follow Christ was used by Robert of Rheims (before 1107) and Pope Innocent III (in 1213); references to Mattathias and the Maccabees are found in Guibert de Nogent (before 1108), Popes Eugenius III (1146) and Gregory VIII

(1187), Jacques de Vitry (*c.* 1216) and Humbert of Romans (early 1270s); the idea that divine aid would enable one fighter to rout 1,000 of the enemy and two to rout 10,000 is found in Gregory VIII, Innocent III and Humbert of Romans; the crusade as God's test of love for him in St Bernard and Pope Alexander III (1169); and so on. It is a commonplace that echoes of biblical passages, to say nothing of direct quotations, regularly recur in a wide variety of works by medieval writers. It is not surprising, then, to find certain passages used and reused in crusade *excitatoria*. For example, another famous sermonizer, Odo of Châteauroux (d. 1273), also used the idea that so much is gained (eternal bliss) for so little labour (the crusade) and, like Jacques de Vitry, he claimed that sufferers in purgatory benefited from crusading vows taken by the living. But Odo added his own touches, in appealing to history; for example, those now setting out on crusade (with Louis IX, in 1248) will, in God's eyes, compare well with 'the ancient noblemen who, coming out of the realm of France, took Antioch and Jerusalem' in the First Crusade. Odo also drew upon natural history, when he asked rhetorically what the hesitant should do.

> You should do what little deer do: when they see the older deer take to the trail, they go after and follow them. That is what you should do, and if you do not want to follow [the departed crusaders] in body, at least you ought to follow them in heart and prayer and alms, and if not now, at least in another expedition [*passagio*].

Even the simplest rustic could hardly fail to grasp Odo's message. In another sermon to would-be crusaders, he says that those who steal and do not pay debts should not take the cross. It is better for a man to follow the despoiled Christ naked than to follow the Devil with a great household. Whoever takes the cross should first do penance, settle any debts and restore ill-gotten gains. The cross is the wood of life: 'Run, therefore, and seize it.' Thanks to preachers like Jacques de Vitry and Odo of Châteauroux, many thousands did.

People responded to the call for many different reasons. Some made their crusade vows because they were moved by the rumoured plight of their fellow-Christians, the so-called desecration of the Holy Land and atrocities allegedly committed by the infidels. Undoubtedly these wild tales infuriated many people, but it is unlikely that righteous indignation alone could have sustained the majority over the long trek east. Though the question of motivation is complex—even for people who went on pilgrimage to local neighbourhood shrines—one easily identifiable motive for the Jerusalem trip was the crusade indulgence promised by preachers and guaranteed by popes. There can be no doubt that the indulgence was a much-prized benefit, or that it prompted hordes of peasants and nobles alike to take their vows to rescue Jerusalem. What was said of an indulgence offered for the ill-fated Fourth Crusade was generally true in all recruitment campaigns: 'The hearts of the people were greatly moved by the generous terms of this indulgence,' Villehardouin reported, 'and many, *on that account*, were moved to take the cross' (emphasis added). Basically the indulgence was thought to lighten the burden of punishment for sin. Beyond this general statement not much had been formulated; Pope Urban II himself had little specific canonical guidance to follow. During the twelfth century, Somerville claims, 'it is impossible to find any fully consistent or clear doctrine' on the subject, and, furthermore, 'it is unlikely in the extreme that the popes themselves had an absolutely clear notion of the sort of remission they were granting' even by the early thirteenth century. The controversy continued long after the Middle Ages. For instance, the terms used by Jacques de Vitry to explain the indulgence in the thirteenth century were condemned by an eighteenth-century pope, Benedict XIV. For the potential crusader, the important thing was what *he* thought the preacher meant by 'indulgence'. When the pope himself promised crusaders full remission of sins and 'an increase of eternal salvation', for example (the words of Innocent III at the Fourth Lateran Council, 1215), this filtered down to the ordinary man in the crowd as a promise of instant heaven, if he died on crusade—or while travelling to the Holy Land. Everyone, whatever his evil past, might thereby wipe the slate clean and perhaps even qualify for martyrdom. It was, indeed, a new form of salvation. Both Moslem chroniclers and Christian writers described their fallen warriors as martyrs for the faith. Neither Moslems nor Christians were, in fact, claiming anything new. In a speech invented for Titus by the Jewish historian Josephus (d. *c.* AD 100), the emperor addresses his men in the following words: after noting the 'immortality of those men who are slain in the midst of their martial bravery', the emperor continues,

> those souls which are severed from their fleshy bodies in battles by the sword are received by the ether, that purest of elements, and joined to that company which are placed among the stars; . . . they become good demons, and propitious heroes.

The average medieval Christian cannot be blamed for coming to similar conclusions, since many preachers hardly discouraged it, as seen in the sermons of Odo and Jacques de Vitry. It is hardly surprising that the indulgence was a standing offer in crusade sermons and propaganda letters. St Bernard, trying to interest the English in the Second Crusade, wrote, 'I call blessed the generation that can seize an opportunity of such rich indulgences.' Not only did preachers promise indulgences, they told little stories to emphasize their value. A sick man rapt in a vision was shown that the crusade indulgence outweighed all the good things he had done in his entire life, according to one *exempla*-collection. In another well-known tale, a man was locked in an upstairs room by his wife, for fear he would desert her and go off on crusade (Innocent III declared that husbands could do so without their wives' consent). But when he heard the great indulgences offered by the preacher in the village square, he leapt into the crowd from his window and was the first among them to take the cross. The indulgence was not the only spiritual benefit promised to potential crusaders. For example, excommunicates could regain Church membership by battling Moslems; or one might substitute the crusade vow for some other, perhaps less palatable, promise, such as the vow of chastity.

Popes, wise in the ways of the world, also offered more concrete, practical rewards for crusaders, and kings usually assisted in their implementation. These temporal privileges began to appear as early as the First Crusade and were well-developed by the early thirteenth century. Generally speaking, the protection that ordinary pilgrims were supposed to enjoy was augmented for crusaders, all of whom were in theory under papal direction: whoever insulted or injured them insulted or injured the pope. The well-organized crusader double-checking his gear before departure would be wise to obtain a papal or episcopal 'passport', just to make certain that his protected status was recorded in black and white. English crusaders also sought royal assistance, as did the Welsh, like Griffith son of Rutherik to whom King Henry III gave (or sold) a letter of protection and safe-conduct on crusade in 1233. The Church also promised to look after crusaders' lands and families left behind, that is, to put them under the protection of the Apostolic See, to use Clement III's terminology of 1191. Innocent III repeated these guarantees in 1215. In England four years later, the Archbishop of Canterbury wrote to the royal justiciar to remind him of this, and to ask him to restore the lands of a certain crusader which were *sub protectione Dei*. Attorneys could be appointed to administer the property of an absent crusader and to look after the welfare and marriage of his heirs should he die on his holy mission. There were also other inducements. If a man wished to terminate bothersome lawsuits before his departure, the law was speeded up for him. No one could sue him during his absence; this even applied to accusations of homicide. For example, it was suggested that a certain Luke, a constable, may have killed someone unjustly. But since the constable was preparing to go on crusade, according to the anonymous scribal bureaucrat who recorded the case,

> The king, compassionating the pious vow of the said Luke. . . to save him harmless, as far as he can of right, grants that if he or any of his household going to the Holy Land, be charged with the deaths, they shall not be outlawed by reason of their absence, nor suffer any injury of their lands or possessions.

Any accusations were to be lodged with King Henry III, who would look into the matter when the constable returned. Alternatively, attorneys were allowed to prolong lawsuits already begun—an activity in which they have always excelled—by pleading crusader status for the absent defendant. An even greater benefit for many Christians was the suspension of interest payable on debts and an exemption from the crusader taxes that non-crusaders had to pay. Naturally there were complaints that some took the cross just to enjoy these privileges, having no intention of going off to risk their necks in some sandy waste.

There were many reasons for going on crusade in addition to spiritual and temporal perquisites and the millenarian dreams whipped up among certain classes by roving enthusiasts. Some men were involuntary members of these armed expeditions, for instance, having been sent there as penance for their sins. An obvious example is King Henry II: as part of the price of his implication in Becket's murder in 1170, he was to support 200 knights for a year in the Levant, and to serve on crusade for three years. Henry, defending his lands from his wife, his sons and the French king, understandably never went. But seventeen years later, the money he had sent was used (unavailingly) to bolster the Christian forces in the face of a new threat from Saladin. By the thirteenth century the enforced crusade or its equivalent was a customary penance. In 1291, for example, John Cleymund of Boston whacked a local priest not once but twice across the tonsured pate with his sword, causing bruises but no bloodshed. For this outrage he was to finance a suitable warrior on the next expedition. In a more serious case, a London cleric involved in the murder of Bishop Stapleton of Exeter was ordered, in 1329, personally to go on the next crusade (*cum fuerit generale passagium personaliter . . . transeat ultra mare*).

The old concept of a penitential pilgrimage was therefore easily extended to the penitential crusade. There were, however, some who went on crusade whom the Church would have preferred to see remain at home. Take this assorted unsavoury bunch, for instance, the

> criminals and pestilent men, wicked and impious, sacrilegious, thieves and robbers, homicides, parricides, perjurers, adulterers, and traitors, pirates, whore-mongers, drunkards, minstrels, dice-players, mimes and actors, apostate monks, nuns that are common harlots, and women who have left their husbands to live in brothels, or men who have run away from their true wives and taken others in their stead.

Such wicked people, Jacques de Vitry lamented, crossed the Mediterranean to take refuge in the Holy Land, only to continue plying their nefarious trades and committing their horrible sins. This was a thirteenth-century criticism, but the problem was hardly novel. During a recruitment campaign at Regensburg in 1147, the historian Otto of Freising—who was there—noted somewhat naively how 'so great a throng of highwaymen and robbers (strange to say) came hurrying forward' to take the cross. Some forty years later, on the Archbishop of Canterbury's Welsh tour, Gerald of Wales observed that some of the most notorious criminals of the area, highwaymen, robbers and murderers, were among the volunteers. There is probably some justification in questioning the sincerity of such people, though a few among them may truly have seen the crusade as a means to wipe away their crimes. The uncharitable, but perhaps more realistic, view is that such people saw the Holy Land and all lands en route as new fields in which to ply their trades, fresh pickings courtesy of the Church. Certainly the behaviour of even some of the crusade leaders suggests this. Stephen of Blois wrote to his wife from Antioch in 1098 that he had gained twice as much silver, gold and other riches as he had started out with; at the fall of Antioch, the crusade leaders boasted to the pope that they had killed the city tyrant and his soldiers, but had kept their wives, children, servants, gold, silver and all other goods. An often-quoted passage from the anonymous *Gesta* sums up this attitude: 'Let us all unite in Christ's faith and the victory of the Holy Cross, for, God willing, today we shall all be made rich.' Anna Comnena, writing her famous description of the western barbarians of the First Crusade, claimed that the simple folk were sincere, whereas the leaders were villains out to capture Constantinople itself. Alongside these motives which reflect the seamier side of the crusade, one can as easily cite examples of unselfish devotion to the cause, a willingness to give one's life for the recovery of Jerusalem. As one Moslem historian wrote of the Third Crusade,

> A Frankish prisoner told me that he was his mother's only son, and their house was their sole possession, but she had sold it and used the money . . . to equip him to go and free Jerusalem. There he had been taken prisoner. Such were the religious and personal motives that drove the Franks on.

Whatever his motives may have been, the action which 'made' a crusader was the taking of a vow. Though few reliable texts of the vow itself have survived, it seems to have involved a promise to visit the Holy Sepulchre in Jerusalem as a member of a general, armed expedition. Once made, the vow was to be discharged, or the defaulter was liable to ecclesiastical or even supernatural punishment. It was a common motif in medieval hagiography that a broken vow of pilgrimage to a saint's shrine was punished in some ghostly manner by the offended saint. Broken crusade vows were often punished in a more direct way. As the Patriarch of Jerusalem wrote in 1098, 'Those especially who have made the vow' were to come to the aid of the Holy Land; 'unless they come and discharge their vows', he warned, they were to be excommunicated and utterly removed 'from the Communion of the Church'. A year later the Archbishop of Rheims said the same in regard to 'all who vowed to go on the expedition and took the sign of the cross upon themselves'. By the twelfth century, surveys were being carried out to discover who had taken but not fulfilled his crusading vow. The 'taking of the cross' was another act, linked to the vow, distinguishing crusaders from ordinary pilgrims. At first this seems to have been something of a makeshift ceremony, although even during the First Crusade the opinion apparently developed that those going to the Holy Land should wear the crosses on their breast but, when returning, on their back. This, however, never became a rule. Bernard of Clairvaux, after running out of prefabricated crosses, cut up his own clothing to make crosses for volunteers for the Second Crusade. In the Third Crusade, in Wales, a local prince burst into tears upon seeing the threadbare cloak of one of his followers, when the cross was about to be sewn on. During this crusade each participating 'nation' wore a cross of a different colour.

By this time, too, more decorous ceremonies had evolved around the rite of taking the cross. These rituals probably developed from the

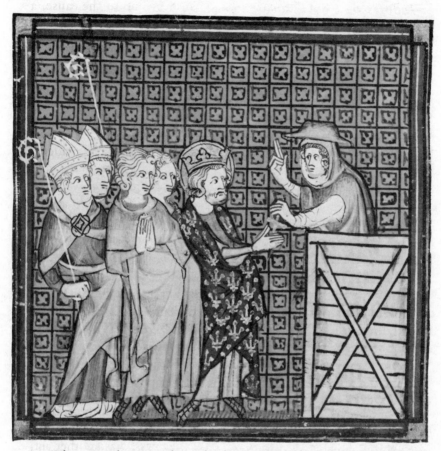

3 When crusaders vowed to 'take the cross' and battle the infidel, the expression was no mere metaphor. Cloth crosses were distributed and sewn to their clothing. Here St Louis of France receives his cross for his second, ill-fated, crusade.
(London, Brit. Library *MS Royal 16 G VI*, f.436ᵛ)

blessings of pilgrims' staffs and scrips. In an English ceremony, the cloak with the cross sewn on was handed over to the crusader to the accompaniment of appropriate prayers. In a continental service, the crusaders prostrated themselves in the form of a cross in the church while prayers were said over a pile of cloth crosses and cloaks, which were placed near the altar. Then, amidst aspersions of holy water and fumes of incense, the crosses were sewn to the cloaks while an antiphon extolling the virtues of the anti-diabolic badge was sung. Such procedures were not dramatic enough for a few crusaders, however, for it was said that some among the common people—including women—cut crosses into their flesh and kept the wounds fresh by applying herbs. It was also reported that a certain clergyman branded his forehead with the Christian symbol in a fit of enthusiasm, showmanship, or perhaps both. There are other references in crusader tales to these self-inflicted signs of sincerity. There must have been many cases of vows taken while under the influence of the enthusiasm evoked by a convincing preacher, or through other more common means.

> When your head is swimming with wine by the fireplace, you take the cross without a summons. Then you would go to inflict great blows upon the Sultan and his people. . . When you get up in the morning you have changed your talk.

The Church eventually acknowledged such basic human weaknesses, and allowed alternatives to excommunication for non-fulfilment of vows. By the thirteenth century, reluctant crusaders could substitute supposedly better-trained fighters, could commute their vows to other pious works, or go on some other 'crusade' called by popes against their European enemies. Finally, it became relatively easy in the thirteenth and fourteenth centuries simply to buy one's way out through the redemption of one's vow. Papal agents drummed up cash, not crusaders.

This introduces what must have been a troublesome subject, that is, how to afford the trip in the first place and, beyond that, how crusading finances in general were managed. The annihilation of the rabble during the popular crusades of the 1090s proved that the pope's fears were well-grounded: it would take more than zealots with elated souls and twinkling eyes to conquer Jerusalem. The requisite planning, logistical arrangements and military dispositions could only come from the experienced, authoritative leaders of feudal society. But an even more fundamental need was the money to set the huge machine in motion. The participants financed themselves in various ways. For instance, Robert, Duke of Normandy, agreed to part temporarily with his duchy in exchange for 10,000 marks (about £6,000) from his brother, King William II of England. William imposed a tax upon the clergy and laity throughout his realm, the rate based upon an

Anglo-Saxon territorial assessment. English churchmen (and presumably laymen) complained, but paid. Little did they know that their successors would be moaning about crusade taxes for the next 200 years or so. All across Europe, various expedients were put in train by all sorts of people. The Bishop of Piacenza, where the First Crusade may have been suggested to Urban II, borrowed money on a piece of property which later embroiled his diocese in tedious litigation. In the same city a loan raised by a leading citizen was eventually paid off by his son. Up and down the social scale, similar deals must have been arranged between enthusiastic pilgrim-crusaders and stay-at-homes, who preferred to help others. Wealthy princes and kings could rely on their own resources, but there are also indications that crusaders sometimes established confraternities and set up common funds, by which they shared the benefits of their pooled reserves of money. On the Fourth Crusade, too, it seems that wealthier crusaders arranged at least partial financing for the poor, while in the midst of the Fifth Crusade, a dying Italian participant made a will leaving, *inter alia*, one bezant 'to the treasury of the commune of the army'. Naturally, the Church tried to facilitate raising money for active as well as prospective crusaders. For instance, when drumming up support for the Second Crusade, Pope Eugenius III decreed that those who wished to go could mortgage their lands without being hindered by the usual feudal customs and restraints involved in such property transfers.

During the twelfth century, kings and popes attempted to rationalize and expand the basis of crusade funding. King Louis VII, probably responding to a bull from Pope Eugenius III after the fall of Edessa, announced to his clergy and noblemen at Vezelay in 1146 that all who did not take the cross would be asked to provide support for those who did. There was resistance from both clergy and laity in attempts to collect, however. Twenty years later Louis again tried to raise money for the relief of the Holy Land, and interested King Henry II of England in the project. The 1166 rate was set at a percentage of the value of movable property. In England it worked out to 1/40th of the value, payable over a period of five years, for which Henry's subjects living in his continental Angevin lands were also liable. Each contributor was to assess the value of his own goods, then place the appropriate sum in a special strong-box (locked with three keys) kept in his parish church. There also seems to have been some sort of attempt to raise money for the Holy Land by Henry II and Louis's son, Philip II, in 1184–85 with (apparently) disappointing results.

After the battle of Hattin, however, all of western Europe was once again aflame with indignation and promises. In late October 1187, Pope Gregory VIII invited royal participation in what became the Third Crusade. Henry II and his son Richard, and King Philip II, agreed to go. Henry and Philip again levied a tax in their respective realms. In (probably) early December 1187, Henry commanded his bishops to arrange that in every parish, on Christmas Day and the two following days, the laity and clergy of England were to be told to determine the value of their movable goods, along with their incomes, and be ready with 1/10th of that valuation by 2 February 1188. On and after 3 February, they were to bring that tithe to their parish church and deposit it in the presence of their priest, a Templar, a Hospitaller, the rural dean and royal, baronial and episcopal clerks. Should there be doubts about the adequacy of the sum deposited, a jury of four or six (seven in France) local worthies would determine the appropriate sum. Those taking the cross were exempt from this 'Saladin Tithe'. Though there was much indignation all round—in France, Philip II had to give up the attempt to collect it—the tax paid off for Henry. In just one of the main collection centres, Salisbury, nearly £6,000 was deposited. Though Henry's life ended in 1189, not in battle against the Saracens but in the midst of warfare with his own family and Philip II, his government had shown the way towards modern taxation; the Englishmen of 1188, who feared that a precedent might be set in the Saladin Tithe, were right.

The papacy, too, encouraged donations by non-crusaders, sometimes, as in the case of Gregory VIII (d. 1187), promising indulgences for such acts (reinforced by the papacy in 1188). When Archbishop Baldwin went on his Welsh preaching tour, he met the inhabitants of Swansea one morning after Mass. Many took the cross, but one old man claimed to be too infirm to go. He offered to pay a tenth of his goods for one-half of the spiritual benefits, to which Baldwin agreed. After further thought, the old man returned with a second tenth, so that he could gain the entire indulgence. Towards the end of the twelfth century, popes were also imposing contributions for the Holy Land as penances, as in the already-mentioned case of Henry II. In addition, some popes, like Alexander III (d. 1181), were moving towards allowing the redemption of vows to go to the Holy Land by sending a substitute or by offering an equivalent money payment. Gradually this notion of convertibility was not only widely accepted, but in some cases made mandatory. For those who died before going on their promised crusade, the sums they would have spent were to be paid by survivors and heirs; this money could support a trained fighter in the Levant, thus discharging the original vow. The income could also be used for general crusading costs, such as transport and provisions.

Several months after returning to England from the Third Crusade in early 1194, King Richard ordered a general judicial visitation. Among other things, the English justices were to find out who had been signed with the cross but died before starting his Jerusalem journey, who now had his property, and how much of it was left. In Lincolnshire in the later 1190s, such an inquisition took place in the flat and watery marshlands around the Wash. At several villages in the Spalding area, the locals were questioned about their neighbours who had taken but not discharged the crusade vow; the returns of this inquiry provide an intimate picture of crusade fervour (and neglect) in a specific corner of England. It was found, for instance, that John Buchart of Wyberton got as far as southern Italy but was turned back by political disturbances. Fortunately, he had a papal document temporarily excusing him. A few miles down the road at the next village, the young John le Borne claimed that he could not afford to go, having produced a family since taking his vow. The local smith, however, could afford the trip, according to his neighbours; perhaps he had made a few too many enemies in the village, who were now taking their revenge. Yet a few miles farther down the rutted lanes, the inquest turned up Richard son of Turstin, who claimed that he had fulfilled his vow and gone to Jerusalem. Unfortunately, he had no proof of this. The same claim was made at a nearby village by William Swift, which he too could not prove. At Wigtoft, a certain Thomas had produced five children since taking his crusading vow, so naturally he was too poor to go anywhere, let alone Jerusalem. In a village five or six miles away, Hugh of Swineshead made exactly the same excuse, five children and all. Ten miles south of this place, it was discovered that Guido's son Hubert took the cross and set out to aid the Holy Land but was robbed of his travelling-money in southern Italy; he had been at loose ends ever since, making his way back to England. Two miles beyond, at Pinchbeck, lived a certain Hugh. He had taken the vow ten years earlier, but was now too old and poor to live up to it. His neighbour Ulf denied ever taking the cross, though the local priest and other villagers thought otherwise. And so on through one village after another, where the enthusiasm and vows of long ago suddenly returned to haunt would-be Moslem killers. In the early thirteenth century, one preacher in England claimed to have a record of the names of 40,000 people who had taken the crusade vow, a potential gold mine in redemptions: those who had failed to carry out their promises could be fined or otherwise penalized, to the great advantage of the Church.

Papal crusading finances radically changed with the advent of Innocent III (d. 1216), as interested in centralizing and strengthening the papacy as he was in recovering the Holy Land. During and after his reign, overall direction of the crusades was a less emotional, far more business-like affair. Papal hearts would have been warmed by the Moslem historian who claimed that all Franks were under the control of the 'Lord of Rome, who held a very high place in their society, so that they dared not disobey him'. At least his prelates and clergy were expected to obey him. Taking his cues from earlier royal and papal techniques, in 1199 Innocent tried (in *Graves orientalis terrae*) to raise money from the clergy by calling for 1/40th of clerical revenues. He also required weekly sermons on the crusade, to inspire laymen to donate as well; the now familiar triple-locked boxes were to be provided in parish churches that did not already have them. Innocent also designated panels (similar to those established by Henry II for the Saladin Tithe) to assist his prelates in allocating sums to needy crusaders who promised to stay at least a year fighting the infidel. They were to bring written certification of their tours of duty when they returned. The pope made similar demands in 1213 and 1215, by which time he also openly encouraged the redemption of crusading vows by a money payment. In this way, even the unfit were able to take the cross, redeem their vows and thus contribute to the effort and gain the associated indulgence. During the thirteenth century the Church began to treat such vows as a regular source of income, which led to criticism, especially when the income was used for non-crusading purposes. Thirteenth-century popes also encouraged laity and clergy to bequeath legacies to the cause: in 1274 Gregory X directed priests to advise, in the confessional, that this would be pleasing to God. Finally, by this time the penitential pilgrimage and crusade had become far more common, it being understood that the 'sinners' would substitute a financial payment for their penances.

Most of the financial aspects of crusading are well illustrated from thirteenth-century English records. The Lord Edward, having seen the baronial threat posed by Simon de Montfort overcome and the government of his father Henry III re-established, embarked on his crusade in mid-1270. At the parliament of April 1270, the English clergy and laity agreed to donate 1/20th of their revenues towards this project. In May 1270, Henry III reminded the Bishop of Worcester of this agreement and ordered the Sheriff of Worcester to levy the tax by force if necessary. Altogether, about £30,000 was collected. A few years later Pope Gregory X called for a crusade at the Second Council of Lyons. At this meeting, attended by some 300 leaders of the Church—as well as sixteen envoys from the Mongols, then seeking allies against the Moslems—the pope authorized the collection of a tax amounting to 1/10th of clerical incomes. In October 1274, Gregory ordered the two papal collectors in England (there were more than two dozen collection-districts in Europe by then) to gather this tithe. The English team were authorized to hire sub-collectors and to keep the papacy informed. On 1 February 1275, the two wrote to the Archbishop of York and, presumably, to other prelates telling them of the pope's orders. The archbishop, in turn, on 16 February ordered the archdeacons of York province to set up alms-boxes in all the churches so that lay offerings could augment clerical contributions. As part of this fund-raising campaign, during 1275 many 'sinful' clergy and laity of the province were assigned the crusade as a penance, which was then automatically commuted to a cash payment. Among the most common charges directed at village priests was ordination by the wrong bishop. For example, Peter Peper the priest, sent to fight the infidel for this offence, was allowed to pay ½ mark instead of going to the Holy Land, a bargain indeed. Dozens of parish priests thus contributed to the crusade effort, each paying, on average, about five shillings. Some were allowed the choice of actually going or paying a higher fine; some even volunteered to pay more than the average, for the sake of devotion. Laymen, too, were involved. A knight who attacked a priest had a choice of paying or setting off eastwards, as did an excommunicate who had assaulted two priests. A knight who had committed adultery with another knight's wife was signed with the cross and given the choice of going or sending a substitute; furthermore, he was to pay £100 to the crusade fund if he committed the offence again.

Twelfth-century money-raising techniques were thus streamlined during the thirteenth century. Relaxation of feudal tenurial restrictions in land transfers was even encouraged by lay powers: King Henry III in the 1230s granted licences to his subjects to alienate their lands, and when Edward was preparing his crusade another spate of licences was recorded. John Lovel leased his manors of 'Elecumbe, Suthmere,

Dokyng and Tychewell' for ten years to raise money for his journey; Herbert de Boyvill was allowed to sell his manor of 'Terling' to the Bishop of Norwich, William de Detling leased one manor for four years, Eustace de Balliol leased out five manors for four years, so that Edward could be accompanied to the East with a proper retinue. In the later 1280s Edward, now King Edward I, planned another crusade. The papal collectors were to keep the money in English religious houses until the king required it. In late 1291, in the aftermath of Acre's fall, a papal bull of 1281—82 was reissued in London in an attempt to determine what had happened to unrealized funds and undischarged crusaders. Diocesan inquiries were to be made in England about these defaulters, using a format of nineteen standardized interrogatories. Once again, as in the inquiry in Lincolnshire in the later twelfth century, peasants, burghers and even lords were subjected to financial pressures, probing questions. In the end, Edward I was unable to go on crusade because of political problems in western Europe, though the money was spent anyway. But by then Edward could claim to be following papal precedents, for Roman pontiffs had discovered that crusade taxes had a great many other uses. The rule-bending was not all on the side of popes and kings: it was alleged that when rumours of a forthcoming crusade began to spread, some took the cross so that they would be immune from paying the crusader tax. Having escaped under this privilege, they then commuted their vows at a lower rate, saving money and gaining an indulgence at the same time.

By the end of the thirteenth century, the call to crusade seemed to many, both clerical and lay, to be no more than a thinly-disguised way to raise money for both kings and popes for a variety of purposes unconnected with the Near East. This was not entirely untrue, but during the heady days of the First Crusade and throughout most of the twelfth century, men took a less jaundiced view of the great adventure awaiting them in the Holy Land. Though they may have been impelled by a mixture of motives, the 'religious' impulse was still the most visible. Many rushed forward to accept their cloth crosses in the sincere belief that Jerusalem cried out to be liberated from the infidel, that their armed pilgrimage would win them the blessings of the Church in this life and the companionship of the saints in the next. Having made their vows, having put on the holy emblem and set their affairs in order, they faced the first of many hazards to come, the journey.

3

The Journey

A dead horse sold for more by far
Than any living steed of war.
They found it all pleasing to the taste,
Even ate entrails, naught did waste.

(Ambroise)

When the ageing Byzantine princess, Anna Comnena, looked back over her father's reign, one of her sharpest memories was of the western rabble arriving at the gates of Constantinople on the First Crusade. At the time, Ekkehard of Aura noticed that most of these miserable, poor creatures passing through Germany were encumbered with wives, children and all their household effects. Like the impoverished farmers of middle America, beaten by famine and the 1930s Depression who migrated to the golden west with all their earthly goods piled on clattering Fords, these medieval have-nots followed their wandering preachers towards an eastern Promised Land. Popes never encouraged this sort of migration, preferring the less zealous but more efficient leadership of the nobility (who actually could afford to take their families) and participation by well-equipped fighting men rather than the motley, desperate crowds. Yet it was difficult to prevent anyone from going and, on the First Crusade at least, the very young, the very old, and women accompanied the crusaders and died with them.

Nevertheless, it was thought to be a man's business to bear arms, a woman's to stay behind and tend the land and family. It is said that when news of Saladin's conquest of Jerusalem reached the West, 'wives urged their husbands, mothers their sons, to devote themselves' to the recovery of the holy city, regretting the weakness of their sex which prevented them from going in person. Usually, however, it is not this Amazonian attitude which chroniclers mention, but the opposite, seemingly more natural ones of regret and sorrow at parting. 'He commended her to the Lord, kissed her lingeringly, and promised her as she wept that he would return.' So wrote a man who went on the First Crusade. This all-too-familiar scene would have taken place in countless villages and towns of Europe in every crusade. According to

Ambroise, when Richard of England led his hopeful heroes through Tours for the Third Crusade, they left behind them many weeping damsels. By the thirteenth century, the theme of sorrow at departures for overseas, *Outremer*, was common in both story and song. The motif of the crusader indulging himself in long, tearful farewells, to make his journey even more difficult and, therefore, more praiseworthy, is found in half-a-dozen collections of thirteenth-century tales. But more poignant are the love songs lamenting what might become a permanent absence:

> If my body goes to serve our Lord, my heart remains faithful to her:
> May God grant me grace to rise so high that I might hold her naked in
> my arms before I go overseas.

Then as now, men suffered even more acutely the pangs of separation when alone in strange lands:

> A hundred times a night I shall recall your beauty:
> It gave me such pleasure to hold your body!
> When I no longer have it I shall die of desire.

> Good Lord God. . . grant her the strength to love me,
> So that she will not forget me in my long absence,
> For I love her more than anything in the world
> And I feel so sad about her that my heart is breaking.

But the women left behind also had reason to weep for their men gone to war:

> O, when they cry 'Overseas', dear God, help the pilgrim for whom I
> tremble, for the Saracens are bad.

Though, as Georges Duby suggests, the eleventh century was an age of departure, this was little consolation to such women. But one need not rely only on the emotional media of song and lore. That bountiful source of information on the Fourth Crusade, Villehardouin, wrote that when the crusaders began to leave,

> Many a tear, as you may well imagine, was shed for sorrow at parting
> from their lands, their own people, and their friends.

By mid-century Joinville himself, preparing to accompany his lord, King Louis IX, on crusade to Egypt, received his pilgrim's staff and scrip and left his castle on foot for *Outremer*.

> And all the way to Blécourt and Saint-Urbain I never once let my

eyes turn back towards Joinville, for fear my heart might be filled
with longing at the thought of my lovely castle and the two children I
had left behind.

On the other hand, it cannot be denied that many men probably
welcomed the crusade as an excellent opportunity to escape the bonds
of matrimony. In Wales, while drumming up support for the Third
Crusade, Gerald claimed that some were so eager to join that they 'left
their cloaks behind in the hands of wives and friends who had tried to
hold them back'.

Whether reluctantly or gladly leaving their sorrowing women
behind or whether taking them along, all crusaders were confronted
with the basic problem of getting to the Holy Land. By the First
Crusade, so many pilgrims had visited the Holy Land that customary
routes were more or less established, though these were sometimes
interrupted by political upheavals. For instance, after the Turks moved
into Anatolia in the 1070s, the flow of pilgrims across that region,
though not blocked, was certainly less smooth. The choice of route
depended not only on current politics, but also on the goals set by
crusade leaders. Some took the direct sea passage to Levantine ports,
while others led their followers overland through the kingdom of
Hungary, then into Byzantine territory. Some, like St Louis of France,
attempted a flanking operation and set out for Egypt. The contingents
of the First Crusade, as noted earlier, followed a variety of routes.
Though there were two waves of marchers in 1096 and 1097, the first
made up of enthusiastic but badly-controlled hordes, then the official
second wave, the goal of both sections was Constantinople, where they
would cross into Anatolia—Moslem territory. At this famous, wealthy
city, a shocked Emperor Alexius, exposed to two extremes of western
society, gladly sent them all off to the enemy. After the first crusaders
had established themselves in Levantine coastal cities, later expeditions
generally favoured the sea routes, though land approaches were still
used. Pisa, Genoa and especially Venice grew rich, envious and
mutually hostile. They battled fiercely for trading privileges in
near-eastern Christian cities and for the lucrative business of
transporting pilgrims and crusaders. There was also a brisk trade in
goods to and from Moslem ports, and in particular Egypt, in spite of
papal invective condemning such dealings with the infidel.

The time required to reach the Holy Land depended upon many
factors: the route itself, the nature and number of the crusaders, the
weather, hostile or friendly action from Moslems and Christians en

4 General view of the Holy Land, with coastal cities, Jerusalem and (top) the
Dead Sea. Bethlehem is shown to the upper right of Jerusalem.
(London, Brit. Library *MS Royal 14 c VII*, f. 5ᴿ)

route, understanding of the geography of the region. For instance, one party among the first crusaders, who left northern France in September or October 1096, arrived in southern Italy by early December but were held up there by winter weather. On 5 April 1097, they set out on the Adriatic from Brindisi, headed for Durazzo about 100 miles away. They arrived on 9 April and began the march to Constantinople, which they reached on 14 May 1097, a total time of some seven or eight months. Another contingent in the First Crusade laboured seven weeks to cover slightly more than 100 miles of wild Balkan terrain during the winter. The actual daily marching-rate of two groups in the First Crusade has been computed at 15.5 and 17.7 miles. Besides difficult terrain, there were a variety of extraordinary diversions. Richard I's fleet, for example (he himself went by land to southern Italy), left England in late March 1190, but did not arrive in Sicily until 14 September, having stopped along the way to attack the Moors at Lisbon. The king then tarried more than six months in Sicily (1190–91), held back by winter weather as well as political intrigue. Finally, he spent a month subduing a petty tyrant of Cyprus on his way to Acre, which he reached at last in early June 1191.

Though some rash crusaders continued their march despite winter snows, most sea-borne expeditions wisely waited for the spring. In fact, one fourteenth-century writer even believed that the storms of winter halted all sea traffic completely. Although this was an exaggeration, those who did venture out on winter seas not only risked their lives, but also spent perhaps twice as much time getting to the east. Crusader fleets usually were composed of a variety of types of ships. When Richard I finally left Messina in the spring of 1191, he and the other nobles travelled in thirty-nine galleys—fast, sleek, sail-assisted warships propelled by rowers. This fleet also included two dozen larger and slower transports, together with some 150 additional vessels. The king's galley led the way, carrying a lantern visible to the other captains, since they sailed both day and night. The eight major sections of the fleet were to stay within trumpet-blast of each other, with individual ships remaining within shouting range of one another. Despite all these precautions, two dozen ships were lost in storms.

The crusades generally stimulated improvements in ship design and navigation. For example, by the fourteenth century, a medieval passenger liner, the 'great galley' of Venice and Genoa, with more space for pilgrims and cargo, was developed. Some of these ships could carry a thousand or more passengers. In addition, the need to transport knights and their valuable horses led to an increased demand for the *usciere*, a name derived from the doors in the stern through which horses were loaded and off-loaded. Villehardouin, arranging transport for the Fourth Crusade, says that the Venetians agreed to provide these '*vuissiers*' for 4,5000 horses and 9,000 squires, along with other vessels for 4,500 knights and 20,000 foot-soldiers, all escorted by fifty armed galleys. During the mid-thirteenth century, Joinville described how a portside door could be opened so that horses could be led directly into the hold of the ship. The door was then carefully caulked, since it was normally below the water-line. When everything was ready, Joinville continued, the captain had the clergy sing a hymn, after which he commanded his crew to unfurl the sails in the name of God and set out on their way. Before undertaking what proved to be his last crusade (of 1270), King Louis IX ordered from the Venetians and Genoese 120 *usciere*, which were to be an average of twenty-five metres long and six broad, with two masts and two complete decks.

Though Louis required suitable cabins for the more important passengers, life aboard such vessels must have been unpleasant even by medieval standards. However, there were occasional exceptions. In 1113, Adelaide of Sicily set out for the Holy Land to join her future husband, King Baldwin of Jerusalem. She lounged about on cloth of gold; her galley sported a silver-and gold-plated prow and enjoyed the protection of two escorting, armed galleys. Seven additional ships were loaded with the riches that made up her dowry. Usually, however, until they were once again on land, even the crusading nobility had to endure Spartan conditions in the midst of an unknown, sometimes terrifying world. Though Villehardouin acquaints us with a crusading nobleman who died and was buried at sea, the hazards of sea travel must have resulted in many less important, unrecorded, deaths and burials in the deep.

Although they may seem incredible now, legends and superstitions amplified the danger and mystery of the sea for contemporaries. For instance, it was believed that a certain ferocious fish, which attacked small ships, could only be frightened away 'by the sight of a man's angry and terrible face'. The *modus operandi* required confronting this monster at water level with a 'bold and terrible countenance'; but care had to be taken, since it could spot a bluff. If the glowering sailor showed any sign of fear, the fish promptly began to chew up the ship. One intrepid seaman lowered himself from his ship on a rope in order to show an angry face at such a fish, 'as is the custom'. Unfortunately, he grew frightened, his scowl slipped, and the fish bit him in half. Behind such ludicrous tales there was a real fear of the sea, especially among those crusaders for whom perhaps the greatest body of water they had ever seen was the village fishpond fed by a mossy brook. They reacted like certain children who are horrified at the mere sight of the vast and uncompromising sea. Humbert of Romans, a thirteenth-century Dominican, recognized that ocean-terror was a real obstacle to crusade recruitment. A century earlier, during the First Crusade, the chaplain to the Count of Toulouse wrote with mixed admiration and disbelief of the English as 'men who dared to sail through the strange and vast surface of the Mediterranean and the Ocean out of love of crusading'. When, during this same crusade, 400 men and women drowned after their ship sank off Brindisi, many crusaders who witnessed this tragedy turned around and went home at once, swearing never again to entrust themselves to the treacherous sea. Fear of the sea was not restricted to ordinary western Christians, for many Moslems shared this horror. When Saladin claimed that he would battle the Franks even if he must take to the sea, his admiring secretary-biographer wrote this down as yet another instance of his wonderful bravery. After his capture in Egypt, King Louis of France joked with his Moslem captor about the near-idiocy of anyone who entrusted his life to the sea; we Moslems, said the Egyptian, do not let such people give evidence in our courts, for they obviously lack plain sense.

Of course, there were obvious reasons to fear the sea quite apart from the possible danger of foundering in a storm or the irrational terror of empty wastes of water. Lion-hearted Richard was susceptible to sea-sickness, for instance. He must truly have wished himself back in his beloved Aquitaine, when his fleet ran into a storm after leaving Messina. In the words of one of the passengers, words all too familiar to those who have made many channel crossings, 'men's stomachs began to feel a qualm and were affected by a violent nausea; and this feeling of sickness made them almost insensible to the dangers around'. A fifteenth-century Dominican named Felix, who twice went to Jerusalem, left a colourful account of his travels. He once made a list of fifteen reasons why the sacrament of holy communion was not celebrated on a ship, ending with 'because of the ease and suddenness with which men vomit there'. It would be horrible if the Body of Christ, subjected to such a fate, ended up floating in bilge or in the sea. Life below deck in these bobbing little buckets was hardly comfortable for pilgrims trying to sleep on a section of plank marked out in chalk, amidst gabbling chickens and spewing companions. One pastime was drinking wine, Felix reports; another was the daily 'hunting and catching of lice and vermin', an activity which must have given everybody something to do. In addition, the rowers were thieves, there was pitch everywhere one sat, and passengers talked all night or snored. Felix once saw the lights of chattering, insomniac pilgrims doused by the contents of a chamberpot hurled by an irate bedfellow. In such hellish circumstances, tempers were easily frayed, angry words and blows were exchanged. Lest God punish the whole ship for such impious behaviour in these holy enterprises, rules and regulations—with more than a tinge of religious overtones—were established early on. Riley-Smith provides a translation of the first surviving example

5 The sea route was favoured in later crusading expeditions. Ships could be fitted with special doors in the hull for quick off-loading of men and horses. (London, Brit. Library *MS Royal 16 6 VII*, f. 409ᵛ)

(mid-twelfth century) in which each ship is likened to a parish, with its own priest and religious observances. There are harsh, eye-for-eye penalties, while the temptations to sin are curbed by sumptuary rules and the restriction of women to quarters. About forty years later, England's Richard I ordained that whoever sailed in his ships on crusade would lose a hand for drawing a knife on someone and be ducked three times for fist-fighting; thieves would be tarred, feathered and cast ashore; a murderer would either be tied to his victim and dumped overboard or buried alive.

Another danger, aside from piracy—always a threat, even from fellow Christians—was the possibility of capture as a result of shipwreck. During Richard's voyage to the Holy Land, two of his ships were washed up on Cyprus. This calamitous event was compounded when the survivors were arrested by the local tyrant, Isaac Comnenus. Isaac, who lorded it over his small domain in the belief that he was the Emperor (Byzantium already had one), hated Latins to the point of even allying with Saladin. When Richard arrived and asked for the return of his men, Isaac characteristically insulted the envoy and refused to discuss the matter. This left the king little choice: he attacked and, within a month, the King of England was also master of Cyprus, which was of great strategic value for future crusading ventures. Though this story of shipwreck had a fortunate ending for Richard, on his way back from the crusade another shipwreck ultimately put him into the hands of his enemy, the Holy Roman Emperor.

Although the difficulties and dangers of the sea route to the Holy Land were real enough, land-bound crusaders had their own problems, which were only slightly alleviated by songs sung along the way, such as 'Wonderful Jerusalem'. Roads were practically impassable in wet weather, for example, and bridges were continually collapsing. Some participants in the Third Crusade were lost when a wooden bridge over the Rhone fell, and in Yorkshire the money (nearly £18) found on some thirteenth-century crusaders, drowned when a bridge gave way, was aptly used for the repair of the offending structure. The practice of fording also hurried many unwary or unlucky crusaders to an unexpected martyrdom, as on the First Crusade, when many people were swept away while trying to wade across a river; the local Bulgars had good reason to call it the 'Demon' river. Even great men fell victim to the powers of nature, for the Emperor Frederick Barbarossa drowned in a river as he led his German host to Jerusalem on the Third Crusade. Other dangers were attributable to man's inhumanity to man. In some cases, crusaders starved because local eastern Christians refused to sell them food. Robbery was another scourge of the pilgrim-and-crusader trails, as a bishop of Norwich found out in the twelfth century, when he was relieved of his money while travelling through Burgundy on his way to combat Saladin. At least he avoided ending up in one of the many cemeteries where his predecessors 'were buried along the footpaths, on the plains, and in the woods'.

Bands of Jerusalem-bound crusaders often created their own problems. The violent and desperate mobs who made up the 'popular front' in the first crusading movement generated retribution and brought disrepute upon later crusaders in various ways. Not content with slaughtering Jews, they also attacked the Christians of eastern Europe as they passed through the kingdom of Hungary, and ravaged Byzantine territories as well. The rabble following Gottschalk, for example, included some Bavarians and Swabians, who went on a drunken, pillaging rampage. When they went so far as to spear a Hungarian youth his countrymen were outraged and the plain of Belgrade was soon filled with the bodies of fellow-Christians. Peter the Hermit's so-called army was attacked by the Bulgars after some German crusaders burnt down seven mills outside Nish. The atrocities multiplied: about 150 men in the group following Walter the Penniless were burnt alive by Bulgars in response to their cattle-rustling, while Peter the Hermit's band was said to have killed about 4,000 Hungarians at Semlin, an unreliable figure which in medieval terms means a great many people. As a result of such rapine, the King of Hungary and the Byzantine Emperor, who had originally provided the Christian newcomers with markets and a safe-conduct, began to regret giving support to such a rabble. Consequently, the later official crusade parties led by noblemen had to regain the confidence of their outraged hosts and co-religionists, a challenge they never seem fully to have met. As William of Tyre wrote, those who arrived in the wake of the rabble were 'put to great trouble to conciliate the favour of the King of Hungary'. It is not surprising that Bulgars refused to trade with Bohemond's group, for 'they feared us greatly, thinking that we came not as pilgrims, but to devastate their land and to kill them. Wherefore'—here the writer is oblivious to the irony of his words—'we took their cattle, horses, asses, and everything that we found.' Raymond of Toulouse's followers had similar problems in eastern Europe. The local population refused to trade with them or to furnish them with guides. Instead, they lay in wait for old and weak crusaders who had dropped behind the main armed body, and butchered them like cattle. Assuming that the crusaders reached Constantinople, even there they encountered supply problems. Godfrey of Bouillon was obliged to make several appearances before the emperor to complain about the high price of food.

Although these examples come from the First Crusade, the rivalry between Roman Christians and Greek Christians plagued later crusades as well, and culminated in the conquest of Constantinople itself. The controversies between the Greek and Roman worlds extended over many centuries and, in a sense, the crusades only served to aggravate and emphasize those differences. Fortunately for historians, the conflict is openly expressed by contemporary writers. For instance, the anonymous author of *Gesta francorum*, a participant in the First Crusade, described the Byzantine Emperor Alexius as a wretch, guilty of 'fraud and cunning', even a fool 'as well as a knave'. It is true that some Byzantine Emperors did assist the Moslems, when it was politically expedient to do so. The abrasive relations between Greeks and Latins are also illustrated in the Second Crusade, when the Greeks, 'tainted with perjury' as one westerner wrote, 'shut up their cities and fortresses and sent their merchandise down to us on ropes suspended from the walls'. Naturally, this forced the crusaders to plunder the countryside and local villages for their food, setting the whole vicious cycle in motion again. Constantinople itself was unflatteringly described as

> rather squalid and smelly and many places are afflicted with perpetual darkness. The rich build their houses so as to overhang the streets and leave these dark and dirty places for travellers and for the poor. Life in this city is lawless. . .

The cleric who recorded that passage also described an incident in a tavern outside the wall of Philippopolis (now Plovdiv in central Bulgaria), which illustrates yet another aspect of the cultural differences between eastern and western Europeans. While some Germans were heartily imbibing their wine and presumably enjoying themselves, a local man came into the tavern and joined them. Though he could not speak their language, after several rounds of drink he decided to entertain the company and produced a pet snake from his pocket. It nestled in his wine glass and performed other tricks. The drunken Germans, horrified and apparently unused to the sight of a snake-charmer, leapt at the unfortunate exhibitionist and tore him to pieces. In their sodden state, they had thought he was trying to poison them. The outcome was a riot in the suburbs of Philippopolis, which resulted in the death of many Greeks and Germans, good Christians all. By the Third Crusade, east–west Christian relations had not improved. Even in Sicily, the followers of King Richard found it necessary to battle the 'villainous' Greeks, who reportedly cheated and

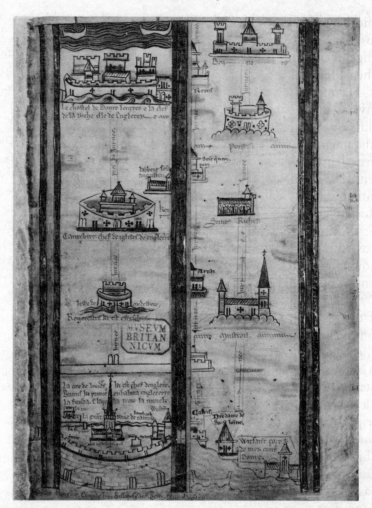

6 Descriptions of routes to Jerusalem became more abundant as pilgrimage
increased. This itinerary shows the English traveller the stages in his journey,
from London (lower left, with St Paul's the central feature) to Rochester,
Canterbury, then Dover, 'key to the rich island of England'. After the
channel, the journey resumes at Boulogne or Calais.
(London, Brit. Library *MS Royal 14 c VII*, f. 2ᴿ)

even killed crusaders, then tossed their bodies down privies. After the
battle of Messina, Richard was able to impose order,

> And there were women taken, fair
> And excellent and debonair.

Another Third Crusade leader, Frederick Barbarossa, met with hostility from Serbian and Bulgarian brigands. The Emperor Isaac Angelus even threw Barbarossa's envoys into prison, but backed down when Frederick began to arrange a crusade against Constantinople.

Having suffered the perils of dangerous seas, inflated prices and physical attack, the crusaders at last arrived in the Holy Land by one route or another. However, even more crushing problems ensued. A fundamental issue confronting crusade leaders was how to get to Jerusalem. Guide-books were useful in a limited way, but they were neither written with mass armed migrations in mind, nor—at least until the later Middle Ages—did they make sufficient allowance for the Moslem habit of cutting off Christian heads in times of hostility. The First Crusade was a land-bound attack. The various parties involved crossed into Anatolia and then, taking a south-easterly line across the mountains and deserts of that inhospitable land, they headed into what is now Syria, the Lebanon and Israel, and finally reached Jerusalem in 1099. The route, carved out by the Byzantines before they lost control of the area, was modified according to the needs of each crusader contingent. Sometimes western perseverance held sway. For instance, when a group of 3,000 men were sent ahead as pathfinders on the way to Nicaea, they literally staked out a route for the others with crosses of metal and wood set up on poles. However, it also was not unusual to ask the natives for assistance: some crusade leaders wandering around Tripoli, for example, had to ask the locals about the best and easiest route to Jerusalem. Although they naturally depended on local Christians for such information, crusaders even followed Moslem guides who had deserted their own side or been captured. Of course, it was risky to trust such a person in this important matter, as both Conrad of Germany and France's Louis VII discovered during the abortive Second Crusade. Their guides seem deliberately to have misled them along a route that took them past the bleached bones of other crusaders, who had travelled that way a few months earlier. It does seem odd, in any case, that as late as 1148, a crusader army in southern Anatolia ended up 'wandering now here, now there, without knowledge of the locality', as William of Tyre reports.

Apart from the risk of getting lost, crusaders were also subjected to many dangers of a harsh, sometimes brutal, environment. Although there is evidence of changes in European climate around AD 1300, it can probably be assumed that modern readings for maximum temperatures in east and west are indicative of the magnitude of temperature differences experienced by crusaders. (The temperature during the hottest month of the year at four European cities—London, Paris, Cologne, and Vienna—is on average nearly eleven degrees Fahrenheit less than the hottest month in Constantinople (Istanbul), Beirut and Jerusalem). Heat and thirst were among the crusaders' worst enemies. Before the bands led by Peter the Hermit were destroyed in Anatolia, they suffered the consequences of their premature departure for the Holy Land and this climatic shock:

> They bled their horses and asses and drank the blood; others let down belts and clothes into a sewer and squeezed out the liquid into their mouths; others passed water into one another's cupped hands and drank; others dug up damp earth and lay down.

Another chronicler of the First Crusade recorded that over 500 men and women died in Anatolia 'overcome by the double distress of intolerable thirst and extreme heat'; pregnant women collapsed by the road to give birth prematurely. Even after the first crusaders reached their goal, they continued to suffer. The Moslem governor of Jerusalem had, very sensibly, blocked or polluted the water supplies outside the walls, leaving only the pool of Siloam, which was dangerously near the city, and other sources five or six miles away. So great was the crush at the pool that crusaders 'pushed one another into it. . . And so when the pool was filled with the crowd and with the bodies of dead animals, the stronger, even at the price of death, forced their way forward to try to slake their thirst'. Sick pilgrims, with swollen tongues and outstretched hands, were left to beg for water on the fringes of the mêlée. Whoever succeeded in bringing water back to the camp could charge any price he wished for the precious fluid. Men died from thirst, as did the animals, the stench of rotting carcases pervading the camp. A pilgrim who landed in the Holy Land in 1102 put the case succinctly: 'Many are cut off by the Saracens, but more by heat and thirst. . . ' Crusaders suffered almost as much from the effects of damp winter weather. Even at Constantinople, Godfrey of Bouillon's men had to endure violent rainstorms, cold and snow, according to William of Tyre. (Again, a comparison of modern climatic differences may help to illustrate this: Beirut, for instance, receives more than three times the winter precipitation of Cologne or even London.) A participant in the First Crusade described how those without tents died in the freezing rains, while in the Third Crusade it was said that the Christians were beaten down by rain and hail: their soaked food rotted; their hauberks—coats of mail—rusted; their clothing disintegrated; their horses and pack animals fell ill and collapsed in the mud. This passage touches on yet another great worry facing all crusaders—the well-being of the livestock. E. Coquet (*Riding to Jerusalem*, 1978) discovered the difficulties facing even modern pilgrims trying to keep their horses in good health on the long, hard journey from France to the Holy Land. A First Crusader experienced mixed reactions when viewing the curious results of the loss of these animals. He could see horseless knights suddenly demoted to the foot-weary ranks, or even perched on the backs of lumbering oxen. In place of their defunct pack-animals, crusaders loaded their goods—clothing, food, equipment—onto goats, rams, dogs, even sows. On another occasion during the First Crusade, on a trek over Anatolian mountain passes, whole strings of baggage animals fell to oblivion from paths made muddy and slippery by the rains. Some of the knights, shuffling about wringing their hands in fear and misery, sold or threw away the heavy armour that encumbered them. The animals were also the first to go when food was scarce. While Barbarossa was on his way to the Third Crusade, the death of his animals caused him to abandon much of his baggage, armour and arms, burning them to prevent the Moslems from using them. His knights, in an attempt to make the best of a bad situation, broke up their lances for firewood, then cooked and ate their horses.

Extreme weather, thirst and exhaustion naturally made crusaders susceptible to a variety of diseases, like dysentery. A twelfth-century Arab historian even claimed that it was 'a disease to be feared and one from which its victim scarcely ever recovers'. One famous victim who did recover was the King of France, St Louis. On the Sixth Crusade in Egypt, his dysentery obliged him to use the privy so often that the lower part of his drawers was cut away to simplify things. There are indications, too, of more serious, epidemic diseases, like the 'pestilence' which is said to have killed 1,500 crusaders from Regensburg after they landed at Antioch's port, St Simeon, in 1098. Another widespread ailment was scurvy. Though it is likely that this was an almost annual affliction throughout Europe, as vitamin-rich foodstuffs were depleted during the winter, its effects were exacerbated in crusade-camp conditions. During the Third Crusade, the victims coughed and spoke hoarsely, and then their teeth began falling out; on the disastrous Sixth Crusade of St Louis, the men's skin turned livid, their gums became gangrenous, and there was haemorrhaging from the nose. Barber-surgeons went about cutting away swollen, rotted gums so that the men could try to eat. Joinville heard the screams resound throughout the camp 'just like the cry of a woman in labour'. Scurvy was a problem because most crusaders' diets were not balanced, to say the least. The sufferers described by Joinville, for example, had only eels for fresh food. Even so, they fared better than many others, who had little or no food at all.

The spectre of famine began to haunt the First Crusade at the very first important victory in Turkish territory, the capture of Nicaea just across the Sea of Marmora from Constantinople. The poorer classes especially, who could not afford the high food prices, 'starved to death for Christ's name'. No doubt it was some consolation to them that 'their souls were triumphantly carried to heaven', where they received their martyrs' robes and where food was immaterial anyway. Conditions worsened when the crusaders moved south and besieged the key city of Antioch from October 1097 to June 1098. Like Old Testament locusts, the Christians picked the surrounding countryside clean. They were soon reduced to meals of beanseeds, weeds, thistles which pricked the tongue, dead horses, asses, camels, dogs and rats. The poor, according to Fulcher, were forced to make do with animal skins, which they made into a kind of soup, and the bits of grain they managed to tease from animal dung. After taking possession of Antioch, the unfortunate crusaders were besieged in their turn, and food was even more scarce. The contemporary Christian sources vie with each other in reporting outlandishly high prices: horse's head (complete with tongue) at two or three shillings, goat's guts for five, a cock for eight to nine shillings, a hen fifteen; an egg two shillings, a walnut one penny—which was what three or four beans cost. Ram's tail went for three to nine pence whereas camel tongue brought four shillings. Back home in Normandy, many crusaders must have reminded each other, a cow with its calf cost around four shillings. The trapped crusaders boiled fig leaves, vines or bark, while some of the knights stayed alive by sucking blood from their horses. Even rotting animals that had escaped the cooking pot the first time around were dug up and eaten. A Moslem historian with an eye for social distinctions noted that 'the wealthy ate their horses and the poor ate carrion and leaves from the trees'. Finally, in a letter to Pope Paschal II (d. 1118), crusade leaders reported that at Antioch 'some could scarcely refrain from eating human flesh', and in later sieges the 'Christian people now ate the putrid bodies of the Saracens'. The letter probably refers to the siege of Maarat an-Numan, south-east of

Antioch, which the crusaders attacked in the winter of 1098–99. The men

> cut pieces of flesh from the buttocks of Saracens lying there dead.
> These pieces they cooked and ate, savagely devouring the flesh while
> it was insufficiently roasted.

According to another crusader, the spectacle of fellow-Christian eating rotten Saracens so horrified some that they left the crusading host in disgust. The Moslems were quick to seize upon such incidents as further evidence of Christian depravity. This cannibalism, as will be shown, may have had a ritualistic aspect to it as well.

The same horrors accompanied subsequent expeditions. At the siege of Acre in the Third Crusade, once again the scarcity of food drove prices to incredibly high levels—in one account a one-penny loaf was said to have cost sixty shillings, though such figures no doubt owe as much to literary as to economic inflation. Starvation reduced once-proud men of gentle birth to dire straits, forcing even them to eat grass wherever they could find it. War-horses were far more valuable dead than alive: attentive crowds watched as the animal was flayed, prepared to pay high prices for a good slice; even the entrails were eaten. Later on, King Richard tried to help those too poor to pay for horsemeat by promising to give a live horse to anyone who freely donated his dead steed to his men. So the foot-soldiers

> Flayed them with a will
> And of the good parts ate their fill.

Finally, in another tale from the siege of Acre, a foot-soldier who had purchased thirteen beans discovered that one of them was rotten. He was said to have walked across a seven-acre field to return it to the vendor in exchange for a good one. On the Fourth Crusade, once again one finds the men who were besieging Constantinople reduced to the necessity of eating their horses as the only food source. After an invasion of Egypt (the Fifth Crusade), the Christians surrendered in order 'that we might be filled with bread'. Not the enemy, but lack of food and the flooding Nile, a participant averred, brought defeat to the crusaders. Food shortages during the Sixth Crusade have already been mentioned in connection with scurvy among the troops of St Louis. In this case, even the careful logistical planning of the saintly king was of little use. As early as 1246, he was stockpiling wine and grain on Cyprus. By 1248 the barrels of wine were piled high as a barn and the mounds of wheat and barley looked like grassy hills, the rains having caused the outer layers to sprout. Yet by 1250, his troops were scorbutic, exhausted, defeated.

Undoubtedly the plight of crusaders was sometimes exaggerated by sympathetic chroniclers. Yet many of these writers were present on the various campaigns and the events they described would have been too well-known to others to permit excessive overstatement. There are, in any case, corroborative sources. For instance, Pope Innocent III (d. 1216) assigned a penance to a certain Robert who had been captured with wife and daughter. The Saracen leader, seeing that a famine was imminent, ordered all prisoners with children to kill them for food. 'This wretched man, urged on by pangs of hunger,' the pope wrote, 'killed and ate his daughter.' Later, another order followed and Robert killed his wife for the same purpose. 'But when her flesh was cooked and served up before him, he could not bring himself to eat it.' After making his way back to Europe, Robert begged forgiveness for these sins. Among other requirements, the pope ordered him to wander about on a three-year penitential pilgrimage. And he was never supposed to remarry, or eat meat, again.

Crusaders met less serious dangers in their new environment. After King Richard's men bedded down at night at a certain camp site, they were attacked by 'swarms of tarantulas and stinging worms'. It was found that one way to drive them off was to raise a tremendous din by beating on helmets, saddles, tubs, pots and kettles, shields and basins. Whenever these swarms were seen creeping up, the crusaders leapt to their noisemakers. In another part of the Holy Land, Richard's people were harassed by flying insects that attacked the face and throat, causing swellings and disfigurement. As a result, for this part of the march they covered their faces with cloths. The scorpion posed yet another entomological hazard. On the way to Jerusalem, a knight and a foot-soldier in Richard's army were said to have died of its sting. But perhaps the most unusual deaths not caused by enemy action on the Third Crusade involved two people who decided to bathe in a river near the camp. They were, so it was reported, eaten by crocodiles.

In spite of crocodiles, scorpions, tarantulas, starvation, heat and thirst, cold rains, exhaustion, sickness, hostile Christians, stormy seas, muddy roads and broken bridges, somehow thousands of people managed to reach the Holy Land. Even more surprisingly, they did it while being attacked by the Moslems. Of all the obstacles confronting them, this was the one they had dreaded most, with good reason.

4

God's Armies

This is war, and the infidel's sword is naked in his hand,
ready to be sheathed again in men's necks and skulls.

(al-Abiwardi)

When Perceval was still a simple country lad, according to the grail legend, he was startled out of his rustic wits one afternoon by the sight of five knights with 'jingling coats of mail and the bright, gleaming helmets and the lances and the shields. . . the green and the vermilion catching the light of the sun, and the gold, blue and silver' sparkling against the forest shadows. It is likely that most ordinary crusaders were just as spellbound in the presence of their knightly and noble leaders at least until the glitter and glamour were erased by the sordid truths of war. This chapter will examine these glittering leaders and their inferiors, their weaponry and tactics, and look at discipline and the place of non-combatants. The composition of opposing armies will also be briefly reviewed.

The knight, one of the archetypal figures of medieval culture, was a very real cornerstone of the military structure built up in the Christian Near East. Marc Bloch noted that the distinguishing mark of these fighting-men was the combination of horse and complete equipment, which throughout the most active phase of the crusading movement consisted basically of the protective hauberk (a shift or long shirt of mail). Made of links of iron, it was hot in the summer, tended to rust in the damp winter and was uncomfortably heavy whatever the season. It was usually put on over some sort of cloth or leather garment, though some of the more earnest knights following Emperor Frederick Barbarossa into the Holy Land during the Third Crusade vowed to wear no clothing at all under their mail. Their leaders intervened, however, to prohibit such a painful display. Surcoats of loose-fitting cloth might be worn over the hauberk–especially in hot weather, to minimize the effects of the hot sun on metal. The knight's head was protected by an extension of the mail called the coif (which could be separable from the hauberk) and, of course, a helmet. The latter gradually became more elaborate: the simple type so well illustrated in the Bayeux Tapestry was eventually replaced by the heavy, visored, sometimes crested helms of the later Middle Ages. An elongated shield completed the outfit. Crusaders fitted out in this manner were well insulated from the relatively minor hazard of Saracen arrows—horse and knight were, in many skirmishes, said to return to camp bristling with arrows. After an encounter in 1119, more than forty arrows were found in the body of one Frankish warrior; during the Third Crusade, an obstinate Christian continued to fight despite having been hit by more than fifty arrows and numerous stones.

The lance and sword were the knights' favoured weapons, though the mace was a useful addition. Their horses were usually protected by some sort of padding, even chain mail, and the saddles were designed to keep the rider seated in spite of powerful lance-thrusts. Knights sometimes fought on foot—as in Europe—but usually avoided travelling *à pied* even if this meant riding oxen or mules. The horse, in any case, was more than a status symbol; it provided the Europeans with the spectacular massed charge, an advantage over their Moslem adversaries. Even Anna Comnena, who hardly qualifies as an admirer of the Latins, had to admit at least twice that the Franks were unbeatable when charging down upon the enemy, which made a magnificent show besides. Clever lady that she was, Anna also recognized the great disadvantage of the massed cavalry attack: when it was over the knights were seldom able to regroup and could be surrounded individually. In addition, if the enemy had both the sense and the time to get out of the way, which Turkish mounted archers often did, then the mighty charge simply removed the knights from the field of battle. Even with these drawbacks, though, the Moslems learned to respect and fear the sight, and the screams and clatter, of hundreds of mailed, helmeted polytheists thundering across the plain in their general direction. About 1149, an Arab historian described a 'famous charge upon the Moslems'; some forty years later, Saladin's personal secretary drew a vivid picture of a charge that took place near Arsuf during King Richard's march south in the Third Crusade:

> I myself saw their knights gathered together in the midst of a protecting circle of infantry; they put their lances in rest, uttered a mighty war-cry and the ranks of infantry parted to allow them to pass; then they rushed out, and charged in all directions.

The kinetic and psychological power of the knight's charge made him an excellent offensive weapon. Foot-soldiers, on the contrary, usually played a defensive role. Normally forming the first lines against attack—standing or kneeling with spears presented—on the march they were often positioned so as to shield the knights (and their valuable horses) and non-combatants. Foot-soldiers usually had leather or padded cloth vests as body protection, with a hood of the same material. They used round shields and wielded spears, pikes, axes and short swords, as well as a short bow which was not, however, very effective. One of the weapons used by 'specialist' infantry was the crossbow. Mercenary archers preferred this instrument, whose penetrative power was only surpassed after the thirteenth century by the famous longbow. The Genoese, in particular, were adept with crossbows, and, consequently, were sought out by *Outremer* barons. (In the West in 1346 there was a famous confrontation in which superior weapons technology played an important part. Genoese mercenaries facing English longbows 'had never met such archers before' and, after a shower of arrows descended upon them, they retreated in confusion, littering the field near Crécy with their crossbows.) The crossbow, at least through the twelfth and early thirteenth century, served the crusaders well. As the ever-observant Anna Comnena remarked, it was a 'truly diabolical machine' of such power that 'the unfortunate man who is struck by it dies without feeling the blow'. Even the papacy tried to curtail its use in 1139, but with as little success as all subsequent arms-control pronouncements. The enemy had a similar weapon, as a sergeant in the Third Crusade discovered. The bolt pierced his hauberk and was only deflected when it struck a small container he wore round his neck. In it, according to Ambroise, was a slip of parchment bearing 'God's names'. This story, *mutatis mutandis*, has probably been told of every battle man has ever fought. The 'sergeant', incidentally, is a difficult figure to define. He seems to have ranked between knights and foot-soldiers and is said sometimes to have fought on horseback, sometimes on foot. They often followed after the knights in battle, finishing off anyone already knocked down by the mounted warriors.

In addition to knights, sergeants, and infantry and archers, later crusading armies were joined by mercenaries from both Europe and the Levant. Christians with greater interests in warfare and its profits than in dedication to crusade ideals even served as mercenaries in Moslem armies and navies. Christian pilgrims were sometimes pressed into service in emergencies, for instance during the twelfth century, when some sailors and pilgrims arriving on their pious trip to

Jerusalem had their plans changed for them and found themselves drafted into the siege of Ascalon, with scant chance to refuse. There were also the military orders, of whom the Knights Templars and Hospitallers were the most famous, both orders papally licensed in the early twelfth century. These permanent fighting forces were crucial: two of the greatest problems facing the lords of Christian territories in the Holy Land concerned manpower, since there was never enough of it and, in the second place, when reinforcements *did* appear, they seldom seemed to do so at the right time. Most men who had taken the crusader vow felt that after they had visited, or attempted to visit, Jerusalem, their obligation was at an end. Popes, for example, were always trying to persuade volunteers to agree to a one-year or three-year term of service. Alternatively, members of the minor crusades and those who came on their own might spend a season chasing about the desert hoping never to meet the enemy, then return to the comforts of home. Even more troublesome were the newcomers who often ruined delicate diplomatic agreements that local resident Christian lords had just made with their Moslem neighbours. Certainly, visiting crusaders were a welcome sight to resident Christians at recurring moments of crisis, but the inevitable time lag between crises and the arrival of organized assistance meant that many recently-landed war bands either disrupted *détente* or got themselves slaughtered. Often the result was mutual distrust between 'resident' and 'visiting' crusader. (It has been argued that Christians resident in the Holy Land were not technically crusaders at all.)

Non-combatants accompanied practically every crusade, though perhaps in larger proportions before around 1200 than after. On the other hand, Kedar claims to have found evidence in a crusade-ship passenger list that the 'popular' element was just as strong in 1250 as at earlier periods. Though the papacy usually tried to discourage the poor and others who could not be expected to fight (at least until the thirteenth century), hordes of paupers and the sick, women and the very young accompanied many crusades. Not only did such people add little or nothing to effective military might, they were often a burden on the Christian warriors who had to protect them and control their progress on the march. William of Tyre writes of a 'helpless throng' of the sick and old of both sexes, who were sent off into the bushes with the baggage during an attack in 1097. In Louis VII's crusade (in 1148), he says that the troops had to guard the rear 'as protection for the non-militant throng and especially for the crowd of people on foot'. However, one group among the desperately poor earned an unsavoury reputation in the crusading movement due to their indiscriminate acts of murder, looting and rape, general viciousness and frenzied barbarity: these were the wild 'Tafurs' (the name is an etymological puzzle) on the fringes of the First Crusade, whom the Turks were said to fear and near whom not even the bona-fide crusaders would camp. Normally, the slight military assistance rendered by poor civilians was limited to the simplest of tasks. In Egypt in 1219 unarmed 'common people' with the women, clergy and less-experienced infantry made themselves useful by carrying water to their defenders. However, as Oliver of Paderborn noted, in a later skirmish, these unarmed 'common people... displayed manifest timidity'. They were not always so ineffective in battle, for in a later crusade led by Louis IX, Joinville reports that the 'butchers and the other camp followers, including the women who sold provisions', began shouting when they beheld the Comte de Poitiers being dragged off to captivity; as a result, he was rescued by armed crusaders.

The clergy have been mentioned among non-combatants, the assumption being that they, along with women and children, would be unarmed. In fact, many clergymen flagrantly disregarded the old ecclesiastical dictum restated by the famous scholastic theologian Aquinas in the thirteenth century: 'It is altogether unlawful for clerics to fight, because war is directed to the shedding of blood.' But the clergy, Aquinas adds, might participate in a just war in order to bring spiritual counsel to others. In any case, not all clergymen were interested in the subtleties of canon law or spiritual counsel. 'The Latin customs with regard to priests differ from ours', Anna Comnena wrote, since 'your Latin barbarian will at the same time handle sacred objects, fasten a shield to his left arm and grasp a spear in his right. . . The race is no less devoted to religion than to war.' Things had not changed much some 150 years later, when, in 1250, Joinville's own chaplain, hiding a spear in the folds of his clerical garb, casually (but carefully) approached some Saracens and, suddenly producing the weapon, chased them away (to the great admiration of the rest of the Christian army). Eventually this bellicose priest was punished, for when the crusaders were defeated, he was unceremoniously slaughtered and dumped into the Nile. At least he met a relatively honourable death, which was not the case for the bishop surprised and killed by Moslems in the midst of his chess game with a lady. There were other disreputable adventures attributed to crusading men of

71

God—and women, such as the nun who seems to have preferred her Saracen lover to the burdens of celibacy.

These, then, were the usual participants in a major crusading force. En route, each evening as they approached camp sites selected by scouts, the various components would disengage from the motley throng and put up temporary shelters. Feudal vassals would cluster round their lords' pavilions, mercenaries round their captains' tents, while the clergy and the mass of infantry and the poor sorted themselves out along lines of kinship, lordship, language, convenience; German-speakers selected their own patch of ground, French-speakers another, and so on in accordance with the usual barriers that divided one western people from another. After this miniature Europe had moved off again, all that remained was litter and perhaps some graves for those who had already found their Jerusalem. If the camp had not been of temporary duration, something else remaining behind would have been the horrible stench such places generated; sometimes armies almost suffocated in their own effluvia.

A standard debating-point among historians of the crusades involves proportions: the ratio of knights to foot-soldiers, armed crusaders to non-combatants, and so on. The simplest answer is that no one knows. There was nothing comparable to a formal register or muster-roll of participants, armed or unarmed, aside from the highest-class leaders among clergy and laymen whose rank earned them history's acknowledgment. As for the other participants, the unreliability of large figures, which is a commonplace of medieval historiography, precludes exactitude. It should be noted, in fairness to the chroniclers, correspondents and speech-writers of the Middle Ages, that even today crowds tend to vary in reported size as a function of an observer's prejudices about their 'cause'. Medieval writers did attempt, at any rate, to suggest the relative numbers participating in particular crusades. William of Tyre, for instance, suggested that when Jerusalem came under siege in 1099, there were 40,000 Christians among the attackers, 20,000 of whom were infantry, with some 1,500 knights—the rest being non-combatants or too ill to fight. Unfortunately, statistics was not one of William's strong points. Compare, for instance, his calculation about Raymond of Toulouse's army, written about seventy years after the event, with the estimate of Raymond's own chaplain. William of Tyre says that Raymond had about 10,000 infantry and 350 knights; the second source mentions 12,000 able-bodied fighters and 1,200 to 1,300 knights. After examining such figures in their historical contexts, Runciman estimated that there were approximately seven infantrymen for every knight in the First Crusade. When the Venetians contracted to take combatants to battle in the Fourth Crusade, Villehardouin says that they agreed to carry 4,500 knights, 9,000 squires and 20,000 foot-soldiers. If the last two categories are combined, this approaches a one-to-seven ratio. In a letter reporting on the Fifth Crusade to Egypt, between 5,000 and 6,000 knights and 40,000 infantry are mentioned, again near a one-to-seven ratio. Of course, this proportion cannot be applied to the whole crusading movement, since special circumstances often varied the balance between knights, infantry and non-combatants. In addition, some of the troops cannot be so neatly categorized, such as the bowmen, who were sometimes dealt with separately from the infantry. Specialists in other war arts accompanied crusaders, such as the pyrotechnicians, found in Byzantine, Latin and Moslem armies, who were responsible for 'Greek fire', an inflammable substance whose exact composition is still a subject of debate. It

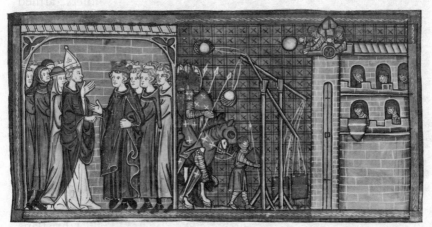

7 Before the advent of proper artillery, medieval siege warfare techniques included battering the walls with huge stones, projected by mangonels or trebuchets. Though simple in concept and design, such machines were often highly effective.
(London, Brit. Library *MS Royal 16 G VI*, f. 388[A])

seems to have resembled modern napalm and could be squirted at the enemy or his ships through pipes, dumped on him from metal pots, or thrown at him in clay hand-grenades. In Egypt, Joinville witnessed a night bombardment of his camp, during which the whole area was lit up bright as day whenever barrels of Greek fire, streaming long flaming tails, hurtled in and exploded among the Christians' tents with

8 Another tactic in sieges was the undermining of walls by sapping (tunnelling under and weakening) them or by physically removing the wall stone by stone. Here the defenders are using wooden stakes, stones and fire against the movable screen protecting the attackers.
(London, Brit. Library *MS Royal 16 G VI*, f. 74^R)

the sound of thunder. Another group of specialists, the engineers, built and operated the ballistic machines so important to siege operations. The medieval propensity to give names to inanimate objects, like Arthur's sword, is found here as well. Two of the catapults used against

Acre in the Third Crusade, for instance, were dubbed 'Evil Neighbour' and 'God's Own Sling'. Walls were also attacked by undermining, work entrusted to sappers who tunnelled under the base of a wall, shored it up with beams, set fire to these supports, then crawled—quickly, no doubt—back out of their burrows. With any luck the section of wall above would collapse or crack and, thus weakened, be easier to breach with missiles or even by hand.

All these miscellaneous bands on the march or in camp, haughty knights and impoverished rustics, pompous clergymen, whores, tough foot-soldiers and little children, all involved in the holy enterprise, must have created a tumultuous, kaleidoscopic spectacle. Fluttering above the throngs, the noblemen's banners served as rallying-points for their vassals and hirelings, or for the different 'nations' or even larger groupings. A Christian writer conjectured that when besieged crusaders undertook a sortie from Antioch (in 1098), Moslem leaders, interrupting a chess game, observed among the flags 'the standard of the great Pope' advancing towards them. Banners played more than a decorative or symbolic role, and did more than mark out proprietary claims, for—in this ambulatory Babel—linguistic confusion could mean the difference between life and death, and banners helped keep like to like. These godly armies were also accompanied by trumpets and drums, as in 1250 when Louis IX's troops set off behind his great flag of St Denis: 'As the royal army began to move there was. . . a great sound of trumpets, kettledrums and Saracen horns.' In the twelfth century, the night that King Richard arrived at Acre the trumpets blared,

> horns sounded, and the shrill intonations of the pipe, and the deeper notes of the tambourine and harp, struck upon the ear. . . and there was not a man who did not, after his own fashion, indulge in joy and praises; either singing popular ballads to testify the gladness of his heart, or reciting the deeds of the ancients.

Richard also directed his army on the march with blaring trumpet signals. Noise, music or shouting of one sort or another seems to have been almost continuous in battle, on the march and in camp. In an engagement during the First Crusade, Raymond of Toulouse's men took their standards into the city shouting the Count's battle-cry, 'Toulouse, Toulouse'. Each noble contingent in the Holy Land seems to have had its own cry, which was also the custom in western Europe. When Bohemond wished to know the identity of a band of crusaders he asked, among other things, about their battle-cry. On that occasion, the anonymous *Gesta* reports, it was the famous 'God's will; God's will; God's will' of the Council of Clermont. Before the crusades began to decline, several other war-cries would be raised in the heat of battle: 'Saint George!' 'Deus adjuva!' 'Saint Sépulchre!' 'Diex aie!' 'Christus!' 'Kyrie eleison!' 'Alleluia!' 'Saint Denis!'—but 'God's will!' was long remembered as the spontaneous outburst that proved Christianity would overcome. Songs, too, lessened the boredom of the march and raised morale. At the siege of Antioch in the First Crusade, Raymond of Aguilers says 'the knights even sang the military songs so festively that [it seemed] they regarded the coming battle as if it were a game'. During the Third Crusade, the English and the French entertained themselves by composing and singing scurrilous verses about each other. The banners, the music, the noble war-cries, the knightly songs and pilgrim chants, all the paraphernalia of dedication and chivalry glitter from time to time through the dust and gloom of deprivation, disease and death. The famous lines penned by Bertran de Born evoke the paradoxical beauty of warfare. Though he writes within a European context, the sentiments and imagery apply as well to *Outremer*:

> I love the mêlée of shields with blue and vermilion tints, flags and pennons of different colours, tents and rich pavilions spread over the plain, the breaking of lances, the riddling of shields, the splitting of gleaming helmets, and the giving and taking of blows.

Some lordly crusaders took with them to the Holy Land many of their accustomed comforts and privileges. When he invited the French king to join the Second Crusade the pope warned that noble participants must not concern themselves with 'costly garments, bodily appearances, dogs, hawks or other such things', which were considered to be signs of loose living. Such regulations were also promulgated by secular rulers, though they usually still allowed themselves all the trappings of their rank. King Philip II of France brought a large white falcon to the Third Crusade, which proved to be a mistake since it escaped and flew to the walls of Acre, where the delighted Moslems captured it and refused to give it back. Though birds of prey were used to bring down the enemy's carrier-pigeons, Philip's valuable mascot does sound rather extravagant. This love of ostentation and the social obligations of conspicuous consumption and largesse, part of the noble ethos, arises again and again in contemporary accounts of the crusades. When the Count of Jaffa arrived in Egypt in 1249, his galley was 'covered, both under and above the water, with painted escutcheons bearing his arms. . . beside each rower was a small shield with the count's arms upon it, and to each shield was attached a pennon with the same arms worked in gold'. The galley flashed by with pennons flapping, drums booming, horns screeching. In proper heroic style it was deliberately run onto the sands and the count and his knights jumped out ready to face the foe.

The Moslems were equally capable of chivalrous display and behaviour. Perhaps the best-known figure in this regard was Saladin, King Richard's enemy. It is sometimes said that the courtesies exchanged by these two leaders, who never met, are the best examples of high chivalry; but when these accounts are examined, it seems that most of the 'courtesy' was on Saladin's rather than Richard's side. Saladin's fame was appreciated by both Moslem and Christian writers: he knew the lineage of all the famous Moslems, all about their battles and the pedigrees of their horses. As for the Christians, he was as capable of respecting as of butchering them. About 1183 while bombarding Raynald of Châtillon's castle, he learned that a wedding was going on inside, so he ordered his engineers not to hurl boulders at the bridal-chamber. After the battle of Hattin a few years later, some prisoners were escorted into Saladin's tent. One of them, the King of Jerusalem, was given a refreshing drink. Another, in fact the young man who had occupied that bridal chamber, was also courteously treated; but the perfidious Raynald of Châtillon was carried from the tent without a head.

As Raynald discovered, life at the top involved a great many risks, of which the 'commoner' had only the vaguest notions, as well as advantages; in particular, adherence to a rigid code of conduct was required. When that code was broken, punishment was swift and often severe. One reason for Raynald's execution was his violation of an agreement not to attack Moslem trading caravans during a truce. Other infractions of the knightly code were punished accordingly. Cowardice, for example, was not to be tolerated. After two knights were chased off the field by a single Moslem their lord, Bohemond II (d. 1130), took away their shields, which he turned into mangers for animals, pulled down their tents and expelled them from camp, calling them women—or so a Moslem historian, for whom this last act was in truth the ultimate insult, reported.

The 'other half', common foot-soldiers, non-combatants and

camp-followers, were constantly reminded of their separate status. First, the customary European social prejudices were often freely expressed. The two major Egyptian crusades of the thirteenth century provide examples of this. At Damietta, a participant noticed that 'the foot-soldiers reproached the cowardice of the horsemen, the horsemen made light of the risks of the foot-soldiers when they went out against the Saracens'. This was hardly the camaraderie conducive to successful military operations, and successful the Egyptian campaigns were not. This was not mere jolly banter to keep up spirits. When St Louis led his men into the same theatre of action some thirty years later, another eye-witness, Joinville, recorded the following example of a nobleman's estimation of his inferiors. Peter, Count of Brittany, while trying to save his own neck by fleeing from the Moslems, was nearly pulled from his saddle by his own men in their panic. 'It would seem', Joinville observed with measured understatement, 'he had a very poor opinion of them; for as he spat the blood out of his mouth he kept ejaculating: "Good Lord, did you ever see such scum?".' In the same way, Christian knights fleeing Antioch in the First Crusade were unceremoniously pulled from their saddles by the terror-stricken Christian rabble around them. Apart from the fact that knights and infantry (to say nothing of most non-combatants) came from different strata of society, another tradition upheld the belief in the 'natural' superiority of knights. The aristocratic Joinville, seneschal of Champagne, reveals this prejudice when describing a skirmish in 1250: it was 'a truly noble passage of arms, for no one there drew either bow or crossbow; it was a battle of maces against swords'. Although there was something unseemly about killing one's man, probably a stranger, with an arrow at a hundred yards, it was perfectly acceptable to mutilate, puncture or decapitate him at arm's length—quite the reverse of modern opinion on this topic. In the sixteenth century another famous French soldier, Pierre Terrail, the seigneur de Bayard, was highly respected for his military feats. Nicknamed *le bon chevalier*, Bayard despised the democratic firearm. This ridiculous instrument allowed the meanest villain, at no great personal risk, to kill even the most distinguished knight. It seemed to be a breach of social propriety, a sentiment which Joinville would no doubt have shared with the chevalier Bayard, who died of a gunshot wound in 1524.

Another social distinction among crusaders was due to the very marked inequality in personal wealth; the poor suffered horribly during times of famine, whereas the rich managed far better. During the Third Crusade it was said that the 'rich still had sufficient store/ But direst want assailed the poor'. After being persuaded to do so by the Bishop of Salisbury and other prelates, the noblemen agreed to set up a fund to help feed indigent crusaders. Aid was distributed according to the rank and needs of starving comrades. The pillage of captured Moslem cities and strongholds was one of the consequences of this poverty. At one point in the First Crusade after taking a Moslem stronghold, Raymond of Aguilers claimed that 'first our poor [*pauperes nostri*] one by one, then our poor footmen [*pedites pauperes*] and finally our poor knights [*milites plebei*] left the scene to return to their tents some ten miles away' loaded with loot. Thus, there was a pecking order even among the down-and-outs. Sometimes looting caused a sudden, albeit temporary, alteration in fortune when grasping Christians hit an occasional jackpot. After a victory near Antioch, some of the poor returned on the backs of Arabian horses, dressed in two or three silk robes, carrying three or four shields. Sometimes the booty was shared out by mathematically-determined means. After Constantinople was captured, the movable wealth was distributed so that 'one mounted sergeant received as much as two sergeants on foot, one knight as much as two mounted sergeants'. After Damietta fell in 1219, gold, silver, pearls and other valuables were divided up according to a similar scheme among clergy, knights, other warriors and even women and children. The poor were usually so anxious for a chance to strike it rich that sometimes they were scrabbling for the spoils while the knights were still killing Turks. This acquisitive urge even led some of them to try to disobey their leaders' orders. At Tyre in 1124, for instance, the 'common people and those of the second rank' heard that their barons were negotiating for a peaceful surrender. They 'became very angry... for, in that case, they would be deprived of the plunder and spoils which would fall to their lot were the place taken by force'.

Finally, these social and economic differences were related to an even more important distinction, a participant's survival rate. Though it is true that the cavalry took offensive roles in battle and, therefore, bore the brunt of enemy action, losses among the more numerous, more tightly packed, less mobile, less heavily armoured infantry—to say nothing of inexperienced, unarmed and confused non-combatants—were far higher. (Survival rate even after capture was better for knights and nobles, since there was a purpose in maintaining prisoners who would bring a fat ransom; the riff-raff, on the other hand, were slaughtered or enslaved.) As for the commoners, even if they had weapons, this did not ensure that they could employ them, for sometimes their weapons were hardly usable anyway. Before they lost Antioch in 1098, the Turks were highly amused over some of the gear such as a rusty old sword, a worn-out wooden bow and a useless lance taken from poor crusaders. The possession of a horse, to be used not to attack but to escape from the enemy, naturally raised a man's survival quotient appreciably. The Turks discovered this at Antioch, for when they were routed by the Christians, only a few Turkish knights perished, whereas practically none of their footmen survived. Fulcher, a participant in the First Crusade, summed it up: 'He who did not have a swift horse was soon beheaded.' The fact that death was often the consequence of a low or modest position in the social and military hierarchy, then as now, is also illustrated clearly in an incident that happened during the Third Crusade. In the push to Jerusalem in 1192 Baldwin was unhorsed and ordered a sergeant to hand over his mount. Baldwin, Ambroise claimed,

> saw presently the head
> Of this same sergeant severed
> Who thus had lent to him his horse...

Though reports of battle deaths are no more reliable than any other medieval statistics, the general trend is clear enough. In the First Crusade at Dorylaeum, 4,000 common and low-ranking people were said to have died but only two of higher rank; in one encounter at Antioch, 500 foot-soldiers were killed, with a mere two knights dead. In the Third Crusade, Ambroise, who often belittles the 'unimportant' infantry, says two upper-class crusaders were killed at Acre versus 5,000 'humbler folk'. Such figures would not have become conventional unless they reflected, however inaccurately, an unpleasant truth.

Besides the social distinctions, which must have been intensified in these mobile populations thrown into uneasy proximity, another source of friction was the traditional hostility towards those who could not speak the patois, dialect or language of one's own village, region or kingdom. Fulcher of Chartres, Baldwin of Boulogne's chaplain on the First Crusade, claimed—with some rhetorical exaggeration—that he travelled surrounded by the babble of Flemings, Frisians, Normans, Lotharingians, Allemani, Bavarians, the English and Scots, Aquitanians, Italians, Dacians, Apulians, Iberians, Bretons, Greeks, Armenians and others. 'If any Breton or Teuton wished to question me', Fulcher remarked, 'I could neither understand nor answer.' Animosity between 'nations' was felt most strongly between the 'Germans' and the 'French'. During the Second Crusade the

> Germans would not allow the Franks to buy anything until they got enough for themselves. From this arose a brawl, or rather a squabble, for when one man denounces another whom he does not understand in a loud voice, that is a squabble.

In their turn, the French taunted the Germans for delaying the expedition as it marched into Anatolia. As mentioned above, the English and French also enjoyed hurling abuse at each other. King Richard's followers exchanged insults with the Frankish troops and Hugh, Duke of Burgundy, composed some verses slandering the English king, which were 'sung widely through the throng'. The Lion-heart in turn wrote his own song, blasting those who vilified him and his subjects. If the various contingents found it difficult to live together, even in death they preferred to lie among their own. At the siege of Moslem-held Lisbon in the 1140s, two burial-places were established for crusaders who fell in battle, one on the eastern side of the city for the men of Cologne and the Flemings, the other on the western side for the English and Normans.

Animosities, in fact, tended to boil over during sieges, with groups of crusaders vying for the capture. On these occasions proprietary rivalries poisoned the already unstable atmosphere surrounding uncomfortable encampments. The incident involving King Richard's men tearing down the Duke of Austria's standard at Acre is one of the best-known examples: since claims were confirmed by the unfurling of banners over a captured stronghold or city, competition for this valuable honour was keen. Raymond of Aguilers, who accompanied the First Crusade, well illustrates the point in remarking that some ambitious men even got out of bed at midnight to go quietly ahead of the others and plant their standards at forts and other sites along the route. Quarrels, some of them lasting for years, over respective claims weakened Christian control in the Levant and contributed to the eventual Moslem reconquest. In the short term, such unseemly squabbles can only have reinforced hostilities between crusading groups who were foreigners to each other. At Lisbon in 1147 (where they were buried in separate areas), the Flemings and Cologne men refused to allow the English and Normans to use the breach they had begun; the English and Normans were forced to make their *own* breach in the wall. Sometimes this selfishness was appropriately rewarded: Runciman describes the Templars holding off other Christians at the siege of Ascalon, demanding rights of first entry in⁻. the breach. They entered and were slain, and their corpses were dangled from the walls while the Moslems repaired the breach. On the other hand, Anna Comnena's comments suggest that there was a positive side to this bickering:

> Having approached Nicaea. . . the crusaders allotted towers and intervening battlements to certain sections. The idea was to make the assault on the walls according to these dispositions; rivalry between the various contingents would be provoked and the siege pressed with greater vigour.

Besides differences between regional groups, even (or especially) among the leaders themselves there were many occasions of controversy and outright conflict, since for them the potential gains were correspondingly greater. The feudal alliances and antagonisms of western Europe, the complex lines of lands and blood, were extended into new regions where the underlying relationships continued, sometimes to hinder and sometimes to promote the great Christian adventure. The very fact that old forms had to be adjusted to new surroundings stimulated a great interest in the complexities of feudal custom so that, ironically, collections of laws compiled in the Levant are useful sources of information on western feudalism. As for the customs themselves, up to about 1125 there was a certain looseness, necessitated by the need to attract recruits from the West, in the texture of relationships between noble and knightly families. In the later twelfth century, however, the great families of *Outremer* tightened the net and began resisting newcomers. Prawer claims that, by about mid-twelfth century, the Christian conquests were controlled by less than a dozen lordly houses. All was not convivial and peaceful amongst such families. A well-known feud between noblemen occurred during the First Crusade, even before Jerusalem was captured, when Tancred and Baldwin clashed in 1097 over Tarsus, which Baldwin successfully claimed. Afterwards he refused to give shelter to some 300 crusaders en route to join Tancred, who, as a result, had to camp outside the walls of Tarsus. That night the Turks killed them all, and caused a near-mutiny among Baldwin's own foot-soldiers, who deplored the deaths of their 'fellow pilgrims'. The feuding went on after Baldwin and Tancred had risen to leadership in the crusader states and prompted a Moslem writer to make a special note (for the year 1111) of an occasion on which these two men actually co-operated, 'notwithstanding their hostility to one another, and their mutual aversion and disagreement. . .'

Although there were vast disparities in rank amongst the nobility, and between knights and infantry, in times of crisis sometimes the forces managed (occasionally with brilliance) to co-operate. Such unity owed a great deal to forceful leadership and effective discipline, which, however, broke down on many crusades. When Peter the Hermit's charisma waned in enemy country during the First Crusade, the result was a failure of direction which contributed to the annihilation of his followers. He managed to return to Constantinople where he blamed the massacres on disobedient brigands and robbers who rejected his leadership. Even the most respected leaders were occasionally perplexed by lack of discipline of another kind—over-enthusiasm. Inside his tent, the quixotic Gautier, just arrived in Egypt in 1249, donned his armour excitedly, took up his weapons and shield and mounted his horse: at his word, the tent flaps were thrown back and, cheered on by his vassals, out he charged, alone, against the massed Saracen devils. That night, when King Louis IX learned of Gautier's death, the future saint remarked that 'he would not care to have a thousand men like Gautier, for they would want to go against his orders as this knight had done'. Since most crusade leaders appreciated the importance of military discipline, penalties for disobedience were usually harsh. During the Second Crusade another French king, Louis VII, was troubled by his 'commoners', who wantonly damaged Greek property outside Constantinople. He relieved many offenders of their ears, hands and feet in an effort to curtail such activities. Ironically, when the Latins during the Fourth Crusade openly attacked and captured the Greek capital, many were hanged for not turning over the booty to their commanders. Then, as now, discipline paid greatest dividends when an army came under attack. The Moslems themselves must have admired the marching crusaders who refused to break ranks even under the heaviest incitement. About 1147, some crusaders on the march were harassed by a rain of Turkish arrows,

> yet our soldiers under the commands given them did not dare to break out of line against them. For if, contrary to the discipline of war, they should break ranks, they would be exposed to a harsh sentence as deserters from their places.

One crusader did break ranks to pursue and slay an enemy leader. He was later pardoned for transgressing the rules, because he was an alien who may have misunderstood the order to maintain formation. When Saladin's troops attacked some Franks in 1183, the latter kept their ranks closed, thereby protecting each other, and continued their march in spite of attempts to disrupt their formation. One of the most famous examples of discipline in the face of enemy fire came—as might be expected—during a march led by King Richard. As his forces were travelling south after taking Acre, Richard's own contingents were in the centre section, grouped around the mule-drawn, four-wheeled cart which carried a wooden mast painted white with red spots. The king's banner fluttered from the top of the mast which ended in a cross, a

9 Contemporary accounts of the Third Crusade describe King Richard's standard flying from a red and white pole mounted on a cart. This mobile rallying point would have been similar to the one shown here. (London, Brit. Library *MS Royal 16 G VI*, f. 174ᵛ)

literal command post and place of refuge for the wounded. This movable flag-pole was the rallying point, a beacon for the whole army, tall enough to be seen above the dust and disarray of combat and sufficiently mobile to be shifted quickly as the circumstances of battle changed. As the army lumbered south along the coast, the mounted knights rode in file between two parallel files of ordinary infantry. The file nearest the sea carried the baggage, while those exposed to the enemy shielded the cavalry. From time to time the two infantry files changed places and duties. The exposed landward foot-soldiers naturally had the worst of it, but their thick felt vests and mail kept the

Turkish arrows from doing much harm. 'I saw some', Saladin's secretary wrote, perched on an elevation safely out of the action, 'with from one to ten arrows sticking in them, and still advancing at their ordinary pace without leaving the ranks.' Richard knew that if he let his knights charge from behind this protective wall of infantry, the mounted Turkish archers would flee, only to wheel and attack when the crusader ranks were thoroughly disorganized and the knights' impetus spent. Therefore, the king kept his men in line. The Moslem war-correspondent continued,

> these men exercised wonderful self-control; they went on their way without any hurry. . . One cannot help admiring the patience displayed by these people, who bore the most wearing fatigue without having any participation in the management of affairs, or deriving any personal advantage.

Ultimately, Richard allowed his army to halt and face the now reckless enemy near Arsuf. The Hospitallers (who had suffered more than other mounted units, covering the rear of the march) led the sudden charge, described earlier in this chapter, which so impressed Saladin's secretary.

The knights' charge at Arsuf is one of the most famous instances of a standard Frankish tactic, but the crusaders employed other, less straightforward, ways to defeat the enemy. In fact, both sides used a number of stratagems of varying degrees of unchivalry in addition to recourse to open battle. For instance, the crusaders were reluctant to leave the corpses of their men on the field of battle or route of march since (apart from religious considerations) they did not want the Moslems to know how many had been killed. Normally they immediately buried them where they died and hoped that the graves would go unnoticed. But on one occasion, around 1147, the Christians propped their dead on camels and other pack animals and marched off with them; the weak and wounded were also put on animals and given swords to make them look dangerous. Both sides also used spies. Richard Lion-heart learned about a Moslem caravan from a Syrian-born spy named Bernard, who knew Arabic and dressed as a Saracen. The king then sent a bedouin into the caravan to discover further information. But conversely, because crusaders were heavily dependent upon local Moslem traders and merchants, Moslem spies found it easy to learn of Christian plans. Occasionally, non-combatant Moslems were rounded up to prevent them from learning or saying too much about a forthcoming campaign. Usually, though, each side could discover the other's plans without too much effort. For instance, the crusader custom of sending heralds through camp to shout out the day's instructions must have made life simpler for spies. Another stratagem for Moslems and Christians alike was the use of disguises. In

10 A study in treachery: three Saracens claiming to desire baptism are welcomed into a crusader camp, while their comrades to the right prepare to attack the deceived Christians.
(London, Brit. Library *MS Royal 16 G VI*, f. 442[R])

one case a force approaching Jaffa in 1101 were identified not as Saracens, but as Franks, only when they began a cavalry charge. Saracens likewise donned crusader clothing and arms to get closer to their prey. The Moslems seem in fact to have had a greater liking or knack for this sort of thing than the Christians. In 1155, for example, an Egyptian naval commander gathered crews who spoke a European tongue, put them in Frankish clothes and sent them off to slay the accursed idolators. Sometimes Moslem sailors even went so far as to disguise their ships by putting on board crosses and pigs, which were most unclean to followers of Allah. Small detachments as well as whole armies disguised themselves, like the fellows who dressed up as women and hung about Frankish camps until nightfall, when they made off with horses, women, even crusaders themselves. There were many other ways to outwit the enemy: unfurl a great display of banners by day, light a great many camp-fires by night 'so that', as a First Crusade source puts it, 'it might appear that the whole host was there'.

Moslem armies presented points of similarity as well as differences when compared with the crusaders. Though in general they were not as heavily protected as Christians, their tunics seem effective enough: Joinville wore one in Egypt and was none the worse after being hit with five enemy arrows. Most Christian bowmen were foot-soldiers, but the Turks relied on mounted archers, who rode up and discharged their arrows into the enemy then just as quickly rode out of retaliatory range, as their offensive team. This hit-and-run tactic was intended to disable as many crusader infantry and horses as possible, then, having weakened the infidel dogs, mounted Moslem lancers and swordsmen along with the infantry moved in for the kill. Though crusaders faced Egyptian armies from time to time (an enemy also capable of effective naval action whenever they could organize themselves), the Turks proved to be a more formidable Moslem force. Their arsenal, which matched that available to the crusaders, included a type of crossbow, Greek fire, sappers and siege machines, in addition to the usual swords, maces, daggers, lances and bows. Other tactics used by Moslem forces included burning the scrub vegetation near crusader camps and armies, thus adding to the confusion with heat and smoke; William of Tyre says that at Antioch in 1098 this was done 'according to their usual methods'. Night-raids into Christian camps, briefly referred to above, were also carried out, for example by the 300 special troops hired by Saladin, who crept in amongst the sleepers and made off with their goods and even living captives. Saladin's secretary Beha ed-Din says some crusaders woke up to find a knife at their throats, their captors making signs to keep quiet and follow. 'The prisoner did not dare to open his mouth' until he found himself in Saladin's camp.

Turkish emirs often faced the same manpower problems as Christian noblemen. Even Saladin occasionally had trouble raising troops and keeping them in the field long enough for effective campaigns. Moslem leaders sometimes had to allow looting, since their troops felt cheated otherwise. Camp-followers plagued Saracen commanders just as they embarrassed Christian leaders and churchmen. At Acre in 1189, when the crusaders attacked a Moslem camp, the Moslems' own servants looted their fleeing masters' tents. Afterwards Saladin ordered restitution. Finally, Moslems, like the crusaders, drew upon a variety of sources for manpower including the

Sultan's or the emirs' personal followings, or perhaps plundering nomads, even Frankish mercenaries.

For Moslems as for Christians, there was a very strong religious justification for the struggle. The famous call for *jihad* or holy war, still heard in some quarters in the 1980s, developed out of the conditions that gave birth to Islam itself. As the Koran teaches, 'When you encounter the infidels, strike off their heads till you have made a great slaughter among them' (sura xlvii). Though this precept, reminiscent of many passages from the Old Testament, was at first not meant to apply to the 'people of the book'—Jews and Christians—these idealistic fine points had become academic by the eleventh century. Just as the Christian clergy harangued in hopes of stirring Europeans to action in the Holy Land, Moslem zealots excitedly preached *jihad*. In 1110, for instance, as Baghdad was preparing to celebrate the arrival of the Sultan's sister, the gaiety was spoiled by the clamour and weeping of holy men from Aleppo, who came to preach and beg for aid for Syria against the Frankish peril. In fact, these enthusiasts caused what amounted to a riot, smashing the pulpit in the Sultan's mosque while bewailing the 'misfortunes that had befallen Islam.'

On the march or drawn up for battle, the Islamic armies, like their Christian counterparts, followed and rallied round their leaders' flag-poles and banners. In thirteenth-century Egypt, a Turkish commander's banner was decorated with the arms of Emperor Frederick II (who had knighted him), the arms of the Sultan of Aleppo and the arms of the Sultan of Cairo. Joinville, who made these heraldic observations, also evokes a scene which would have exhilarated Bertran de Born:

> It was a sight to enchant the eye, for the sultan's arms were all of gold, and where the sun caught them they shone resplendent. The din this army made with its kettledrums and Saracen horns was terrifying to hear.

Drums and horns were used to direct Moslem army movements as well as to throw the enemy into a general state of psychological confusion. During Saladin's campaigns there are repeated references to rallying to drum-beats and to ordering different sections of the army about by drummed signals. While Richard besieged Acre, the trapped Moslem garrison's drums pounded out replies to Saladin's drummers up on the protected high ground. From time to time they also communicated with their distant leader by smoke-signals. Another communications system, remarked on by many crusade chronicles and bemused pilgrims to the Holy Land, was the pigeon post. Even in peacetime, Moslem cities kept in touch through carrier-pigeons; their value during war was clearly to the Moslems' advantage. Occasionally these birds were shot down or caught by Christians; their messages augmented crusaders' intelligence of enemy plans. Finally, aggressive Moslem armies were just as vocal as their Christian enemies. As one non-linguist on the First Crusade put it, the Turks

> began, all at once, to howl and gabble and shout, saying with loud voices in their own language some devilish word which I do not understand.

As far as this observer was concerned, they were 'shouting like demons'. The Moslems no doubt thought the same about Christian war-cries. After a victory or beneficial shift of fortune in battle, Moslem camps and ranks were filled with screams of the *tahlîl* and the *takbîr*, the acknowledgment that 'there is none but God' (or 'there is no other god but God, Allah'), and 'God is mighty!'

Echoes and images of this curious commotion, seas of turbaned heads, incomprehensible shouts and the endless din of horns and drums, were taken home by many a crusader. Perhaps, as he could almost hear them again while recounting his experiences (once more) to friends in the safety of his own manor hall or village tavern, the clashes took on heroic dimensions and the details of battles grew sharper with passing time and repetition. One of the reminiscences of war was caught by a Moslem writer—a moment of dreamlike suspension foreshadowing Agincourt:

> Each army could see the fires of the other; we heard the sound of their bells, and they heard our call to prayer.

On the other hand, it is just as likely that most crusaders would have agreed with the poet of King Richard's crusade, for whom the enemy were 'black men hideous', obnoxious to God and nature. Yet even this xenophobe, who often refers to Moslems as 'base cattle', could not help admiring how the Turks moved 'fearsomely/ With their red headdresses on high/ Like ripely laden cherry trees'. Deadly fruit, as many crusaders would discover.

5

Fighting and Dying

A year later I crossed the battlefield, and saw the land all
covered with their bones, which could be seen even from a distance,
lying in heaps or scattered around.

(Ibn al-Athir at Hattin)

During the First World War, the strange sight that greeted an East
Anglian farm boy sent to the Dardanelles was 'a great muddle, carnage
and men without rifles shouting "Allah! Allah!"'. Other Europeans,
including East Anglians, faced the same cries, confusion and
bloodshed when they arrived in unfamiliar eastern Mediterranean
lands eight centuries earlier. Due to the similarity in detail of many
crusade battles, historians (like Riley-Smith) usually, and quite
understandably, choose to concentrate on the outcome and significance rather than the bloody minutiae of such military encounters.
Even so, it was through battle in the Holy Land that most crusaders
fulfilled the role they had chosen. Ideology was literally embodied

11 The crusaders managed to install themselves in the Holy Land by the
piecemeal reduction of walled towns, though such operations could be a
major drain upon the limited resources of the invaders.
(London, Brit. Library *MS Royal 16 G VI*, f. 168ᵛ)

in physical conflict with the Moslems. It was more than bravado that prompted a crusader at Antioch to ride alone to certain death in the midst of the enemy: before departing, he invited his comrades to join him in this carnal meal, as Fulcher's story goes, for soon he would be supping in Paradise. Among the rank-and-file, who seldom had the opportunity for such heroics, the drudgery and danger of the conflict were just as significant a part of their crusading commitment. In this chapter, through anecdote and eye-witness accounts, the atmosphere of battle will be re-created, the excitement as well as the indignities and horrors of war that so many discovered while serving the Prince of Peace.

For convenience, the military encounters recorded by contemporaries will be divided into three categories: skirmishes and limited assaults, full-scale field clashes between armies, and sieges. The first type usually provides many examples of dramatic deeds of valour. For instance, when King Richard attacked Cyprus en route to Acre, his fully-armoured knights, with archers and crossbowmen, left the galleys to be rowed ashore in small boats, firing as they went. Though the enemy had built a makeshift barricade on the beach, the training and discipline of the attackers gained them the victory; by nightfall, Richard had ordered the horses brought from the galleys to bolster the assault, which resulted in the conquest of the island. The first attack on Constantinople in the Fourth Crusade followed similar lines. Knights leapt from their ships, lances in hand, accompanied by archers, sergeants and crossbowmen. While the Greeks fled at the sight of this mass of men wading ashore, sailors opened doors in the transport vessels and led the horses to the beach, where the knights mounted and the rest of the army assembled. Surprise was an important element in many skirmishes, and once again Richard's crusade provides good examples. In his last battle in the Holy Land, his men were caught unawares by the Saracens, who launched a dawn attack on Jaffa. Richard had fewer than sixty fit knights and only a few thousand foot-soldiers. The king and his men, half-asleep, scarcely had time to arm themselves; some even fought without their breeches on, which—according to Ambroise—caused them greater distress than the wounds they received. Even so, the Saracens, hooting and yelling as they fired, encountered a well-disciplined body of men: the front ranks knelt behind shield and lance; between and just behind them were the crossbowmen with their loaders, and then the knights. Saladin's troops, although they greatly outnumbered the defenders, eventually gave up after several attacks. One of Richard's men, the victim of surprise at an earlier combat (at Acre), was discovered in even more undignified circumstances. He was just squatting to yield to nature's

12 In his last engagement in the Holy Land King Richard 1 of England withstood repeated attacks by Saladin's forces against Jaffa in 1192. The Mamluk sultan Baibars took Jaffa after a one-day siege in 1268.
(*The Holy Land*, vol 2, London 1843. Oxford, Bodley Mason EE68)

needs when spied by a Turk, who set his lance and spurred full-speed at the target.

> It was most cowardly and base
> To take a knight thus unaware
> While occupied in such affair.

When nearby crusaders shouted a warning to the knight

> He scarcely had the time to rise
> But managed to get to his feet
> And left his duty incomplete.

Even so, he was able to kill the Turk, and ride his horse into the crusader camp.

Occasionally, the surprise tactic succeeded on a grand scale and involved not merely individuals or separate contingents, but entire armies. Normally, the general position and movements of huge armies were usually known to both sides, though sometimes there were disastrous exceptions. While Peter the Hermit was conferring with the Byzantine emperor, his rabble decided to press on into northern Turkey, blithely ignorant of the dangers they faced. They ambled along shouting and making quite a commotion, encouraging each to avenge colleagues slain by the Turks. Albert of Aachen, writing a generation later but probably recounting eye-witness reports, says they finally emerged from a forest to find spread out before them the army of Sultan Kilij Arslan, alerted by their noisy behaviour. The crusaders, amazed and no doubt suddenly quiet, were at once charged by a wave of screaming Turks. Recovering at last, the Christians shook off their terror and raised their own war-cry, but their horses were already being shot from under them, and soon they were retreating in confusion. The victors pursued, cutting them down as they fled back to camp where the disabled, priests, old men, women and children had been left. The Turks burst into the undefended camp, killing everyone in sight except the good-looking girls and boys.

Since large armies usually had preliminary notice of each other's probable route and intent, stalemate sometimes resulted. A Frankish army encountered an Egyptian force in the twelfth century and, as Runciman expressed it,

> For three months the armies faced each other, neither side daring to move; for everyone, in Fulcher of Chartres's words, liked better to live than to die. At last the soldiers on either side dispersed to their homes.

When one army thoroughly defeated another in the field, it was often the consequence of errors in tactics, or failure of discipline, or both. The Turks annihilated the Byzantine army at Manzikert in 1071 (precipitating, in some ways, the chain of events which led to the First Crusade) because, among other things, the Greek commander's order to pull back turned into a panic-stricken rout, always a dangerous possibility in such a manoeuvre. On the other hand, one of the worst defeats suffered by a twelfth-century crusader army, at Hattin in 1187, was brought on in the first place by one group of leaders imposing their will upon another, who should have known better. In addition, R.C. Smail, the military historian of the earlier crusades, suggests further proximate causes of defeat. In its origins, the crusader expedition that ended at Hattin was a reply to an earlier movement of Moslem troops against Tiberias. The ranks of attacking Islamic warriors were described by Imad ad-Din (one of Saladin's secretaries), a man very fond of exploiting the ornate twists and turns of Semitic rhetoric: for him, the massed battalions created a 'second sky of dust. . . in which swords and iron-tipped lances rose like stars'. With his usual rapid shift of metaphor, he then claims that the whole area was changed into enchanting flowerbeds and orchards

> by crescent swords like arches of myrtle, by *Yemeni* blades like garden trees, by yellow banners like unfurled pennons of jasmin. . . by helmets gleaming like sweet-smelling many-petalled camomile flowers. . .

These deadly flowers cut the crusader army to pieces. In order to recover Tiberias from Saladin and rescue the besieged wife of Raymond III (Count of Tripoli and Prince of Galilee), the crusader army had to cross the waterless expanse of Galilee, moving from Acre eastwards to Tiberias. Though some, including Raymond III himself, advised against so dangerous a march in the hottest season of the year, King Guy of Jerusalem let himself be persuaded to make the attempt. By 3 July, the crusaders ground to a halt near some peaks called the Horns of Hattin, ironically, by tradition the famous Mount where Christ preached his best-known sermon of peace. Saladin's army of perhaps 18,000 at maximum, against at most 15,000 Christians, moved up to block their progress towards Tiberias on the Sea of Galilee, less than ten miles away. The Moslems surrounded the crusader encampment, firing the dry grass to torment the thirsty Christians with the heat and smoke, a standard Moslem tactic. Throughout the night, the crusaders could hear their enemy's incessant cry, the *tahlil* and *takhbîr;* the Moslems knew victory would be theirs, as the next day was to prove.

Whether the fighting occurred in small-scale skirmishes or extensive confrontations involving thousands, as at Hattin, the face-to-face cutting and thrusting of sword and lance seem to have done more damage than the volleys of arrows. In any case, as suggested in the previous chapter, the bow and arrow was not yet a gentleman's weapon, at least not among westerners. In most warrior-aristocracies, heroic deeds, tremendous wounds inflicted and received, quickly passed into the realms of legend—as in the brain-gushing spear thrusts so carefully, even lovingly, described in the *Iliad*, or Roland's bloody skill with his relic-hilted sword, Durendal. In the same way, historic crusade leaders were believed to have been gifted with superhuman strength and prowess. At Antioch in 1098, Duke Godfrey of Lorraine performed a famous deed 'worthy of remembrance forever', as

William of Tyre reports, when he sliced a Moslem in two, even though
the latter was encased in armour. The top part of his victim fell to the
ground, while the lower section continued riding into the city whose
residents, William somewhat unnecessarily adds, were frightened and
amazed. While on the Second Crusade, King Conrad III of Germany
was said to have removed an enemy's head, neck, left shoulder, arm
and part of his side, again with one blow, even though the Moslem was
wearing armour. Not to be outdone, Richard Lion-heart's sword split
Moslem heads 'to the teeth', or so Ambroise claimed. Certainly many
encounters were bloody enough without requiring poetic magnifica-
tion to epic proportions: the horrors of combat are more convincingly
conveyed in the simple, realistic prose of day-to-day mayhem. A
survivor of Saladin's capture of Jerusalem in 1187, for instance, recalled
the Saracens blowing their trumpets and shrieking 'Hai, Hai' as they
attacked. 'I myself', he adds, 'was wounded in the face by an arrow
which struck the bridge of my nose. The wooden shaft has been taken
out, but the metal tip has remained there to this day.' Noses seem to
have been especially at risk, for in a fight in Egypt about 1250, a
crusader's face was slashed, leaving his nose 'dangling over his lips'.
The frenzy of battle is also well illustrated in two accounts from the
period just after Saladin's victories. During a skirmish outside Acre,
one Frank seized a Moslem by the hair while another Frank, in an
attempt to cut off his head, missed and amputated his colleague's hand;
in the confusion, the prisoner escaped. As mentioned in the last
chapter, Baldwin ordered a sergeant to give him his horse, having lost
his own to Moslem aggression. Afterwards, Baldwin was knocked
down yet again and beaten senseless with clubs, the blood streaming
from his nose and ears. A knight who came to his rescue was unhorsed
as well, and beaten even more terribly: the enemy stood round
pounding him with their iron toothed maces until a leg was completely
detached from his body.

 During lulls in the fighting, combatants repaired their defences and
looked after their wounds, even traded impressions and information
with their opponents. The courtier-writer Usamah described an
encounter (about 1120) with the Franks, in which he drove his lance
through the back of a fully-armoured Christian knight with such force
that the point emerged from the chest. Incredibly, the knight survived.
It was such an astounding case that the Franks sent someone across the
lines to discuss it with Usamah himself. Such interpersonal exchanges
were not always conducted with regard for the rules of chivalrous

behaviour. Outside the walls of Acre during the Third Crusade, a Welsh and a Turkish archer agreed to a trial of skills. Each promised to stand still while his adversary took a shot at him. The Turk fired and missed, then suggested they allow themselves two shots each. The Welsh archer—says the Norman poet Ambroise—agreed, but while the Turk was getting his second arrow ready, the Welshman took careful aim and shot him through the heart:

> 'You kept the pact not,' so he spoke,
> 'So, by Saint Denis, mine I broke.'

The third major category of confrontation involved siege warfare. Though walls and the siege have featured in western history down to the present century, it is not easy for modern, highly-mobile Europeans to appreciate earlier sentiments associated with a city wall. For many of our predecessors, the wall was more than just a protective shell or a customs barrier. Though the symbolic and psychological associations of the wall are manifold, in the present context, these alternative aspects must give way to an examination of the defensive function only, for the siege was a significant form of military activity during the crusades. Indeed, it was only by moving from city to city that the first crusaders were able to secure the Holy Land, linking one successful or threatened siege with another. Crusaders had a wide repertoire in their siege techniques. Inspired, perhaps, by the crumbling walls of Jericho, they sometimes called upon the supernatural by offering prayers and processions before a major assault. Alternatively, subterfuge and treason were employed, though on a level rather more sophisticated than the Trojan horse. By the twelfth and thirteenth centuries, in fact, both Christian and Moslem armies drew upon skills and tools that might have impressed, or at least interested, the author of *De Bello Gallico* himself. In general, siege warfare was a relatively unexciting, humdrum routine interspersed with moments of high drama. The attackers often had to defend against relief forces, while pounding and undermining the walls at the same time, in most cases hoping that despair and starvation would force the defenders to give up. Though the Moslems might protect their walls with sacks of straw and chaff, ropes and tapestries, huge wooden beams and mattresses stuffed with silk, still the crusaders hammered away. At Acre, a priest stood by one of the siege weapons preaching and soliciting money to pay the people who brought stones for heaving at the enemy. At that same siege, a boulder King Richard brought all the way from Messina in Italy killed twenty people. In their turn, the attackers had to guard against damage (for example by naphtha-bombs) to their siege weapons, the mangonels and more effective trebuchets, battering rams and roll-up towers. In addition, they could suffer serious harm from sorties by a city's defenders suddenly rushing from the city and driving the invaders back, sometimes into their own camps. At one stage during the siege of Antioch, in fact, the Christians piled huge logs and rocks up *against* a gate to block troublesome sorties. A sortie of another kind was reported at Acre during the Third Crusade, when Christian sappers digging towards the wall broke through to a counter-mine being dug by Moslems with captive Christian labour. In the confusion of this subterranean confrontation, the captives escaped and the Moslems sealed off their tunnel. Christians unfortunate enough to be present in a city under crusader attack were sometimes forced by Moslems to shoot at the besiegers, though one may suppose without much accuracy. Since Christians inside besieged Moslem cities might also take more active measures to help their co-religionists on the outside, they were sometimes disarmed and put under curfew. The besieged were in some ways better off than those outside. Provided their supplies held out, at least for the moment they had solid shelter and the advantage of height, which some defenders used (at Maara in 1098) to hurl down stones, fire, quicklime and beehives upon Christian heads. Defenders not only fired arrows and dropped various articles, but on occasion grappled and hoisted sundry objects over their walls. A Christian knight killed outside Nicaea in 1097 was snagged with iron hooks, hauled up the wall, stripped of valuable armour, then flung back to the helpless throng below.

Another defensive tactic, mentioned earlier, was the sending of spies and raiders by night into the Christian camp outside a besieged city. William of Tyre says that spies possessed of great facility in various languages and disguises were everywhere. In order to discourage spying, Bohemond ordered some prisoners strangled and trussed as if for roasting for a meal and decreed that this would be the fate of all his enemies. The spies quietly left his camp. In addition to discovering what the enemy planned, one's own forces of course had to maintain communications. We have seen that the Moslems used drums, smoke signals and pigeons, but occasionally more dramatic means were employed. Saladin, with a field army outside Acre, sent a diver, by night, into the harbour underneath Frankish ships to carry money and letters to the besieged Moslem garrison. The brave swimmer carried three pouches water-proofed in oiled silk containing gold and documents. A messenger-pigeon was sent from Acre to Saladin confirming the diver's arrival. Regardless of such heroics, the city could not be held and the garrison surrendered, only to be murdered *en masse* on King Richard's orders. This introduces the most unsavoury aspect of crusading warfare in the Holy Land, the massacres, tortures and other atrocities chronicled by Christian and Moslem writers alike.

Historians still wrangle about this bloody deed at Acre in 1191 and Richard's justification. Some view it as a practical decision forced by the exigencies of war, but for others it was yet another example of the king's sanguinary nature. However it may be interpreted, there is little doubt about the deed itself, reported by contemporary Franks and Moslems. In the words of Ambroise

> Two thousand seven hundred, all
> In chains, were led outside the wall,
> Where they were slaughtered every one. . .
> For this be the Creator blessed!

Saladin's confidant-biographer Beha ed-Din naturally had his own point of view:

> They brought out the Moslem prisoners, whom God had pre-ordained to martyrdom that day, to the number of more than three thousand, all tied together with ropes. The Franks rushed upon them all at once and slaughtered them in cold blood. . .

Although Saladin had treated captives with courtesy and even kindness, after this slaughter he usually killed all captured Christians of both sexes. Even centuries later, Richard's bloody massacre of helpless, bound prisoners was still vividly recalled by Moslem writers. It should not be assumed, however, that Richard's was either the first or the last example of such behaviour. The Christian garrison of Marash (in 1150), who had been promised their lives upon surrender, were slaughtered after agreeing to the Sultan's terms; the Templars gave up one of their castles in 1266 on condition that they would be spared, only to lose their heads after quitting the place. Nor should it be thought that Christians were the inevitable perpetrators or victims of such treachery, for rival Moslem factions were not averse to committing such atrocities on each other. In any case, Richard's act was avenged exactly a century later with the fall of the last major Christian stronghold in the Holy Land which was, fittingly, Acre. In 1291, the Moslems besieged and took the city after the garrison were granted their lives. When they surrendered, however, about 2,000 men were slain. A fifteenth-century Moslem writer (Abu l-Mahasin), drawing upon contemporary sources to describe the fall of the city, refers first to Richard's twelfth-century campaign at Acre, when the Franks 'promised to spare the lives of the Muslims and then treacherously killed them'. Then, one hundred years later,

> God permitted the Muslims to reconquer them... the Sultan gave his word to the Franks and then had them slaughtered as the Franks had done to the Muslims. Thus Almighty God was revenged on their descendants.

Even after 1291 the bloody atrocities continued: Sultan Bayezid slew 3,000 Christian prisoners the day after their defeat at Nicopolis in 1396, avenging 30,000 of his own fallen troops.

The brutalizing of the human spirit through war, whether ancient, medieval or modern, is all too evident a fact of life. Religious rivalry, when added to all the other marks by which the 'enemy' is identified, only widens the gap: the enemy becomes something not really human; the likelihood of torture, atrocities and—even in a military sense —pointless slaughter increases. In the crusading era there is ample evidence of this zeal, which sometimes exploded into throbbing fanaticism and glee at the destruction of the enemy whether Christian, Moslem or Jew. Crusaders slaughtered Jewish families with relish as they headed for the Levant. When they arrived, they slaughtered Moslems with equal relish: 'Now the land stank with Moorish blood, and the aqueduct was choked with their corpses. It was a delightful sight,' as one satisfied eye-witness, Raymond of Aguilers, put it. For their part, the Islamic foe were always ready to break out in song and dance whenever Christian idolators were sent to hell. When the defenders of Acre learned that Emperor Frederick Barbarossa had drowned en route to the Holy Land they cavorted about the battlements, taunting the Christians below. A grim celebration of death was also carried out when cities fell after a long or difficult siege. Even Caesar, master of discipline, allowed his frustrated troops to take pitiless revenge upon the stubborn inhabitants of Bourges. During the crusades probably the most famous example of urban storm and slaughter visited upon civilians was the one that really mattered, the taking of Jerusalem. In mid-July 1099, the city fell to the armies of the

First Crusade. Three important contemporary sources (the anonymous *Gesta,* Raymond of Aguilers, and Fulcher) emphasize the goriness of the day's work. The author of *Gesta* claimed that the crusaders waded up to their ankles in enemy blood (*in sanguine. . . usque ad cavillas*); Fulcher also mentions bloody ankles, but Raymond goes one better. In his version, the blood reached to the crusaders' knees and their horses' bridles (*usque ad frenos equorum*) as they rode or waded through the streets of the city. Raymond's editors point out a similar phrase in John's *Revelation* (14.20), which may have inspired Raymond's more colourful description. This is possible since, like Fulcher, he was a clergyman. Some seventy years after the event William of Tyre—drawing upon earlier versions and exercising his craft as a writer—claimed that even the victors were horrified at the carnage. In a chilling, dramatic flourish he adds,

> It was not alone the spectacle of headless bodies and mutilated limbs strewn in all directions that roused horror. . . Still more dreadful was it to gaze upon the victors themselves, dripping with blood from head to foot, an ominous sight.

The sources agree that the crusaders, nobles and commoners alike, stormed through the city taking what they could of booty and slaves. Many poor men became rich, as Fulcher says, and many rich noblemen became richer by planting their banners at particular houses and sections of the city (Tancred was outraged when some of his captives, who took refuge at 'Solomon's Temple', were killed by other crusaders). Having conquered Jerusalem and indulged in a blood-bath, the crusaders processed with happy spirits to the Lord's Sepulchre where, exulting and weeping for joy, they offered up prayers of thanks. They had much to be thankful for; in the words of Raymond of Aguilers

> it was a just and splendid judgment of God that this place should be filled with the blood of the unbelievers. . . The city was filled with corpses and blood.

Atrocity on a grand scale was balanced by individual acts of torture carried out by all sides against their enemies. Anna Comnena accused Peter the Hermit's followers of chopping up babies and impaling others on spits to roast over fires, while the elderly were subjected to a variety of tortures. Anna, it must be added, also accused her fellow-Greeks of atrocities committed against Turks, only here the babies were tossed into pots of boiling water. About a generation later, after a Frankish defeat the captives were taken to Aleppo and tortured to death in the streets to the great delight of the populace. Around the same time (in 1123) some fifty Armenians disguised as monks helped a crusader escape captivity, but they in turn were caught. William of Tyre claimed that some were flayed alive, some sawn apart, others buried alive or used as targets for archery practice. At least these Moslem tortures exhibit a certain ingenuity, nothing so obvious as the Third Crusade knight who spread-eagled a Turkish emir and incinerated his genitals with Greek fire. During his term in Egypt with

13 Both Christians and Moslems fired human heads into besieged cities, hoping to inflict psychological damage through the macabre bombardment. (Paris, Bibl. Natl. *MS Fr. 2630* f. 22ᵛ)

King Louis, Joinville saw a Moslem instrument called the 'barnacle', which consisted of two pieces of ridged wood between which the legs were placed; pressure was then applied until the limbs were crushed and, after the legs had become inflamed, the operation was repeated, a near-eastern version of the Inquisitorial 'boot'. Atrocity stories are notorious propaganda devices, but it would be naive to discount them completely, since they tend to reflect and influence what foes want to believe about each other.

One of the more gruesome aspects of crusade fighting was head-hunting. Like Indians and frontiersmen of the Wild West, both Christians and Moslems scalped or decapitated both the living and the dead, collecting the heads as trophies, a custom noted from the First to the Sixth Crusades. Outside Antioch in 1098, for instance, after a crusader victory some 500 Moslem heads were carried back to camp. About 200 of them were shot into the city and the rest set up on stakes in view of the defenders, to add to their distress. On this occasion, Stephen of Blois wrote to his wife that the heads had been brought into camp so that everyone could share in the rejoicing; for a crusading bishop who was present, the impaled heads furnished a joyful spectacle for the people of God. It would seem that the Moslems of Antioch were able to render payment in kind, however, since (Fulcher asserted that) they killed Christians who were still in the city and hurled their heads out over the walls into the Christian lines. Conceivably, there were moments when Moslem heads were flying into Antioch while Christian heads were on their way out; the catapulting of heads into and out of besieged places occurred elsewhere, for example at Nicaea and Tyre. Apart from their utility as projectiles and morale-boosters—like the 1,000 Christian heads taken in triumph to Aleppo after a battle of 1133—heads were valuable collectibles for Moslems since their leaders sometimes paid a bounty on them. At Damietta during the Sixth Crusade Moslems used to sneak into the crusader camp at night to take their gory treasures, for which the Sultan paid a gold bezant each. The Moslems also took scalps, as did some contemporary Europeans in the course of battle in the West.

No catalogue of indignities would be complete without mention of a custom which was noted, appropriately enough, at the siege of Jerusalem described by Josephus some five centuries before Mohammad's time. In AD 70 the city, which was still then the Jewish capital, was under Roman attack. In the course of this operation local non-Romans such as Syrians and Arabians were discovered dissecting

102

Jews and plucking gold coins out of their bellies or cutting up living Jews who came to them as suppliants, pulling 'the filthy money out of their bowels'. Christians were following the same practice a millennium later. En route to Jerusalem, the riff-raff of the First Crusade sliced open corpses in search of gold coins among the entrails. Ironically, in Guibert de Nogent's version, Pope Urban II at Clermont reputedly accused the Moslems of giving purgatives to Christians or ripping open their stomachs to obtain money. After Jerusalem fell, the Moslem dead were split open or burnt so that the gold could be more easily recovered from the ashes. A few years later the same procedure was followed at Caesarea, where the crusaders also discovered some Moslems carrying their money in their mouths ready for swallowing if necessary. Hence arose the custom of suddenly striking prisoners in the neck in the hope that coins would spew forth. An even more outrageous search was reported at Caesarea: the women 'shamelessly hid bezants within themselves in a way that was wicked and which is more shameful for me to tell', as Fulcher blushingly recounts it. He assumed, of course, that the shame was in the hiding, not the seeking.

In the aftermath of battle one of the more pressing requirements was the disposal of the dead. After major engagements, thousands of corpses might litter the area. At Acre, where Saladin's secretary *Beha ed-Din* claimed that he saw cartloads of bodies dumped into the river, some estimated that 7,000 Christians died, though Beha ed-Din himself thought about 4,000 was a more realistic figure. After another major clash a year later, also at Acre, Beha ed-Din attempted to count the dead crusaders laid out in five rows, but 'there were so many that I could not reckon them'. A soldier carrying out a body count had come to about 4,060 corpses in only two-and-a-half rows. Regardless of the apparent sense of precision conveyed by such figures, medieval estimates concerning large numbers of dead were as subjective as those concerning large numbers of living; in general, they are opinions about relative magnitude rather than absolute determinations. In addition, such figures can be deceptive, since it made a great difference whether one lost two hundred foot-soldiers or two hundred knights. On the whole, Fulcher seems to have had the right idea in concluding that

> the truth regarding the number of dead or wounded in this or any other battle cannot be determined since large numbers can only be estimated.

Whatever the exact figure, large numbers of bodies rotting beneath the summer sun presented obvious problems, one of which is apparent from the many references to the terrific stench generated. When Fulcher visited Jerusalem in December 1099, he was disgusted by the odour of death both inside and outside the city walls—and this was some five months after the slaughter of the inhabitants. The earliest Arab historian of the crusades, Ibn al-Qalanisi, claimed that the bodies of dead Franks and their horses outside Damascus stank so powerfully that birds nearly dropped from the sky. Arabic exaggeration is taken much farther in the flamboyant prose of Imad ad-Din, who claims to describe the battlefield at Hattin in July 1187, where the crusaders were crushed by Saladin's army. Our rhetorician, who would have been more than sixty years old at the time, asserts that he wandered about the carnage inspecting

> heads cracked open, throats split, spines broken, necks shattered, feet in pieces, noses mutilated, extremities torn off, members dismembered, parts shredded, eyes gouged out, stomachs disembowelled. . . arms pulverized, lips shrivelled, foreheads pierced. . . their very ghosts crushed.

Concluding this anatomical litany with a final touch of malicious word-play, he notes that many 'Trinitarians' were cut in two. The noxious air lingering over fetid corpses was itself thought to produce disease, a concept as common in the Middle Ages as in Hippocrates' day and in nineteenth-century Europe. A Moslem historian (Ibn al-Athir, d. 1233) remarked that the smell of dead Franks outside Acre caused infections that began to affect the health of the army; a Christian chronicler said the same, in fewer words, about the siege of Damietta: 'The dead killed the living.'

Though disposal of the dead was a matter of self-protection, this did not pose a problem when the bodies lay out in the wilderness far from camp, castle or city. In such cases, it would seem that combatants were concerned only about proper burial rites for their dead; the enemy could rot, bones bleaching in the sun. Fulcher lamented over the skulls and fleshless limbs he saw scattered across the plain beyond Nicomedia, a remnant of Peter the Hermit's rabble massacred in the 'popular' crusade. On the other hand, some of Peter's 'crusaders' might have made a contribution of sorts to the war effort after all. The bones of these misguided Christians, piled into mounds outside Nicaea, may have been used by a later wave of crusaders to build part of a fortification. It still stood in her day, the aged Anna Comnena claimed, with its wall built of mixed stones and bones. Even after Jerusalem fell in 1099 the road from the coast to the holy city was littered with what the pilgrim Saewulf (in 1102) took to be Christian bones. It was unsafe to stop to bury the dead, he thought, for the Saracens often ambushed pilgrims. Thus 'a number of human bodies, both in the road and by the side of it, lie all torn by wild beasts'.

Though there was usually little regard for the enemy dead in the field, for obvious reasons they had to be removed from residential areas. At Jerusalem the Christian victors forced survivors to haul the dead out through the city gates and stack them in heaps like cords of wood, where they were cremated in huge bonfires. It may be that crusaders themselves, as a form of penance, were encouraged to help carry the bodies out of Jerusalem. Concerning one's own dead, in any event, they were buried where possible with due ceremony. Following an engagement in Egypt in 1250, King Louis IX hired a hundred toughs to break up a log-jam of corpses at a bridge. They flung the circumcised—therefore Moslems—over the bridge, letting them float away on the current, while the rest, presumably Christians (the corpses had been in the water for more than nine days), were buried in great trenches with proper rites.

There are numerous examples of violation of the dead by both Christians and Moslems. For instance, Moslems were reported to have suspended dead, stripped crusaders from the ramparts of their walls during the Third Crusade; earlier, at the siege of Ascalon (1153–54) the Moslems 'shamed us', as William of Tyre noted, by dangling Christians from the battlements. Eventually a truce was arranged so that the dead could be exchanged and funeral rites held. Even partial recovery of one's dead was better than none at all. A Frankish leader was killed during the Third Crusade and his friends sent to Saladin for the body; it was returned except for the head, which could not be found. Moslems besieged in Portugal in 1147 had to contend with the opposite problem. The crusaders displayed eighty heads on spears outside the walls, at which the Moslems came out tearfully begging for them so that death rites could be performed. Taking them up, they carried the heads back into the city; the crusaders heard weeping and cries of mourning throughout the night.

Many Moslems and Christians joined the heavenly host as martyrs, so they believed, through honourable death amidst the dangers and heroism of battle. Others, however, endured only the shame of captivity. Inhuman treatment was sometimes accorded prisoners already suffering the indignity of defeat. We have witnessed how, on many occasions, avaricious crusaders mistreated the inhabitants of captured towns. At Ma'arrat on the way to Jerusalem during the First Crusade, many Moslems were said by a Christian writer to have jumped down wells to their deaths to avoid torture by crusaders hoping to discover hidden treasures. But the Christian rabble were not the only ones to deal viciously with their captives. For example, when the great German pilgrimage to the Holy Land (1064–65) was attacked by Moslems, Bishop Gunther of Bamberg—one of the leaders—advised setting their Moslem captives out naked in chains to take the force of enemy missiles. Indeed, the human shield was a most useful device, though not always effective. In order to deter Godfrey of Bouillon from his siege of Arsuf, the Moslems tied up one of his friends, Gerard, and slung him over the wall. Gerard shouted down to Godfrey begging him to spare him, but Godfrey claimed that he would attack even if his own brother were hanging there. After being punctured by twelve arrows, Gerard was reeled in by the Moslems and, amazingly enough, was able to recover, thanks to Moslem medical care. The next year, Godfrey rewarded him with the fief of Hebron as compensation for those terrifying moments spent as a wriggling target. The use of live Christians as shields was balanced, during the First Crusade, by employing live Moslems as projectiles. When the crusaders caught a Saracen sent to spy upon their siege weapons (says the priest Peter Tudebode, who accompanied the crusaders) they tied him up and put him into one of these very machines.

> They thought that with all of their might they could propel him within Jerusalem. They found it impossible, for he was ejected with such force that his bonds broke before he came to the walls and he was dismembered.

Such behaviour was not limited to Levantine sieges. During the 'Anarchy' of the twelfth century King Stephen of England graciously withstood the suggestion that his enemy's young son be catapulted into a castle.

In general, the treatment of prisoners varied according to their value to the captors. For example, noblemen and women normally fared best and were treated well during the arrangements for their ransom. In the aftermath of the First Crusade, there was one aristocratic prisoner, at least, who seems to have borne his confinement relatively well: Bohemond of Antioch, whom Anna Comnena hated and admired, was rumoured to have enjoyed the favours of various

Moslem women during his captivity. On the other hand, when Baldwin refused to exchange important cities for the captured lord of Galilee, this lord was forthwith murdered and scalped. Alternatively, an offer of payment did not always secure the release of noble prisoners. When an important Frankish leader was taken during the Third Crusade his captor, afraid that the other crusaders would mount a major attack to recover him, killed him and tossed him down to his friends in spite of their attempts to buy his life. Upon seeing his corpse, the Franks threw themselves on the ground and 'covered their heads with dust', as Beha ed-Din reported. Saladin's treatment of captives was at first the very model of chivalrous courtesy. High-ranking Franks were accorded great respect, given fur robes against the cold, fed at banquets, allowed to send for their clothing from their camp and to write letters, before being sent to Damascus under escort on Saladin's horses. After Richard's slaughter of the Acre garrison, however, Saladin's attitude changed abruptly, and his troops shared his fury. Two captured Franks were brought to him and beheaded on the spot, their bodies cut to pieces by his soldiers to satisfy their lust for revenge. Two more were captured and 'put to death in the most cruel manner' since Saladin was terribly wroth at the massacre of the Acre prisoners, as his secretary explained. Another captive Frank was 'so well made', with a distinguished bearing, that even Saladin's advisers admired him, yet Saladin put him in chains and reproached him for the Acre killings. 'He acknowledged that it was an abominable act, but said that it was the king alone who had decreed and commanded it to be done'—the time-honoured excuse for participation in atrocities. After further reflection and prayer, Saladin had him executed. Eight more Franks were captured and killed, then fourteen (of whom one was the daughter of the 'well-made' crusader). All were decapitated. Saladin's biography continues in this vein as prisoner after prisoner was brought before him, asked to provide military information such as the price of provisions in their army, length of stay at marching-stations, numbers of dead and wounded, numbers of horses lost—then beheaded at Saladin's command.

These unfortunate victims of Richard's decision and Saladin's wrath were deprived of the preferential treatment of upper-class prisoners, evident in many accounts such as that by Joinville, writing of his own experiences during King Louis' Egyptian crusade of 1250. In the midst of a battle on the Nile, Joinville found himself aboard a Saracen galley where he was nearly killed, only managing to save himself by claiming to be the king's cousin. The Moslem captain and his men then stripped him of his armour and gave him one of his own wraps and a belt; at his request they brought him some water. Afterwards, during an interview with the commander of the galleys, the latter told the good seneschal of Champagne that his lie about kinship with the king had saved his life. The commander and Joinville then dined together. Some four days after this, as Joinville and other defeated Franks were debarked from the ship, the weak and badly wounded among the lesser crusaders were summarily murdered and dumped into the water. The Moslem commander with whom he had dined then told Joinville that his crew had embraced Islam, an attempt to demoralize and tempt the seneschal which did not succeed: in the end, both the commander and Joinville agreed with a remark attributed to Saladin that 'one never saw a bad Christian become a good Saracen, nor a bad Saracen become a good Christian'. After this interview, Joinville was taken to a large tent, which housed the sultan's scribes who recorded prisoners' names and presumably other particulars. After being added to the POW register he was taken to another large pavilion, which apparently served as a holding area for all captives. Noblemen among them cheered when they saw the seneschal brought in, for they had lost track of him in the confusion. Eventually, a party of Moslems entered and ordered all the 'chief men' to go into yet another tent. This left only the lower ranks and non-combatants, at least some of whom were herded into a mud-walled pen. They were taken out one by one, commanded to become Moslems, and decapitated if they refused. Meanwhile representatives from the sultan came to the noblemen's tent and (through translators) discussed conditions of release. When the crusaders refused to hand over various castles in the Holy Land, talks broke down and the Saracens left, uttering ominous threats which seemed about to be implemented when a party of armed youths burst in upon the noblemen; however, the group soon left without harming anyone. Finally the sultan's agents returned with the news that King Louis had obtained their release through a cash payment and the surrender of Damietta. But Joinville was not yet in the clear, for he was to have other dangerous encounters in Egypt, as well as becoming involved in various diplomatic arrangements for the king.

As for the lower orders, though in some cases by co-operating they would then be sent away as refugees, the prospects for those who had resisted were not so good. When the possibility of a ransom was unlikely, the aged and weak of both sexes were killed and the remainder enslaved, though they could still be used in the bargaining process. Some Moslem writers claimed that slave-dealers were financially embarrassed when large hauls of Christians glutted the markets and drove prices down. Like the Italian merchants with whom they traded, Moslem slavers were very careful businessmen, even drawing up compilations of rules governing their trade and manuals for the careful slave buyer. Among the Moslem documents collected by Bernard Lewis there is, for example, an eleventh-century tract warning would-be buyers to beware unscrupulous traders and their tawdry wares, particularly with regard to female slaves. The first of many injunctions seems sensible enough: 'A lecher should not shop for slave-girls' since 'if he feels an urgent need, he will make a choice at first glance,' which could disappointment him later. Novice buyers were also advised to avoid fly-by-night operations at fairs and festivals, where slavers ply their worst tricks. These deceptions provide some idea of current standards of beauty or at least of what was thought desirable in slaves:

> How often has a scraggy girl been sold as plump, a dirty brown as a golden blonde, an ageing man as a full-bottomed boy, a bulging paunch as a trim, flat waist, a stinking mouth as perfumed breath. How often do they dye blemishes in the eyes and leprous sores on the body, and make light blue eyes dark blue. . . dye yellow cheeks red, make thin cheeks fat, enlarge small orifices, remove hair from cheeks, stain fair hair jet black, curl lanky hair, whiten brown faces. . .

The catalogue ends by reproving merchants who sold sick slaves as healthy or boy slaves as girls, the discovery of which must have been a surprise to the buyer when he returned home and unwrapped his purchase. Customers were encouraged to investigate the previous owner and his reasons for selling. It was also prudent to ensure that prospective purchases were not pregnant, though even menstrual flow was not a positive sign since clever girls 'insert other girls' blood in their private parts'. However, the seller was also given some advice along other lines: 'Never send a slave-girl from your house to the slave-dealer, except during the menstrual flow. Otherwise she is likely to become pregnant in the slave-quarters and claim that it is yours.' All of this concern about physiological detail is a reflection of Moslem custom concerning female slaves, which entailed preferential treatment for a slave whose owner admitted or could be shown to have fathered the child. According to some jurists, she could not be sold or transferred to another, and when her master died she was to be emancipated with her child. So important was this in contemporary Islamic society that the rules provided for almost every potential paternity conflict including, in addition to the owner, the owner's father and grandfather, if they may have had access to her; there were also regulations about paternity in the case of co-owners, and so on. Much red tape also complicated the process of emancipation. One of the customs recalls contemporary Christian teaching about marriage between kin: if a Moslem came somehow to own a slave who was related to him within 'the prohibited degrees' then emancipation was automatic.

Ordinary prisoners who survived the shock of battle and its immediate aftermath were distributed among the victors, though sometimes Saladin—at least before the Acre incident—freely allowed them to return to the crusader camp. His generous treatment of many poor Christians at Jerusalem was praised by Moslems and Christians alike. Even so, regardless of isolated notices of kindly treatment of prisoners, such as the old Saracen who used to carry one of Joinville's injured men to the privy whenever required, the lot of the average captive was an unenviable one. After one mid-twelfth-century battle, the defeated Christian knights (some on camels) rode into Damascus carrying their standards from which dangled the scalps of their comrades; foot-soldiers, roped together in bunches of three and four, walked dejectedly at their sides. When they reached Damascus the whole city—old men and young, women and children—turned out to cheer and revel in what God had granted. Someone composed a poem for the occasion—blessing the day 'when the shame of capture, defeat and disaster' engulfed the Franks.

As mentioned, Hattin was one of the worst crusader defeats recorded; there were many prisoners, and one Moslem was said to have taken away thirty captives tied together with a tent cord. Perhaps some of these prisoners were seen in later years by the crusaders who went on pilgrimage to Jerusalem under the peace terms agreed by Saladin and King Richard. According to Richard of Devizes visitors saw Christian prisoners

> chained together in companies, their feet ulcerated, their shoulders flayed, their buttocks goaded, their backs scourged; they carried material to the stonemasons to make Jerusalem impregnable against the Christians.

As early as the First Crusade, Christians used forced Saracen labour to help build siege machines used against Jerusalem, and, as noted, Christian captives were forced to dig counter-mines from Acre during the Third Crusade. Christians also put Moslem women to work, their legs in iron chains. Some of these prisoners, even poor ones, were ultimately released through ransom or other arrangements. For example, the religious order of the Mercedarians (or Nolascans), founded about 1220, was dedicated to aiding and freeing Christians and even taking their places as hostages until a ransom was paid. Fortunately, many were freed immediately after capture thanks to their ability to pay. In 1187 Saladin allowed the Christians of Jerusalem to ransom themselves at the rate of ten dinars per man (about two months' earnings for skilled Levantine craftsmen), five per woman and two (or perhaps one) for children. The same price ratio was mentioned some five years later at Jaffa. Regardless of such neat price categories, corrupt officials at Jerusalem seem to have released prisoners for whatever they could squeeze from them, turning a blind eye to Christians lowering themselves over the city walls on ropes or hiding in outbound baggage or disguising themselves as Moslems. It was said by Moslem historians that out of more than 100,000 inhabitants of Jerusalem, all were ransomed or released *ex gratia,* with the exception of about 7,000 men and 8,000 women and children sent into slavery.

Of course, Moslem prisoners too were detained until bought back by relatives or benefactors, even though philanthropy was sometimes rewarded with ingratitude and deceit. Between mid-century and 1187, a certain Abu Sa'd went with his friend Musallam to Nablus (Nābulus), where Abu Sa'd made a partial payment for the release of Musallam's sister, leaving a balance of sixty dinars. Afterwards Musallam and his sister went to Egypt, ostensibly to raise the rest of the ransom money, but nothing more was heard from them. 'And now', a worried Abu Sa'd wrote to his own brother in Egypt, 'the payment of the sixty dinars has fallen due' and the Frank had come to collect his money. He therefore begged his brother to search for Musallam and have him send 'either the gold or the girl' to satisfy the Frankish creditor. Interestingly enough, a recently-published letter reveals the reverse situation: it had been sent by a Nablus prisoner to his kin in Egypt during the twelfth century (and presumably before 1187 when Saladin captured Nablus from the crusaders). The prisoner seems to have been an ordinary victim of crusader aggression, perhaps an illiterate hoping to be ransomed for whom someone else wrote the letter:

I haven't had any news from you and my heart is in anguish for I don't know who is alive or dead. . . yet my heart is with you. Reply at once to this letter to comfort my heart. . . Don't neglect me, for you know that I am a captive.

We shall probably never know whether Musallam's sister ever returned from Egypt to Nablus, or whether the other captive was able to go from Nablus back home to Egypt, but these two twelfth-century episodes illuminate, however briefly, the fate of many ordinary Moslems and Christians caught up in the holy war; like their co-religionists bleaching in the desert at Hattin or rotting outside the walls of Acre, they were victims of an insoluble dilemma. It has been suggested that Moslems and crusaders could never have lived peacefully in the Holy Land, given contemporary religious and social differences. If so, Christian justification of war as a means to attain peace was meaningless from the start. Though there could be no fundamental compromises between the two great religions, in many ways Christians and Moslems shared a common universe of belief; that was the terrible irony behind the bitter grief and pointless slaughter engendered by the great Christian adventure.

PART TWO

Zealots and Infidels:
Religious Ideologies in Conflict

6

Searching for God: Christian Enthusiasm, Moslem Beliefs

He said, 'I am only a messenger of thy Lord, that I may bestow on thee a holy son.' She said, 'How shall I have a son, when man hath never touched me?'

(Koran)

The modern age of the common man has witnessed many mass demonstrations in pursuit of innumerable dreams; in the Middle Ages, too, crowds gathered in the open air to pray for the salvation of their souls and for protection against the arbitrary powers that surrounded them. In France by the year 1000, such rallies were addressed by ecclesiastics whose conciliar legislation and prophecies of peace instilled enthusiasm, especially in the *pauperes*, the baffled people lacking power or patrons, oppressed by puzzling, frustrating changes in family, society and economy. Through their massed prayers, these crowds willed not only the curbing of unruly knights, rapacious lords and the chastisement of greedy married priests, but also an end to floods, famines and plagues. Since their universe—human, social, natural and spiritual—was a unity ordained by the Creator, they cried to God to end the evil acts of men as well as the disorders of nature. Their prayers were enhanced by the power surrounding saints' relics carried into their midst from monasteries, which were drawing more and more pilgrims to their holy shrines. Even as they prayed, some fell writhing to the ground, clutching crippled legs that painfully and bloodily straightened under the awesome influence of the saints, as a Burgundian monk wrote.

The monk, Glaber, also described the promises to turn to God, the rousing shouts for 'Peace, Peace, Peace' that the crowd sent heavenwards as they raised their hands to the skies. That was about 1030. Immediately after this the monk says that the promises were not kept, for within a few years the great, then the ordinary, men of both clerical and secular society fell back into their avaricious ways. At the same time, 'an innumerable multitude from the whole world began to stream towards the Saviour's tomb at Jerusalem', more than could ever have been expected. Perhaps Glaber's juxtaposition of these three

115

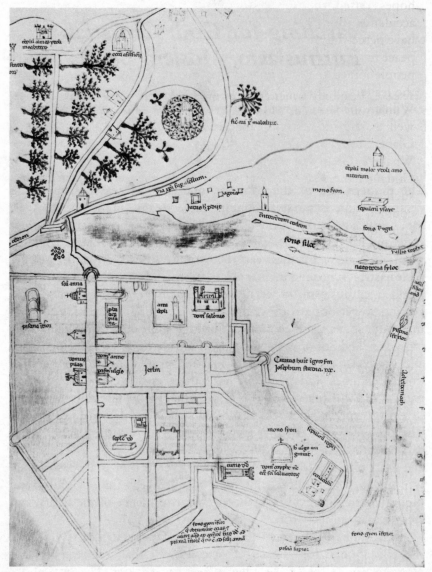

14 Plan of Jerusalem, emphasizing the Christian Church of the Sepulchre, and the sepulchre itself, centre-left. The fig tree cursed by Christ is shown, isolated in upper centre.
Oxford, Bodley *Tanner 190*, f. 206ᵛ.)

things, the enthusiasm of this Peace of God assembly, the failure of hopes raised there, and the mass pilgrimage to Jerusalem, was accidental. But (though he is vague here on chronology) he may well have perceived the pilgrimage to be a result of disappointed hopes for peace in southern France. In any case, he says that at first the common people joined the pilgrimage, then the middle-range folk and finally the leaders of society such as Duke Robert of Normandy, father of William the Conqueror. Even women went along, the most noble as well as the most humble—in numbers that must have impressed Glaber, for the Jerusalem pilgrimage by women was hardly novel. Whatever Glaber's perception of the relationship between the Peace of God movement and the pilgrimage to Jerusalem, for modern historians such as Cowdrey, the enthusiasm generated by such assemblies, coupled with the Church's concept of the holy war, would ultimately contribute to the armed pilgrimage known as the First Crusade: paradoxical as it may seem, the cry 'God wills it!' of 1095 is an echo of 'Peace, Peace, Peace', of the 1030s.

The enthusiastic, visionary, miracle-seeking *pauper*, the powerless man, was swept into the Holy Land at an early stage in the movement, for the most part well in advance of the 'proper' armies. He was encouraged by prophets like Peter the Hermit, revered by the common people as a miracle-worker and messenger of God—after all, Peter was supposed to have received a letter direct from heaven. While he and other poverty-loving preachers evangelized, spreading their new gospel of salvation through the crusade, God seemed to will nature itself to co-operate in mass recruitment. It was believed, for example, that the animal world joined the popular crusades either as leaders (like the inspired goose and the perspicacious goat associated with German rampages) or as followers (herds of cattle meekly organizing themselves to accompany and feed the crowds). Just as God had shown his presence in peace rallies through miraculous cures, on the verge of the First Crusade even the skies gave clear proof—for those who would recognize it—of the Lord's accompaniment. Armies were seen fighting in the clouds and herdsmen saw a city (presumably Jerusalem) in the air, says Ekkehard of Aura. The birth of prodigies such as infants who could speak, or two-headed creatures, also seemed to prove that the old order was about to pass away. Meteor showers prefigured a myriad of souls en route to salvation, just as the crosses that appeared by the sun signified God's concern. As Rousset says, nature was mobilized to encourage man; co-operative celestial and spiritual forces jolted the

117

senses and the inner visionary eye as well. Heaven and earth merged, as did past and present: in the minds of enthusiasts, Jerusalem became at once celestial and earthly. Social, natural and spiritual forces interacted synergetically through the lesser ranks, bursting out from time to time to hurry dilatory knights and quarrelling noblemen on to their goal, Jerusalem. This is clearly seen among the masses who joined the First Crusade under Raymond, Count of Toulouse: whereas the premature popular crusades of northern Europe and the Rhineland ended in catastrophe in the Balkans or Anatolia, many of the poor of southern France joined the official crusade, which may have been crucial for the success of the whole enterprise.

By the time the crusaders reached Antioch in October 1097, they had suffered the physical hardships of the Anatolian trek and were feeling the consequences of internal rivalry as their leaders grew more interested in personal gain: then, after capturing Antioch, they found themselves trapped in the city with no apparent means of escape. In these circumstances, strong undercurrents of visionary enthusiasm came to the surface. For instance, a cleric trying to flee the city was stunned by a vision of Christ himself, who encouraged him and promised aid. A crusader letting himself down the walls on a rope under cover of darkness was turned back by his dead brother, who declared that God would come to the rescue. A cleric reported a vision confirming Christ's special love of the poor, his chosen people. Rescue was, in fact, to come from these despised, inferior ranks: the most famous outbreak of the supernatural at Antioch was linked to an insignificant, semi-literate visionary named Peter Bartholomew. His story is intimately connected with the rivalries among crusade leaders. Peter was a lowly member of the Provençal group led by Raymond of Toulouse. Raymond's main rivals were the Normans of northern France led by Robert (of Normandy) and the Normans of southern Italy, under Bohemond (of Taranto). Since the visionary, Peter Bartholomew, travelled under Raymond's banners, naturally Robert and Bohemond and their followers tended to discount his apparitions and tales of visions.

These visions, which first occurred while the Christian armies were still besieging Antioch in 1097, were recorded by Raymond of Aguilers, the sympathetic chaplain, historian and namesake of Count Raymond. Apparently St Andrew came to Peter Bartholomew and told him that the lance that had pierced Christ's side at the crucifixion was buried in St Peter's church in Moslem-held Antioch. The saint

15 and 16 Two views of Antioch and its walls. Site of their first major military engagement in the Holy Land, the crusaders were miraculously assisted by the discovery of the Holy Lance within the well-fortified city. (*Syria, the Holy Land, Asia Minor*, illus. by W. Bartlett et al., London, 1836–38. Oxford, Bodley 20606 d. 47.)

indicated where Peter should dig (after the crusaders had captured the city) to retrieve the sacred relic, which would assure continued victories. Some time afterwards, this vision was repeated with additional special instructions for Count Raymond, but when Peter tried to convey these wonders to the noble Raymond he was rebuffed. After all, not only was he not a clergyman, but even among laymen Peter also seems—for whatever reason—to have been something of an outcast. In any event, the crusaders took Antioch by 3 June 1098. Once inside, however, they were in turn besieged by the Moslems; as hope faded and desertions deepened the gloom within the walls, Peter Bartholomew continued to have visions. After the failure of a sortie on 9/10 June, Raymond of Toulouse finally decided to listen to Peter's most recent revelations. Hearing about St Andrew and the lance, Raymond at once took it to be a true heavenly visitation. He ordered a search of the specified church and, at mid-month, after workmen had dug all day beneath the floor, Peter Bartholomew himself emerged from the excavation holding what he claimed to be the holy lance. Neither the papal legate, Adhèmar of Le Puy, accepted Peter's visions, even though Adhèmar was closely associated with Count Raymond, nor did some other crusade leaders who were not associated with Raymond. Yet, among the ranks of fighting men in general and the southern French in particular, the lance was a token of victory that restored their hopes, their optimism and consequently their morale. The leaders put aside their squabbles and scepticism about the relic and prepared to take advantage of the revitalized spirits of their armies. Peter reported two more visions extolling the lance and promising victory; finally, on 28 June, after a three-day fast and procession, the crusaders launched an attack against the encircling Moslem ranks. As the Christians left the city, they were blessed and encouraged by vestured priests standing on the walls holding crosses and calling on God's aid. As a further indication of crusader zeal, in the distance, some Christians thought they saw white banners and men on white horses riding down from the mountains, the angelic troupe led by St George, St Mercurius and St Demetrius (or perhaps St Theodore), all warrior-saints. The sortie was a success, rolling back the enemy; many attributed victory to the lance, proudly carried into battle by Raymond's forces. At this point, Peter Bartholomew's popularity and credibility reached its zenith.

Peter was certainly not the only visionary among the crusader host. Another supernatural intervention at Antioch involved a priest called

Stephen. About the time that Peter had his vision of the lance and reported it to Count Raymond, Stephen had a vision of Jesus, the Blessed Virgin Mary and St Peter, which he described for the papal legate, Adhèmar. Although Adhèmar had refused to believe in simple Peter's visitation, he fully accepted priest Stephen's. In the vision, Jesus complained that the lewd sexual behaviour of the Christians in Antioch had caused a great stink—*immensus foetor*—in heaven. After Mary and Peter begged Christ to soften his wrath, he promised to help the crusaders, provided they would amend their ways and sing part of Psalm 47 every day for five days. Using this vision, Adhèmar obtained from the noble leaders an oath to co-operate and not to attempt to flee the city. This greatly encouraged the rank-and-file. As in the case of the holy lance, what began as the imagery of a real or invented vision was translated by others into practical action at the highest level.

Though Antioch was now Christian, chronic jealousies among the nobles soon resurfaced in the form of argument about whether Bohemond or (as Raymond of Toulouse suggested) the Byzantine Emperor Alexius should be lord of the city. In the midst of these aristocratic disputes, Adhèmar, the one universally respected figure who had been able to keep tempers relatively cool, died on 1 August 1098. Two days later, Peter Bartholomew reported another vision in which Adhèmar himself appeared and confessed that he had been punished after death for disbelieving the story of the lance. In addition, Adhèmar's co-apparition, St Andrew, suggested to Peter Bartholomew that Bohemond should have control of Antioch and Raymond of Toulouse ought to lead the crusaders on to Jerusalem. Unfortunately for Peter Bartholomew, this vision stirred up animosity all round, since it seemed to slander the highly-respected Adhèmar, and at the same time it discredited Raymond Count of Toulouse because he had withstood Bohemond's control of Antioch. From this point on, Count Raymond slowly disengaged himself from Peter's circle, though he continued to believe in the lance. As for the visionary, whether Peter acted through sincerity, stupidity, or a desire for attention, his vision probably summed up the unstated wishes of the anxious, ordinary folk who were afraid that their push to Jerusalem would be forever delayed by squabbling noblemen. The net result was continued disputation between Frankish northerners and southerners and between leaders and followers. Hoping to relieve the pressure, in October 1098 Count Raymond launched an attack on nearby Albara–ignoring yet another vision granted to Peter urging that the leaders get on with the march to the holy city. By the first week of November, while the great men were squabbling as usual (in the church of St Peter in Antioch) an impatient crowd demonstrated outside and threatened to tear down the city walls and head for Jerusalem with or without the nobility. The ever-diverging interests of the enthusiastic masses on the one hand, and their calculating leaders on the other, could not have been more clearly expressed.

During December the capture of Maarat provided another place over which Bohemond and Raymond of Toulouse could argue. Finally, after the poorer crusaders decided to destroy Maarat's walls to force a decision, it was agreed that Bohemond would retain Antioch while Raymond—with full control of the crusade, which he had desired all along—would lead the majority of the participants on to Jerusalem. The march began in mid-January 1099, some fifteen months after the armies had arrived at Antioch. By mid-February, the crusaders had travelled approximately 130 miles to the south, where Raymond halted to besiege the town of Arqa. Once again, the movement bogged down as Raymond stubbornly refused to give up the siege. During the first week of April, Peter Bartholomew had yet another, and this time fateful, vision, which commanded an immediate attack on Arqa. By now many ordinary crusaders wished to abandon Arqa and go on to their sworn destination, and, in these exasperating circumstances, to hear contradictory advice from Peter Bartholomew's private pipeline to the other world was the last straw.

His vision contained five sections. In the first part of the vision, Peter claimed to have learned that Christ's five wounds represented different types of crusader, three praiseworthy and two disreputable, those interested only in personal gain, and those who actually fled the battles; Christ also encouraged the plan to assault Arqa. In the second part of the vision, those who disbelieved Christ's—that is, Peter's—messages were condemned. Part three illustrates the tenacious xenophobia and incipient anti-semitism of the crusades, for Peter Bartholomew reported that Christ hated Jews. A fourth and more practical visionary recommendation called for a general peace-keeping organization within the crusader ranks, made up of several judges who would sort out conflicts in the camp. Finally, Peter claimed that Christ declined to return his literacy to him (there was speculation about the extent of his learning), since his native intellect and belief were sufficient. Raymond of Aguilers, Peter's spokesman and defender, found that many were not willing to believe that Christ had spoken these things to such a lowly person. In addition, the complex vision raised again all the old issues concerning the validity of Peter's original claims concerning the holy lance. Raymond of Aguilers and others of his party arranged a confrontation, inviting those who had had, or knew of, visions about the lance to present their testimony to the ecclesiastical leader of the opposition, Arnulf of Rohes, chaplain to Robert of Normandy (and eventually first patriarch of Jerusalem). Some time during the first week of April 1099, at least four priests and a bishop came forward to relate visions confirming the truth of the lance story. One of the priests even volunteered to go through the ordeal of fire to demonstrate the truth of what he said, an offer which may have planted a dangerous idea in the minds of onlookers. Having heard this evidence, Arnulf claimed that he was now convinced of the truth of the lance-visions. He promised his superior, the Bishop of Albara (an appointee of Raymond Count of Toulouse), to confess publicly his earlier errors, thereby indirectly bolstering Raymond of Toulouse's leadership and Peter Bartholomew's reputation. At a subsequent crusade council, however, Arnulf backed down and claimed that he wished to confer with his lord, Robert of Normandy, before accepting penance for his scepticism. At this reversal Peter Bartholomew flew into a rage and, artless man that he was (*sicut homo simplex*), demanded to be put to the ordeal by fire so that his visions would be believed once and for all. This was arranged by Raymond of Aguilers and others pleased with the idea (*placuerunt haec omnia nobis*, Raymond writes), who ordered Peter Bartholomew to fast and prepare himself for the test.

On the day appointed—Good Friday, 8 April 1099—Peter came out to face two rows of dry olive branches some thirty or forty feet long and four feet high, with only the narrowest space between (the manuscripts say *quasi unius pedis*, about a foot). The army and vestured priests watched as the fires were lit and Raymond of Aguilers addressed the kneeling crowd, specifying the terms of the ordeal: if God and St Andrew had truly spoken to Peter Bartholomew about the lance, let him pass without harm through this fire; if not, let him and the lance which he will carry be burnt. Peter then knelt before the Bishop of Albara and asserted the truth of his vision, denied any falsehood, asked forgiveness for his sins and requested the prayers of the bystanders. The bishop handed the lance wrapped in fine cloth to Peter, who arose and went into the blazing corridor.

When he emerged he was holding the lance up for all to see and shouting for God's help. The excitement was so great that the surging crowd nearly crushed him, but he was rescued and taken to Raymond of Aguiler's (or perhaps, as Alphandery suggests, Count Raymond's) quarters. Many people saw burns on his legs and serious wounds on his body. Yet he was alive, and for some—Raymond of Toulouse and Raymond of Aguilers for instance—the lance was vindicated. Unfortunately, the experiment did not end neatly, for Peter Bartholomew died some twelve days later; by neither expiring amidst the fires nor living to a ripe old age, he destroyed the certainty expected of a divine judgment. On the other hand, the incident did provide a way to resolve a deadlocked confrontation and, as Peter Brown has remarked, such decisions made by God and not man saved face, one of the social functions of the medieval ordeal. Ambiguity lies at the heart of every ordeal: here, even after his death his (and Raymond of Toulouse's) enemies could claim that Peter Bartholomew was a fraud, while his allies could continue to support him. There are a few other curious points about this famous ordeal. In particular, there is a strange accusation which the dying Peter levelled at a certain Raymond, one of the chaplains of Raymond of Toulouse. As Alphandery noted, it raises a question about the 'spontaneity' of the whole operation. Peter called the chaplain to him and asked him why he had wanted him to go through the fire to verify the messages received from God, adding that he—Peter—was amazed (*miror satis*) that the chaplain had desired so dangerous an *experimentum*. Raymond of Aguilers says the chaplain then broke down in tears, at which Peter Bartholomew forgave him. Perhaps Peter finally realized in his agony how his visions had been manipulated, for example by this chaplain and by Raymond of Toulouse, the nobleman who had a clear interest in the matter of the lance. The chaplain may even have been Raymond of Aguilers himself, who had admitted that he liked the idea of the ordeal, and who seems to have promoted it. In the last analysis, Peter Bartholomew was a victim of crusader rivalry: not only were his veracity and reputation a matter of dispute between the southern and northern Franks, but in the end his life itself may have been sacrificed to baronial pressure and pride. After Peter was buried at Arqa, Count Raymond gave up the siege and marched on to Jerusalem. As for the famous Antioch lance (there were others), it was officially rejected by the Church in the eighteenth century; many claims have been made, but no one knows what became of it. Though there is no reason to doubt Peter Bartholomew's sincerity, his visions may well have changed through suggestion and feedback to suit the policies of the Count of Toulouse. Nevertheless, his original visions and the lance discovery certainly did raise morale among the besieged crusaders at Antioch, and he was prepared to announce visions that favoured Bohemond, while urging Count Raymond to lead the crusaders on towards Jerusalem. In this he faithfully reflected the anxieties and deep emotional drives of many a hopeful, enthusiastic *homo simplex*.

Though Peter's death should have been a warning to others, men on the First Crusade continued to report supernatural visitations. During mid-May 1099, in the vicinity of Tripoli, a priest named Stephen (who had also experienced a vision at Antioch, noted above) claimed that the dead bishop Adhèmar struck him with his staff and ordered the lance to be carried before the crusaders. Adhèmar also wished to have Christ's cross, which context suggests was his own episcopal cross, borne in the forefront of the Christian host. The vision (the dead prelate was accompanied by the Virgin Mary, St Agatha and another virgin holding two candles) seems to reaffirm the spiritual nature of the expedition rather than to confirm the secular leadership of Raymond of Toulouse. Finally, yet another priest (Peter Desiderius) had a visionary encounter during the siege of Jerusalem in July 1099. He, too, had experienced an earlier apparition, announced at the great pre-ordeal debate in Arqa where he claimed that Adhèmar's beard and hair were singed by hellfire because he had doubted the lance. Now, before the holy city itself, Adhèmar's ghost appeared to him a second time. The spirit urged the leaders to forget their differences, then ordered the army to fast and go in procession before the walls of Jerusalem. This was done, thanks to the encouragement of the dead bishop's brother to whom the vision was reported: there was a three-day fast, a barefoot procession (duly parodied by whooping Moslems prancing about on the walls) and finally a marathon preaching session at the Mount of Olives (the roll-call of preachers is interesting, including Peter the Hermit, Arnulf of Rohes and Raymond of Aguilers). The righteous indignation generated by all of this spiritual heat may have helped the crusaders to breach the wall and pillage the city a week later. Just before this final triumph, a mysterious warrior brandishing a splendid gleaming shield, another supernatural sign, was seen on the Mount of Olives. Even when taking the city, the crusaders had further visitations, for many saw the dead Adhèmar scale the walls and lead the attack. After the combat had finished, William of Tyre records, others who had died were seen visiting the holy places of Jerusalem alongside the living; since they had assisted in the enterprise, the dead were permitted to share in the spoils of victory.

17 A seventeenth-century Dutch version of Christians bathing in the Jordan, a ritual common to pilgrims and crusaders alike. (*Naukeurige Beschryving van gantsch Syrie*, O. Dapper Amsterdam, 1677. Oxford, Bodley Mason T. 128.)

Though faith and hysteria alone were not enough, without such occasional manifestations of enthusiasm the vast enterprise might well have failed long before the holy city was even sighted, as Hagenmeyer suggested long ago. Even in victory, invisible authority continued to aid the Christian cause. After the crusaders took Jerusalem, Arnulf of Rohes, who had resisted the influence of Peter Bartholomew and the lance, was elected patriarch. In order, perhaps, to emphasize the legitimacy of his and his party's position in the matter of that controversial relic, Arnulf 'found' an even more potent object. After making inquiries about the cross pilgrims once venerated at Jerusalem, he discovered the True Cross itself, buried in the floor of a church; by these non-visionary means he neatly counterbalanced the influence of Peter Bartholomew's popular support. In other words, the Cross and the official Church gained equality in stature with the lance and the laity.

Primitive urges of another order, in the broad anthropological sense similarly associated with man's confrontation with the holy, are also evident during the First Crusade. In his classic study, Norman Cohn treated the Tafurs (mentioned in an earlier chapter) as an aberrant image of the millennium-seeking, displaced poor, an image partly literary and partly historical. A paper published by Rouche in 1981 provided another interesting interpretation of these infamous bands, which re-emphasizes the importance of non-rational forces during the First Crusade. Apparently a substantial contingent of the Peoples' crusade survived the east European and Anatolian massacres to find their way into the Holy Land, where they fell in with the official crusade led by Bohemond, Robert of Normandy and the others. 'Fell in with' because they had no desire actually to join the organized military bands, and held themselves aloof, proud of their poverty, a special corps under a Norman knight who had exchanged his armour and sword for rags and a scythe. Like St Francis over a century later, this knight, who had accepted voluntary poverty, insisted that his followers remain poor or be ejected from the group. They were to carry only the simplest weapons such as pointed sticks or clubs or, better still, none at all. Their name, Tafur, may have been nothing but a distorted version of their leader's name. The zealous band was always in the forefront of battle, where their berserk attacks made them feared by Moslems and crusaders alike. At other times they greatly assisted the knights and foot-soldiers by bringing ammunition, manipulating siege machines or carrying impedimenta. Perhaps Peter Bartholomew was thinking of them in his last pre-ordeal vision when he described a third category of fighters, who brought stones and javelins to the first ranks. When any attack was launched or a narrow pass was to be taken, the Tafurs were in the vanguard, gnashing their teeth as if they would devour the Moslems.

Most of the foregoing has been commonly attributed to the Tafurs for some time, but Rouche's discussion of specific aspects of their behaviour strikes off in other directions. According to him, the Tafurs and their leader took spiritual guidance from that magical figure, Peter the Hermit, who had rejoined the First Crusade after the slaughter in Anatolia of his eager followers in 1096. Now, in 1098, he once again found himself the elected prophet of a simple yet determined rabble. Rouche has suggested that Peter the Hermit inflamed the Tafurs' eschatological dreams and fed them with spiritual sustenance based upon the Old Testament model of God leading the Chosen People through the desert. In addition, in a kind of macabre re-interpretation of those Old Testament texts, Peter urged the Tafurs to make ritual meals out of dead Saracens, 'new manna' that would sustain them until they reached the Promised Land of 'milk and honey'. Thus, at Antioch and at Maarat, they cut the flesh into pieces, cooked and devoured it—saving bits for later—not just to avoid starvation, but also to enhance spiritual life through a shared ceremonial sacrifice. The revolting behaviour of the Tafurs, then, was actually sacred cannibalism carried out by a closed community of the poor dedicated to throwing themselves, without inhibition, against the enemy in the hope of reaching either the earthly or the heavenly homeland of God. The sealing of their dedication to this goal by eating the dead was perhaps a ritual of reversal in which pollution would lead to power, as described by Mary Douglas:

> When someone embraces freely the symbols of death, or death itself, then it is consistent. . . that a great release of power for good should be expected to follow.

Whether the Tafurs embodied 'power for good' is a moot point, but in any event, Rouche concludes that the Tafurs personified that poverty and messianic animation which was the very soul of the First Crusade: their sacred cannibalism was 'one of the effectual causes of the crusade's success'. This may be attributing too much to too little, though it becomes more convincing when combined with the other outbursts of popular enthusiasm described above. Without such emotional impulses, crusading energies might well have dissipated long before the armies had reached Jerusalem.

After the First Crusade ended, this spirit of enthusiasm grew progressively attenuated, though some of the old fire revived at the start of the Second Crusade. Playing a less important role after this, there are, however, some examples in later centuries of popular enthusiasm, like the omens that continued to presage changes in the crusader states, or to announce forthcoming expeditions: Innocent III stirred up interest in a crusade at the Fourth Lateran Council (1215) and by 1217 German peasants were seeing crosses in the sky, while a lunar eclipse witnessed by crusaders in Egypt in 1218 was further 'proof' that the Saracens would be defeated. Preachers naturally drew upon the world of marvels to stimulate their audiences. In the early thirteenth century, Jacques de Vitry related the story of two brothers from Scotland who took the cross. Though one of them died before completing the crusade, his grave was opened some time afterwards and he was found to be wearing the habit of a palmer, as if his armed pilgrimage had been carried out after death. Such stories could not have failed to strike an appreciative chord in the hearts of *illiterati*. The crusade even featured in visions of the night in northern England. A labourer, injured in a building accident in the 1170s, went for a cure to the shrine of the hermit Godric of Finchale (d. 1170), near Durham. During incubation there (common practice in medieval Europe), a saint appeared to him saying that after his cure he should take the cross and go to Jerusalem, for he would be accompanied and protected by Jesus and the Blessed Virgin. Then, using three fingers, the vision-saint drew a cross on the man's right arm. A tiny cross, as if made of two dazzling white threads, seemed to be inscribed into his flesh. Even in the midst of King Richard's bellicose venture, there are indications that spiritual dedication had not entirely deserted the laity. During the march south after the conquest of Acre, each night as the camp prepared for sleep, someone called on the holy sepulchre three times in a loud voice. Ambroise says the whole camp repeated the cry, everyone raising hands to the heavens. And when an abbot gave what was purported to be a piece of the True Cross to King Richard, everyone tearfully rushed to worship it. Ambroise adds, significantly, that after this excitement the poor and humble grew impatient to get on to Jerusalem.

The 'official' Church continued the attempt to modulate these spiritual demonstrations. Processions, for instance, were organized at crucial moments: before the break-out at Antioch in 1098 and prior to the charge against Jerusalem in 1099. Just before the attack on Acre in 1189, the army formed up in procession with King Guy of Jerusalem at the centre, preceded by the Gospels carried reverently beneath a satin canopy. Processions were ordered at Damietta in 1249 to hasten the arrival of overdue crusaders; the legate preached and granted full indulgences to all on these occasions. As far as was practicable, the liturgical and canonical forms were observed: at King Richard's siege of Acre an English bishop imposed penance upon starving crusaders

129

who had eaten meat during Lent, while an English archbishop gave the crusaders a general absolution before an important attack on the city. Even the crusaders about to assault Constantinople in the infamous Fourth Crusade were asked by the clergy to confess their sins and draw up their wills, which they did 'piously', as Villehardouin claims. Though they tried to modify the spiritual excesses of the laity, the clergy themselves were sometimes just as eager as the meanest peasant to possess relics. In the course of the Fourth Crusade, a certain abbot

18 Relics of the Holy Land were prized by both crusaders and clergy, as violently demonstrated in the Christians' sacking of Constantinople in the Fourth Crusade. Here St Louis receives (what purport to be) the Crown of Thorns, True Cross, Nails and Holy Lance, all principal relics of the Passion. (London, Brit. Library *MS Royal 16 G VI*, f. 395[R])

Martin bullied an old Greek priest into opening his relic-chest. The abbot thrust both hands in, scooping up as much as he could carry away with his chaplain's help. The clergy could be as demonstrative as laymen, too. During the next crusade—the Fifth, at Damietta— the patriarch of Jerusalem himself prayed humbly in the dust before the True Cross, while around him the barefoot clergy sent their prayers skyward. As suggested above, while the lance had become the special totem of the poor, the True Cross (there were many 'fragments') found a natural haven with the official hierarchy as well as with the laity. Saladin captured what was said to be the True Cross in 1187 at Hattin; crusaders sent out afterwards to look for it on the fields of battle found no sign of it—'il n'i trouverent rienz'; nevertheless purported pieces of this holiest of relics continued to be revered throughout Christendom to the end of the Middle Ages and long after. In 1483 Caxton printed a prayer calling upon God to remove the Cross from unworthy hands and restore it to its rightful owners. Within a century most Protestants were to treat these so-called relics of the Cross with as little respect and as much vilification as the Moslems themselves.

All of the practices and underlying beliefs previously discussed are aspects of one religion, Christianity. There was and is great variety in the ways that Christians internalize as well as express their beliefs. Today's weeping cripples hoping for miraculous cures at Lourdes are no less Catholic than Jesuit theologians. In the Middle Ages the same rich spectrum of religious behaviour is observable among the Moslems with whom the crusaders came into contact. It could even be suggested that most crusaders would probably have been surprised, if not disconcerted, to see how far Moslem religious practices resembled their own; the similarities even extended to certain limited aspects of theology as well. Recognition of these similarities slowly made its way into medieval Europe as more and more Arabic writings (including the Koran) were translated, and as political relations between Moslems and Christians changed during and after the twelfth century.

Islam, which some crusaders castigated as 'paganism', an idolatrous, infidel corruption of the sacred truth, was in fact based upon an uncompromising monotheism. However, the framework within which Mohammad's ideas developed was structured along lines of conflict involving many competing forces—religious, political, economic, familial: Judaism and Christianity, Byzantine factions and Persian, townsmen and bedouin, Medinans and Meccans, clan and hostile clan. Sixth-century Mecca was a commercial centre under the hegemony of Mohammad's clan (or tribe) the Quraysh, who exploited the pan-tribal pilgrimage to the ancient Arabian shrine in Mecca, the Ka'ba. At this time, too, both Jewish Arabs and Christian Arabs had settled their own villages in the region, relatively undisturbed by followers of the indigenous pantheon of Arabic gods, goddesses and assorted sprites. Tension was never absent, however, because client-patron relationships, which constantly dissolved and reformed in new patterns, often entailed religious altercation. When the Christian Abyssinians began to encroach in central Arabia with

Byzantine connivance, for instance, Meccan leaders reacted by reinforcing the importance of pilgrimage to the Ka'ba and emphasizing its function as a centre for polytheism. This revitalization was in full swing at the time of Mohammad's birth around AD 570 in Mecca. As a young man—for reasons best left to the psychohistorians—he had been drawn to Judaeo-Christian traditions and repelled by tribal polytheism. His business career, as well as his mystical inclinations, brought him into contact with these alternative streams of Semitic thought, though precisely how and when is not known. The result was Islam, the religion of submission to one god whose nature and plans for mankind were embodied in the suras or chapters of the Koran.

The one god of Mohammad was the god of Abraham, Moses and Jesus. The followers of these earlier prophets had distorted or ignored their messages and Mohammad, the last of the prophets, was now re-presenting monotheism in its pristine form to the Arabic world. Because Judaism and Christianity both touched upon the truth, however, not only their great spiritual leaders but also their writings were respected, even revered, by Moslems. Abraham was most highly honoured, while Jesus, the Messiah as the Koran calls him, was second only to Mohammad himself for later generations of Moslems. Not only does the Koran (in suras iii, v and xix, for instance) sing the praises of Abraham, Isaac, Jacob, Moses, Aaron, Ishmael and Enoch, it also describes the angelic annunciation to the Virgin Mary, her flight and the birth of the Messiah who announces himself as God's prophet. Some of the childhood miracles of Jesus—based upon apocryphal Christian writings long in circulation in the eastern Mediterranean world—are recounted, and some of the details of his later life. The many places visited by the virgin and Christ, as well as sites linked with Adam, Noah, Abel and other biblical figures, were honoured throughout the Islamic world. Moslem attitudes towards Christ prompted behaviour which puzzled and attracted the attention of various crusade chroniclers such as Joinville. He claimed that an envoy sent by St Louis to the Old Man of the Mountain, leader of the Assassins, found a book of 'sayings of Jesus' at the Old Man's bedside. Earlier in the thirteenth century, Oliver of Paderborn reports that Moslems in Jerusalem venerated and kissed the Christian New Testament because of the wisdom of Jesus that it contained; they especially revered the gospel of St Luke, which told of the angel Gabriel's annunciation to Mary. In Moslem belief Gabriel had also been sent to Mohammad, bringing him the Koran.

Although it was once fashionable to attribute Mohammad's visionary encounters to epilepsy or to wrapping himself in a blanket and hyperventilating—just as some believe that it is possible today to blame ergot-infested rye bread for New England witchcraft or the French Revolution—most historians no longer favour such explanations. Mohammad's vision-quest was quite in keeping with an older, extensive belief-pattern within Semitic culture and need not be accounted for in mechanistic terms. In his day it was believed that angels and *djinn* roamed the desert, and thus they were perceived to do so! The celestial messages dictated to Mohammad by Gabriel and written down by Mohammad's friends and followers were said to be inscribed in an eternal, heavenly exemplar in God's keeping. An earthly copy of things celestial, the Koran of thousands of verses in 114 chapters or suras was, *inter alia*, the culmination of earlier Jewish and Christian teachings. As in the case of Old and New Testament textual history, however, different versions of the Koran were circulating soon after Mohammad's death in 632. According to tradition, the third caliph (Uthman) ordered the collation of written and oral variants, followed by the publication of an authoritative text. After this all other versions were to be burned so that Moslems, as a ninth-century writer explained it, would not argue about scriptural canonicity 'like Jews and Christians'. Even so, not everyone accepted this official version and some Moslems resisted it for centuries, just as St Jerome's Latin Bible—the Vulgate, used throughout the Middle Ages—was not officially adopted by the Catholic Church until the sixteenth-century Council of Trent. Alongside the Koran, numerous oral traditions grew up, purportedly reaching back to the Prophet. These *ḥadīth* themselves soon came to be written down, but the variations and contradictions among them were tremendous, increasing with each passing generation. Some scholars spent their lives in Koranic exegesis (*tafsīr*), while others toiled away trying to simplify the tangled strands of traditions, distinguishing authentic from spurious *ḥadīth*. Much the same process (which still goes on in all three religions) also marked Jewish and Christian exegetical investigations. The average Christian likes to believe in the three wise men, the manger and shepherds, just as the average Moslem accepts the story of Mohammad's magical night-ride from Mecca to Jerusalem, regardless of the fastidious reservations of scholars.

Passing from the writings and traditions to the doctrines and daily practices of Islam, these were few, simple, but essential. Mohammad required first of all that believers must acknowledge the omnipotence of God and the helplessness of man. In fact, this led Moslem scholars into the free-will-versus-predestination labyrinth, which also bemused their Jewish and Christian counterparts; yet, for the screaming rank-and-file of Moslems rushing toward a line of crusaders, it was encouraging to know that they would not die that day unless God had willed it. On the other hand, most crusaders do not seem to have benefited from a similar fatalistic sense of security; if they were defeated or killed it was not so much God's will, which was unavoidable, but their own sinfulness, which was avoidable. Other pillars of Islam were almsgiving, pilgrimage, a holy period of fasting rather like the Christians' Lent, and prayer, which was to occur three, then later on five, times daily. Prayers could be offered anywhere and at any time in addition to the traditional hours. Saladin's secretary mentions a group of Moslems standing on the beach at Acre, encouraging three of their supply ships through the Frankish blockade by baring their heads and praying most fervently, with rewarding results. Wherever possible, however, Moslems prayed in their mosques, led by the *imam*, facing the *mihrab* or niche that marked the direction of Mecca. Unlike the churches used by crusaders in Europe and the Holy Land, mosques, although all-purpose community centres, were not necessarily areas of sanctuary (*ḥaram*). The tendency was to treat them as special, though not sacred, places. When the crusaders launched their ridiculous attack on Damascus during the Second Crusade, for example, the citizens gathered in the Great Mosque for safety and prayer. An ancient, priceless copy of the Koran was brought out, the people sprinkled ashes on their heads and shed tears of supplication, which were answered. Mosques also functioned as educational areas ('institutions' is misleading) insofar as teachers decided to settle near by, sometimes encouraged by pious men of wealth. Patronage was important, as in the medieval West. A fourteenth-century sultan, for example, endowed a mosque and college at Tlemcen (in modern Algeria) with gardens, houses, plots of land and arable fields, orchards, mills and bath houses. In addition to the usual parishioners, so to speak, and students milling about a mosque, the buildings and grounds were also frequented by merchants, soldiers and jurists, as well as the poor, who slept there wherever they were allowed; blind men, for instance, are said to have been sheltered in the Baghdad mosque. Just as in the Christian churches and cathedrals of Europe, however, it was sometimes necessary to do a bit of house-cleaning: in 1415, some 750 poor people were ejected from under the arcades of the Cairo mosque, where their kind were supposed to have dwelled ever since its foundation. In addition to being places of prayer, shelter, study and what Michael Rogers calls secular ceremonial, the mosque was also a venue for preaching. Nominees of the local ruler delivered their sermons every Friday (when attendance was compulsory) from an often elaborately decorated *minbar* or pulpit. Because early mosques were founded by particular ruling families, the subject of discourse was not limited to Koranic themes, but often strayed into the political. When Saladin took Jerusalem, for instance, he had a famous scholar preach a celebratory sermon of victory in the famous al-Aqsa mosque, which redounded as much to Saladin's reputation as to God's. On the other hand, when the Christians regained Jerusalem by treaty in 1229, a respected Moslem preacher ascended the *minbar* in the Great Mosque at Damascus to bewail the loss of the holy city, recounting its glories and history; all Damascus was in mourning that day. Just as, according to William of Tyre, Urban II had lamented Jerusalem's subjection to superstitious, pagan Moslems in 1095, in 1229 the Damascus preacher grieved for pious believers still in Jerusalem, caught up in the desolation of Christian polytheism.

Since Mohammad was influenced by many Judaeo-Christian teachings, it is not surprising to find echoes of these in other Islamic doctrines, for example in those concerning the after-life. At death, deserving Moslems enjoyed the rewards of heaven whereas the wicked and unbelievers were punished in hell, a place of fire, scorching winds, boiling water and black smoke. At the Last Judgment, when Jesus the Messiah will return, all the graves will open at the trumpet's blast and the final disposition of every human being will occur. As in Judaism and even more so in Christianity, such doctrines provided Moslem scholars with topics of analysis and argumentation for centuries. For many others, however, the message was accepted as a literal truth. Jonaid, a tenth-century mystic, saw the souls of martyrs drawn up on litters to heaven as their bodies fell in battle, while a twelfth-century Moslem writer claimed that a certain freethinker was seen after his death being tormented by two snakes. As for the pleasures of heaven, the Koran promised shady gardens through which rivers of the purest water flow, fruits, vineyards and wine which did not intoxicate; bracelets of pearl and gold, and green silken garments with brocade; girls with swelling breasts who remain forever virgins, as well as the cheerful company of one's family, in eternal peace. Moslem cosmology shared with other near-eastern systems a belief in seven heavens of ascending purity, with angels as links between those worlds and this one. In addition, there were *djinn*, creatures of fire midway between angels and men, some of whom were good, others who were evil or demonic. Finally, most crusaders would probably not have expected to hear many of their own Commandments enjoined in sura xvii, which elaborates upon the message delivered by God to Moses.

Internal conflict was another characteristic both of medieval Islam and of Christianity. The crusaders who vandalized the suburbs of Constantinople during the First Crusade were acting out an old suspicion of the Byzantine or Greek Church which, as westerners knew, was not *really* Christianity. The same was true of their reactions to Armenian and other near-eastern Christians; how could brown-skinned gabblers possibly be proper Christians? Another source of internal Christian discord was heresy, which would result in the establishment of the European Inquisition by the thirteenth century, when enemies of the faith need not be sought beyond the Bosporus or the Pyrenees, and the south of France became a new crusading battlefield. Islam also suffered from internal dissensions which, it is generally agreed, is one of the reasons for the astonishing success of the First Crusade. Not only were the two great factions of Sunnites and Shi'ites at each other's throats, but further sub-divisions within the two groups presented inviting opportunities to crusaders for diplomatic and military intervention. The fission had significant repercussions long before 1095, as Richard Bulliet has emphasized in a recent controversial study. In the tenth century, as an example of intramural animosities, members of one of the Shi'ite factions raided Mecca and made off with the Black Stone (which was later returned). This was more than a symbolic removal of authority, as in Edward I's taking of the Stone of Scone from Scotland to England, for the Black Stone was itself a holy object. There are many examples of schism within the major parties; a radical wing of the Shi'ites caused problems not only for their Moslem enemies but for Christian leaders as well. Even the Sunnite Saladin himself was threatened by these Assassins. Earlier in the twelfth century, when one of their leaders was overthrown in Syria, he was 'dissected by swords and knives', his head and hands removed as trophies, according to the *Damascus Chronicle*. In a sense these rivalries were as much political as religious and, in any case, Islam made no great distinction between the two realms. In other internal conflicts the religious aspect seems dominant, and these more closely resemble the battles between heresy and orthodoxy in medieval Christendom. As in the case of the Christian West, Moslem unorthodoxy took various forms, such as the learned heresies or innovations, an overflowing of debate between rationalists and fundamentalists. Over the question whether the Koran had existed from the beginning of time in heaven, or was created, an inquisition was established in ninth-century Baghdad, where further battles between conservatives and rationalists erupted in the tenth and later centuries. The medieval West was to experience similar clashes over the place of reason in religious belief.

Another area which caused problems for each of the two religions was the potentially dangerous lure of mysticism. The danger stemmed from the independence of those who communicated with God by divine illumination and thus bypassed the clerical structure which knit believers together. These worries would assail medieval Europe, especially in the fourteenth and fifteenth centuries. Though it is true that, unlike Christianity, Islam did not support an articulated hierarchy (priests, bishops and pope), nevertheless analogous sources of political-religious authority, hierarchical and lateral structures of subordination and control, certainly existed. These controls seemed to be flaunted by some mystics not only in their apparently blasphemous claims, but also through their seemingly peculiar behaviour (particularly among some of the dervishes). Mystics, known generally as Sufis from their coarse wollen garments, became a troublesome party especially from the end of the eighth century. By then Islam, so successful in conquest and expansion, had of necessity involved itself in the world it ruled. Some mystics looked upon this as a turning away from the fundamental purposes of Islam, the recognition of and acquiescence in God's supreme authority. Though there are many to choose from, only a few of the more well-known mystics will be mentioned here. Abu l'Hosain al-Nuri (d. 908), for instance, was said to have wandered about for days and nights on end carrying a brick in his hand and muttering only the words 'God, God'. His mystic thirst had driven him out into the desert, and he once claimed that he had gazed upon a light gleaming in the Unseen until he himself had become that light, a claim that would be repeated by late-medieval European mystics. Reactions to Sufis were often harsh. Amr ibn Othman was executed in the early tenth century and his ashes scattered to the winds; al-Hallaj was killed in Baghdad about the same time—his hands and feet were cut away, eyes plucked out, ears and nose removed, tongue sliced off. After being decapitated and burned, his ashes were thrown into the Tigris river. His sin had been to claim that he was The Truth. That some mystics invited misunderstanding, even fear, among ordinary Moslems is illustrated by the case of al-Shebli (d. 846), as reported in Arberry's collection. It was claimed that he had been seen running about Baghdad with a burning coal in his hand, saying he was going to burn down the Ka'ba so that men would care only for the Lord of the Ka'ba and not the physical shrine. He was also allegedly seen brandishing a piece of wood burning at both ends to be used, he declared, to set heaven and hell on fire so that men would worship God without concern for punishment and reward. Such puritanical-iconoclastic motifs were common among many Moslems: about 400 years later, Joinville reported that an Arabic-speaking Dominican in Damascus, around 1250, saw an old woman carrying a bowl of flaming coals and a flask of water. She told the Dominican that she planned to burn paradise with the one and quench the fires of hell with the other to force Moslems to love God regardless of heaven and hell. Though most Sufis eventually ceased to behave as if God-intoxicated, and though mysticism was defended by as great a writer as al-Ghazali (d. 1111), the movement continued to evoke hostile reponses from the more orthodox; in 1191 the chivalrous Saladin had a Sufi 'heretic' strangled and suspended from a cross for three days.

Thirdly, and finally, many jurists, mystics and philosophers objected to what they thought to be the purely mechanical or ritualistic religious behaviour of far too many Moslems, which seemed at times to degenerate into gross superstition. Here again the parallel with the medieval West is obvious, and most crusaders would have been very familiar with such activities in a Christian context. Before describing some of these practices, however, it must be reiterated that they were and are as important in the overall structure of Moslem belief as theological or juristic doctrines. For some years now historians have realized that the glib phrase 'popular religion' must be used very carefully—if at all; the closer the concept is scrutinized, the more devoid of meaning it becomes. In the present study such beliefs and rituals are mentioned only to suggest similarities with medieval crusader belief and rite, not to segregate them from 'real' religious behaviour.

Pilgrimage to holy places seems to be a universal practice associated with all religions. In a sense, even the solitary, stationary mystic is engaged upon a journey—from exterior to interior and from inferior to superior, in St Augustine's phrase. This movement from mundane to divine, whether physical or symbolic—when a normally profane space is redefined and reapproached as sacred, for instance—is always preceded by forms of preparation. As Toufic Fahd succinctly puts it, a Moslem setting out to visit the Ka'ba at Mecca 'se prépare à être un autre homme'; this transformation into another person entails an open (public) commitment to go, involving confession of sins, payment of debts, fasting and prayer. The similarities between Moslem and medieval Christian pilgrimage and crusade include more than separation rites, for pilgrims of both religions honoured many holy places in common. Of course Christians did not visit the central holy place of Islam, Mecca. As noted earlier, this was an Arabic pilgrimage centre long before the advent of Islam. The Black Stone appears to have been the focus of communal veneration, but the paraphernalia of other tribal deities were also kept in the Ka'ba. Mohammad removed the deities but left the stone, around which Islamic traditions soon gathered: the stone, once dazzling white, was believed to have been created by God and venerated by Adam at a proto-Ka'ba after his expulsion from Eden. The stone was hidden in a mountain during the Deluge, then, through Gabriel's intermediation, used by Abraham to refound the Ka'ba. Eventually the touch of sinful men turned it black or, alternatively, as the eye of God it grew clouded and dark in looking out over human depravity. It once had great curative powers, but by the later Middle Ages these were diminished, though not altogether dissipated. The entire area around the stone was *ḥaram*, sacred, into which no one could enter unless in a state of ritual purity, having changed into simple white garments and abstained from all unbecoming activities. At Mecca the pilgrim also visited the wells of Zemzem, whose waters were morally and physically restorative. One could buy small quantities to take home, just as pilgrims to Canterbury or Walsingham in medieval England and at countless other European shrines could purchase ampoules of miraculous water for later use. There were subsidiary holy places around Mecca such as Mina, or the memorial to Adam, which sometimes drew such huge crowds that people were crushed to death. But these were secondary, for the Ka'ba was thought to be *ṣurrat al-arḍ* by Moslems, just as Jerusalem was *umbilicus terrarum* for Christians and Delphi had been ὁ ὀμφαλός for the Greeks—in each case, the navel of the universe. Mecca was the only place of pilgrimage required by the Koran.

Soon after Mohammad's death, however, tradition added two other sites to which pilgrimage became a moral, though not a scriptural, requirement. Medina and Jerusalem were both associated with Mohammad, the former his burial place around which an elaborate shrine-complex grew, the latter the site of his miraculous ascent into heaven, as well as the city associated with biblical figures mentioned in the Koran. Moslem veneration of their founder's tomb is self-explanatory, although some Islamic jurists claimed that undue reverence should not be shown to the dead, nor should their graves become shrines, precepts universally ignored. As for Jerusalem, there were two main holy places for Moslems, both located in the area that had once been the sacred Temple precincts of the Jews: the mosque, al-Aqsa, and the Dome of the Rock, an Islamic shrine since the late seventh century. Many traditions grew up around the large, irregular lump of stone venerated and anointed by generations of Moslems. These traditions can be reduced to two streams of thought, which flow together at various points to create a confused *mélange* of images. As described by Alfred Guillaume, in one of the traditions Mohammad took a magical night journey on his flying beast, *Burāq,* from Mecca to Jerusalem; there he met Abraham, Jesus and other prophets, then returned to Mecca. The second tradition places Mohammad at Jerusalem, where Gabriel brought him a ladder and led him into the celestial heights, whence he was able to see hell and the punishments of sinners; then he ascended through each of the seven heavens where he saw, among others, Jesus, John the Baptist, Moses and finally Abraham, after which he returned to his people. (The widely-held view that this story inspired Dante's *Commedia* is in need of revision, according to Sir Richard Southern.)

The marking of holy sites with stones or pillars was customary in the ancient world, both eastern and western. Though later religions would reinterpret this tradition in a Jewish, Christian or Islamic manner, the older lithic foundations literally and symbolically underlay them all. At Jerusalem the Rock, whatever may have been its archaic religious associations or functions, was interpreted in some early Jewish traditions as being an altar built by Adam and rebuilt by Abraham, as well as the place where Abraham nearly sacrificed Isaac. It was also thought to be the site of Jacob's dream or vision of the celestial ladder. After the vision, according to tradition, Jacob raised a pillar there and anointed it with heavenly oil; God stepped on it, pushing the rock into the earth. Solomon's temple was built upon this foundation stone or world-navel. (Patai and Graves suggest that the site of Jacob's vision was arbitrarily transferred from Bethel to Jerusalem at some unknown date after the seventh century BC.) Such pre-Islamic Jewish traditions may have influenced Mohammad and later generations of Moslems. In folklore, then, the rock at Jerusalem had religious significance for Jews long before the advent of Christ or Mohammad.

The history of Jerusalem sheds further light upon the traditions about the rock. Jerusalem was destroyed by the Romans in AD 70 and, following yet another rebellion, Jews were prohibited from entering the city after AD 135 except on the anniversary of the city's destruction. When they revisited the Temple area on those occasions, they lamented the destruction of their holy shrine and anointed the rock. This was still the case, Wilkinson notes, even in the mid-fifth century AD. Contemporary Christians, meanwhile, seem to have avoided the Temple area because of Christ's curse upon it. Eventually, perhaps by the sixth century, the site was used by the Jerusalem Christians as a rubbish dump. The Moslems arrived in 637. According to tradition, the caliph Umar (d. 644) built a mosque on the Temple site, either at the suggestion of a Jew who had converted to Islam or at the prompting of the Christian patriarch of Jerusalem, Sophronius. Umar himself was said to have bent down, gathered up some of the filth and carried it away in the folds of his garment. Other Moslems assisted him and, in this way, the site was cleared and the rock once again exposed to view. In any case, it is fairly certain that a mosque was, in fact, built on the Temple site though not, apparently, over the rock. According to one of the first Christian descriptions of Jerusalem after the Moslem conquest (from Abbot Adamnan of Iona, based upon an account by Bishop Arculf, a Jerusalem pilgrim about 680), the Saracens had built an oblong house of prayer over some Temple ruins, obviously a temporary structure, since it was pieced together with planks and beams. Only a few years later, this ramshackle building was re-erected in a much finer style. During the 680s, the new caliph of Damascus, Abd el-Malik, as part of his strategy in a feud with a rival caliph at Mecca, prohibited pilgrimage to Mecca and redirected the faithful under his influence to that other holy place, Jerusalem. In attempting to create a rival to Mecca, he enshrined the Jerusalem rock in a wonderful dome and claimed that circumambulation of this holy object was as effective as circumambulation of the Black Stone of the Ka'ba. He completed the Dome about 691 or 692 and, by 702, had also rebuilt the nearby mosque (al-Aqsa). Henceforth the Islamic world had in Jerusalem a third centre of pilgrimage, along with Medina and Mecca.

Moslem legend spoke of Adam founding and Abraham refounding the Ka'ba (a reflection of Jewish legend, described above), using a stone—in which, moreover, some believed that the impression of Abraham's foot could be seen. In developing the magical flight between the two shrines, Islamic lore linked Mecca with Jerusalem (and the two rocks) even more closely. The 'footprints' in the Jerusalem rock were believed by some, such as the eleventh-century writer Nasîr-i-Khusrau, to be those of Abraham, as at Mecca. Most Moslem pilgrims, however, attributed them to Mohammad himself, the veritable jumping-off point for his heavenly visit. By the time the crusaders had rampaged through the streets of Jerusalem, then, a legendary resonance had long been reverberating between Mecca and Jerusalem, assimilating the two foundation motifs. The Christian newcomers now broke the connection and, during the twelfth century, reinterpreted the Jerusalem rock and its markings in their own way, thereby creating new traditions: the Viking pilgrim Saewulf sums it up in claiming that Solomon had placed the Ark on the rock, which also still displayed the footprints of Jesus. Ironically, the site had never been associated with Christian pilgrimage at all, and had only become an attraction to Christians *after* the First Crusade. Finally, when Saladin captured the city, he removed Christian altars in the Dome of the Rock as well as marble slabs that the Christians, after hacking away generous portions to take back to Europe, had placed over most of the rock itself. Henceforth, the Dome was jealously guarded by Moslems, though some adventurous or foolish infidels did manage to slip in from time to time.

In addition to the al-Aqsa mosque and the Dome, Moslem pilgrims—like Christian pilgrims—had many other holy places to visit in and around Jerusalem. The main exception, the Holy Sepulchre, was also the most crucial: just as Christians could not attribute sanctity to the Ka'ba, the most precious Christian shrine of the Holy Sepulchre could not be venerated by Moslems, since the Koran taught that Jesus was never crucified. Moslems did honour other places associated with his life, however, such as a Jerusalem well where he was said to have washed; the place from which he was believed to have ascended into heaven; the site where John baptized him; or springs at which the Virgin Mary washed him during the flight to Egypt. Like Christ, the Virgin Mary as mother of the Messiah was highly honoured in the

Moslem world. There was even supposed to have been a picture of the Virgin with the infant Jesus in the Ka'ba itself, which Mohammad allowed to remain, though it was removed in a later redecoration— perhaps as a result of growing conventions against depicting created beings in art. As in the case of Christian pilgrims who tended to see Christ's footprints in many places, some very curious Christological 'shrines' were revered by Moslems, such as the cradle of Jesus in a Jerusalem mosque marking his birthplace. During labour, the Virgin had gripped one of the columns in the mosque; the imprint of her fingers was still there. Just as in medieval Christianity, there was competition between certain shrines. Some Moslems claimed that Noah's tomb was near al-Karak, others that it was at Jerusalem. Though Abraham was 'buried' in a number of places, the *Damascus Chronicle* bolsters Jerusalem's claim by noting that, when his body was discovered in that city, it looked as if it had not suffered from decay. The legend of uncorrupted 'saintly' bodies was a standard motif in Christian hagiography as well, persisting throughout the whole of the medieval period. Another figure revered by both religions was John the Baptist, and in both religions various cities contested possession of his head. In the Islamic world, Damascus and Aleppo each claimed the honour, while that fourteenth-century compendium of Christian fact and frivolity, 'Mandeville's' *Travels,* notes that the head was said to be in Christian custody at Amiens in France, although Constantinople, Rome and Genoa were also supposed to have shared it. 'Mandeville' takes the safest way out (as did Moslem writers in a similar predicament) by concluding 'I wot never, but God knoweth'. Many other biblical prophets, saints and holy sites were also shared by the people of both faiths. Ibn Jubayr claimed that outside Acre at the place where God produced the cattle for Adam, both Moslems and Christians assembled, each turning to their own place of worship to pray. He praised God for keeping it safe for Moslems, and for instilling a proper sense of reverence into the Christians. The Christian Ludolph wrote some 200 years later about a church the Moslems had turned into a mosque. He was surprised to see that they had not defaced the inscribed (apocryphal) story of Anna and Joachim and the birth of their daughter the Virgin Mary. In fact, Ludolph used to hear Baguta, an old Saracen woman living near the mosque, 'explain' the representation to interested Christian pilgrims. She told them that the figure of Joachim was Mohammad and the trees in the background were part of Paradise, where he kissed girls (according to Ludolph's selective memory). She glorified Mohammad with such fervour that tears came to her eyes.

As Arnold suggested fifty years ago, Moslem strictures against representing living creatures in art tended to relax, especially in the Levant, after the thirteenth century. Some of the Moslem artists who depicted the Blessed Virgin Mary and Christ had to rely for their exemplars upon Christian works of art. There were, of course, some cross-cultural alterations: the birth of the Prophet Christ took place not in a stable, but under a palm tree; the Virgin's head was surrounded not with a halo, but with flames (a mark of the Moslem prophet); and Jesus, the only one of the major prophets to stay celibate, was sometimes shown as a Sufi in Moslem illuminated manuscripts.

Mohammad was only the greatest of the 'saints' of Islam. The famous or holy Moslem dead were honoured in every country of the Islamic world from Spain to Persia. There were Sunni saints, Shi'ite saints, Sufi saints and even some saints that were not allied to particular sects. Local cults also developed around individuals of doubtful piety, though it did not deter people from wishing to be buried near a sumptuous but unmarked tomb, which could as easily contain a forgotten saint as an unknown sinner. Like the early Christians, Moslems hoped that burial near spiritual leaders or martyrs would provide extra protection on Judgment Day. As in medieval England or France, saints worked miracles, sent messages in dreams or visions and were 'seen' near their shrines. The Islamic world had nothing equivalent to the screening process of papal canonization, and many Moslems spoke out against abuses and 'superstitions': in the fourteenth century, Ibn Taymia condemned the belief that pilgrims could see Moslem saints walking in or out of their tombs (a habit also attributed to dead saints in twelfth-century northern England, for example), because, he explained, the apparitions were actually demons and not the dead. Though many went to shrines in the pious spirit advocated by al-Ghazali in the twelfth century, out of love for God, to give thanks for a cure, or to expiate a crime, many others went only to collect the powers dispensed automatically—one prayer equalled 25,000 prayers if said at Jerusalem or 50,000 if at Medina or 100,000 at Mecca, according to Nasîr-i-Khusrau—or to gape at such wonders as the head of Husayn, within its silver shrine that glistened in the candle-light.

In the Moslem as well as the Christian world, many subsidiary activities were associated with pilgrimage. Curative wells, for instance, were sought out by pilgims of both religions, as were incubation-sanctuaries where one might receive visionary advice from the saints.

In the early thirteenth century at Constantinople, Robert de Clari saw Christians rubbing against a column in Hagia Sophia in order to cure kidney ailments, while his contemporary al-Harawi saw Moslem pilgrims performing the same activity for the same reason in Damascus. Moslems, like Christians, practised bibliomancy, saw visionary warriors (dressed in green, the Moslem colour of martyrdom) help them in the midst of battle, waited for auspicious days to launch attacks against the enemy (Saladin favoured Fridays), used spells and enchantments. (Raymond of Aguilers reported Moslem 'witches' trying to cast spells over the crusaders' siege machines at Jerusalem in 1099.) Warriors on both sides went into battle wearing amulets recording God's names and other potent spells and, as in the Christian West, one could be strengthened by writing scriptural verses on parchment, then washing the ink off and drinking it. Though many other beliefs were also held in common by both sides, for example that menstruant women defiled holy places, that nocturnal emissions required purificatory rites, that those who insulted the saints were liable to physical punishment and so on, death rites form a fitting end to this brief overview. In death, some Moslems and Christians were expected to be able to glimpse the fate awaiting them in heaven or hell, while Christian and Moslem saints were supposed to meet death humbly, even austerely, with pious sentiments on their lips; there were prayers from bystanders, the use of rosaries and sometimes of ashes by the dying, and a last rite in both religions. In Islam, however, water replaced the oil used in the Christian rite; Joinville even assumed that Moslems believed that they could be saved after a sinful life if only they were ritually washed with water in their final moments. Zemzem water from Mecca was kept for the dying, and pious pilgrims dipped their shrouds in these holy wells near the Ka'ba, then put them away until that ultimate day. When the moment of death came, God's angel descended and—as in Christian iconography—gathered up the good soul amidst a sweet odour, pulling the spirit slowly from the body. The corpse was gently washed (a meritorious task, as the ninth-century al-Bukhari emphasized), then, after further prayer, was sent for burial. Sometimes, deceased holy men indicated the place they wished to lie by supernaturally halting the cortège at a particular spot. Although tombs were supposed to be simple, the famous usually attracted living and dead suppliants and their offerings. (On the other hand, not many dared to be as extravagant as a certain Ismaili leader who promised to return from the dead, and whose followers therefore kept a saddled horse always ready at his tomb in anticipation of that happy event.)

Regardless of many shared customs and beliefs, however, the two religions were divided by insurmountable theological barriers; though they may have touched at certain points along the periphery, they did not coincide at the centre. For all the mutual respect of Old Testament patriarchs and prophets, the veneration of the Virgin Mary and her son the Messiah, and the sharing of so many public and private rituals, there were irreconcilable differences. Sura iv of the Koran sums them up: 'Yet they slew him not, and they crucified him not, but they had only his likeness... and they did not really slay him, but God took him up to Himself.' The Jews ('they') were mistaken, having actually crucified Simon of Cyrene or perhaps Judas himself, while according to the Koran Jesus ascended, living, to God. The Christians too were wrong, for Christ had neither died the cruel redemptive death for man nor had he resurrected from that death to join God his father; he was not a sharer in divinity, but only an apostle of God. As sura cxiv proclaims, only infidels say that the Messiah, Ibn Maryam (son of Mary), is God. Nor did Moslems accept the Holy Spirit as God, the third part of the Christian Trinity; the same sura also brands as infidels those who claim that God is one of three—for there is but one God, not three. Thus Moslem writers such as the twelfth-century Ibn al-Qalanisi habitually refer to the crusaders as polytheists, even heretics. Some non-theological Moslems, in addition, preferred to express themselves less subtly by urinating on crosses—so crusaders claimed—and referring to the followers of Christ as pigs, an unclean animal.

Bernard Lewis draws attention to other differences besides the theological, for instance that Islam, almost from the start, was an aggressive, successful movement of expansion in which 'politics' and 'religion' were not relegated to different compartments within Moslem society as in the medieval West. Mohammad, as Lewis says, was his own Constantine; power was good, a sign of God's blessing, amply showered upon the Prophet at the end of his life. This tide of success eventually began to recede as the Moslem world grew so large that particularism started to weaken it and as newcomers finally drew relgious leadership away from political, though never completely separating them. As Bulliet has made clear, the relationship was seldom static, never simple. In the end, in spite of the apparent similarities and of the fact that some intellectuals, both Christian and Moslem, learned to exchange ideas and even to appreciate each other's theologies, the essential differences could not be modified no matter how many Christian and Moslem pilgrims might drink at the same curative well.

7

Christian-Moslem Interactions

'What I advise is that we should all let ourselves be slain,
 for thus we shall go to paradise.' But we none of us heeded his advice.

(Joinville)

Though Moslems and Christians followed many similar religious
practices, even worshipped at the same holy places and venerated the
same Old and New Testament heroes and heroines, there were
insurmountable barriers to true community of belief. The very fact
that each shared something of the other's spiritual universe may well
have aggravated their mutual hostility: at the fault-line where the two
worlds met, running from Spain across southern Italy and eastwards
through the Holy Land, religious similarities tended to invite
animosity rather than to allay it. Yet, according to R.W. Southern, this
hostility was not constant at all times and in all places. He suggested
that the Christian-Moslem relationship passed through four
stages—from the Christian point of view—between the seventh and
the fifteenth centuries, during which western attitudes varied from
ignorant rejection to sympathetic, informed attempts to understand
Islam. In this chapter, Southern's scheme is simplified by reducing the
overview to three stages, while at the same time providing a few
examples of concurrent Moslem attitudes towards Christianity.

During the first period, from the expansion of Islam in the seventh
and eighth centuries to the eve of the Council of Clermont in 1095,
Christians expressed a variety of opinions, both positive and negative,
about this new religion. As is to be expected, the earliest reactions
occurred in those areas where Christian-Moslem confrontation first
took place. When compared with the scurrility and hysterical
hyperbole of Christian writings of the second period (at the height of
the crusades), many of these early responses are tame and generally
level-headed. For instance, among the Oriental Christians discussed in
Moorhead's recent article, the Armenian Bishop Sebeos, writing in the
660s, described Mohammad as a merchant and an expert in Old
Testament law who began preaching and teaching his people to

147

recognize the one God of Abraham. The bishop accepted the ancient identification of Mohammad's people with the descendants of Ishmael, Abraham's first-born son by the Egyptian slave Hagar. (Since at least the days of Josephus (d. *c.* AD 100) this had been the traditional genealogy of the Arabs. It was taken up by Spain's Isidore of Seville (d. 636), emphasized by Mohammad himself and popularized in the writings of Britain's Bede.) Bishop Sebeos also claimed that the Jews had been instrumental in helping the early Moslems in their combat with the Byzantines. On the other hand, Sebeos was hardly an unqualified admirer of Mohammad, calling him a satellite of Antichrist. About a decade later, an anonymous Nestorian Christian monk also assumed that Moslems worshipped the one God of Abraham and were descendants of Ishmael; like Sebeos he 'located' them firmly within a monotheistic, biblical context.

Hostile views of Islam were also expressed in this early period, for instance by an Egyptian bishop (John of Nikiu) for whom Mohammad was a beast, the Moslem invaders of his land God's enemies and idolators—a curious charge. Other Christian ecclesiastics around the eastern and southern Mediterranean were equally outspoken: one denied that Moslems were monotheists, another purportedly told Caliph 'Abd al-Malik (d. 705) that Islam was a belief enforced by the sword and unsupported by miracles. A third bishop, according to an eighth-century Greek chronicler, was executed for deriding the 'myths' propagated by Mohammad. By the ninth century, certain Egyptian Christian writers seem to have concluded that Moslems could not be saved from eternal damnation in spite of their monotheism, or rather because of it, since they rejected the Trinity and the sacraments. Anti-Moslem propaganda broke out about the same time (mid-ninth century) in that other region affected by the Moslem tide, Spain, where some Christian writers again associated the rise of Islam with the approaching time of Antichrist. In spite of such criticisms and rejections of Islam, however, the overall tone seldom fell to the post-1095 depths. Although this impression may only be due to the fact that a few Christian tracts happen to have survived from this early period, nevertheless these writers had direct experience, though perhaps not full comprehension, of Islam. Consequently their attitudes and the forms in which they were cast present interesting views of contemporary Christian-Moslem relations. At the same time, it could be argued that, because these writers were for the most part subject to Moslem control, self-preservation encouraged them to follow a relatively moderate line; Moslems hardly countenanced public condemnation of the True Faith. Conversely, the well-known conflict between Christian Byzantium and certain other eastern Christian groups probably rendered the latter far more tolerant of their new Moslem masters. In view of these variables, it is worth briefly examining the attitudes of Christian writers of this period, who did not live under the direct threat of serious Moslem retaliation or regulation.

No place in Europe could have seemed more distant from the battles and turmoil of Arab conquests than Northumbria, but the remoteness of northern England was merely geographical. During the late seventh and early eighth centuries, Northumbrian monasticism enjoyed a golden age, stimulated to a great extent by ideas and men from Europe. At Jarrow, for instance, the monks prayed in a church decorated with Mediterranean, possibly even Coptic, motifs, enjoyed the beauty of glass windows designed and coloured by experts from Gaul, chanted their services according to the custom followed in Rome and tended lamps flickering before holy icons of Moses and Christ, in the Byzantine tradition. Their books came from Europe, too. Bede, the most famous monk of Jarrow, spent nearly all his life there in prayer or studying and working in the scriptorium. He wrote the invaluable *Ecclesiastical History,* upon which so much of our understanding of Anglo-Saxon society and culture is based. But Bede (d. 735) wrote a great many other things as well, with occasional comments about the Moslems whose empire was increasing during his lifetime. How then did this intelligent, articulate northman perceive the Saracens? R.W. Southern's view, that Bede treated the subject without the rancour and hostility of later writers, requires some modification in the light of Wallace-Hadrill's discussion. When first encountered in Bede's writings, the Saracens were, indeed, dealt with in a relatively neutral manner. In his later work, however, particularly after the beginning of the conquest of Spain in 711, Bede's moderation gave way to denunciation: Moslems were enemies of Christ, followers of Lucifer, an errant, dangerous people. For Bede, these descendants of Ishmael who had wandered the deserts ever since Abraham's rejection of his first-born son, were a horde, of uncertain abode (*incertisque sedibus*). Bede's emphasis upon Saracenic rootlessness may have been influenced in part by the circumstances of his own stable, sheltered life—he seldom left his monastery and probably never went beyond the borders of Northumbria. For him (though in certain circumstances the life of the wandering Christian in self-imposed exile or *peregrinatio* might be meritorious) a whole people in a state of perpetual *instabilitas* must be inherently unnatural—to say nothing of their blasphemous religious claims. In the same vein, during the 350s Ammianus Marcellinus had described the Saracens as *sine sedibus fixis aut legibus* (without settled residences or laws), reflecting a Roman distrust of the wanderer and at the same time associating *sedes* with *leges*, settlement with law and order. In our own society, this attitude is summed up in the police-docket jargon 'no fixed address', which categorizes automatically. But then conflict between settlement-dwellers and free wanderers has been with us from Neolithic to modern times, when, for example, enlightened English communities move 'gipsies' on from one public rubbish dump to the next.

In any case, it is clear that Bede's attitude hardened as the Saracens seemed to pose a more serious political threat to Europe. Even so, his writings show little evidence of the hysterical Christian zeal that becomes common enough after 1095. This relative neutrality is also evident at the end of the eighth century in the annals and histories of the Carolingians. The Franks, unlike the English, had actually engaged in conflict with Moslems during Charles Martel's era, though the danger was not, perhaps, acute. The reign of Martel's grandson Charlemagne is especially interesting because he contended with Moslems on two fronts, in Spain and in the Near East. Not only that, but the manner of engagement differed as well: in Spain he was involved in sporadic military actions against a breakaway Umayyad dynasty, whereas he welcomed the political overtures of Haroun al-Rashid, Abbasid caliph in Baghdad; Haroun needed the Frankish counterweight to Byzantium, but he could also be useful to Charlemagne in his own dealings with the Greeks, who called themselves Roman Emperors. In three of the sources for the period (the so-called *Royal Frankish Annals* and the biographies of Charlemagne by Einhard and Notker), the western Moslems are *Sarraceni*, belligerents from Spain, or they are 'Moors' who periodically ravaged Corsica and Sardinia (*a Mauris*). But among the easterners, Haroun is respectfully referred to as Aaron the king (or sometimes emperor) of the Persians, *Aaron rege Persarum*, and Notker even calls him satrap of satraps, thereby emphasizing his superiority to the 'other' Moslems of Spain. In both cases, however, little is said about religious differences and once again there is none of the scurrility or rampant xenophobia of many later crusade chroniclers. There *is* one passage in which Notker mentions the misery of Holy Land Christians who begged for assistance, but he does not elaborate. Few twelfth-century writers will be as reserved.

To sum up, at least as suggested in the few sources cursorily examined from this point of view, early Christians reacted in a relatively moderate manner to the rise of this new power. It is true that there is condemnation of Islam as a false religion (as well as recognition of its monotheistic basis), especially among Oriental Christian writers, and there is awareness of the political dangers in both eastern and western sources, but neither our Levantine nor Frankish writers, neither Bede nor the Christians of north Africa, seem to have felt it necessary to express themselves in abusive or violent language. This will change in the wake of the First Crusade. Certainly objective, political alterations occurred between the ninth and late eleventh centuries, which might have encouraged Christians subjectively to move from reasoned hostility to outrage: there was Caliph al-Hakim, who persecuted Christians and Jews and destroyed the Church of the Holy Sepulchre in 1009; there was the arrival of Seljuk Moslems in the Holy Land in the later eleventh century, which prompted Pope Gregory VII (in 1074) to try to help endangered eastern Christians. But it has become apparent to most modern historians that the general condition and circumstances of most Christians inhabiting, or on pilgrimage to, the Holy Land had not significantly deteriorated in the pre-1095 decades. Reasons for this shift in Christian attitude lie not so much in the Holy Land or even in the new-model Moslems, but in the West, in the Christians themselves. Before pursuing this point into the second period (from 1095 to *c.* 1200), a glance at early Moslem attitudes towards Christianity may help to establish a balance in the historiography of Christian-Moslem relations.

Mohammad had suggested that the people of the book, Jews and Christians, were to be allowed, under certain conditions, to practise their religions. At the same time, these faiths were defective insofar as they rejected many of God's precepts as well as the holy doctrines set out in the Koran; hence Jews and Christians were second-class citizens, under legal protection (the *dhimma*), but socially vulnerable to occasional abuse. On the whole, indigenous Christians who agreed to accept their inferior status were unmolested, while foreign Christians on pilgrimage to the Holy Land also do not appear to have been unduly harassed. As Wallace-Hadrill remarked *à propos* a Jerusalem pilgrimage by the Frankish Bishop Arculf around

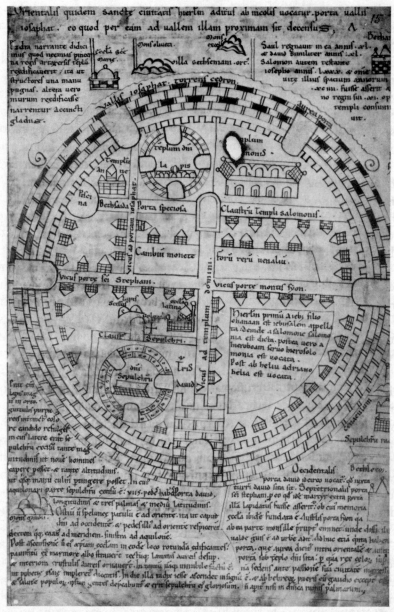

19 In his schematic Jerusalem the medieval draughtsman has portrayed the round 'Temple of the Lord' or Dome of the Rock (upper left)—even drawing the rock itself, *Lapis*—as a counterbalance to the round Church of the Lord's Sepulchre (bottom left).
(London, Brit. Library *MS ADD 32343*, f15^r)

680, the fact that he was able quietly to carry out his holy journey indicates how tolerant Moslems then were towards (at least some) Christians.

The seventh century witnessed such a tremendous expansion of Islam that the movement was still in process of pushing down its doctrinal roots in the eighth and ninth centuries. During this early phase, there are indications of a certain ambiguity or lack of confidence in some areas of Islamic interaction with the older, established religions, just as the early Christian response to Islam had itself varied. For example, it has been suggested that al-Malik may have modelled his famous late-seventh-century Dome of the Rock in Jerusalem on the nearby dome and Church of the Resurrection or Holy Sepulchre, perhaps hoping to borrow some of the older church's established legitimacy. Or, doctrinally, in the seventh century some claimed that Mohammad had intended his religion only for his own people, but by the eighth century this had been overturned by a shift towards universalism loosely analogous to the Pauline approach to Christianity. Similarly, early commentators claimed that because Jews and Christians hid or misinterpreted parts of the Old and New Testaments, which foretold the coming of Mohammad, Moslems were not to read the Bible or to discuss scripture with Christians or Jews. By the eighth century, however, Moslem scholars were prepared to approach those writings in a more critical and confident manner, for Islam was clearly the superior religion and need not be forever glancing nervously backwards.

Another indication of the need to remove ambiguities generated by a swiftly-victorious Islam is the regulating of Christian-Jewish behaviour within the new socio-religious context. Various codes developed over the centuries, issued and reissued throughout the Middle Ages, institutionalized the new minorites in both a negative and a positive sense. For instance, Christians were not permitted, *inter alia* (and there is some difficulty in dating these regulations, as well as apocryphal interpolations), to perform religious ritual in public, but when they *were* in public, they were to dress and behave in a distinctive manner when moving among their Moslem 'protectors'. In the pre-crusade rules collected by Bernard Lewis, aside from obvious ones about paying the poll tax and not aiding the enemies of Islam or striking, cheating, robbing or fornicating with Moslems or selling them forbidden things like wine or pork, the regulations withdrew Christian religious practices from Moslem society, while separating and subordinating Christians as members of that society. Christians were not to build new churches or convents, not to teach or practise their faith publicly or display crosses or books, or use bells or raised voices in their churches or when in funeral processions, or to bury their dead near Moslem graves. Nor were they to inhibit their fellows from becoming Moslems. The desire to differentiate Christians clearly from Moslems is seen in prohibitions against their wearing Moslem clothing, riding horses or carrying swords, using Arabic inscriptions on their seals or even cutting their hair Arab-style. They were to wear a distinctive belt or sash (known as *zunnās*) outside—never under—their clothing. Sometimes these dress regulations were very specific: according to one list, Christians were to wear honey-coloured hoods and belts, with two buttons on their caps, while their slaves were to wear two honey-coloured patches on their clothing, one in front and one behind, each patch to be four fingers long. (Similar patches were later worn by heretics and Jews in western Europe, and a mid-thirteenth-century inquisitor's manual specified that the yellow crosses worn on the breast and shoulders were to have strips three fingers in width.) Christians wearing turbans must use only honey-coloured ones, and their women were to be veiled in the same colour. Finally, this early collection even required Christians to nail wooden images of 'the devil' to their doors. The pre-crusade rules which aimed at social subordination of Christians were equally catholic in approach, including such points as banning them from government jobs and closing Moslem schools to their children, requiring them to offer travelling Moslems shelter for three days, to give up one's seat for a Moslem, to give them preference in the buying of slaves, not to build houses higher than Moslem houses, not to take up the middle of the road while travelling or the good benches at markets. Social subordination followed Christians even after death, for, unlike Moslem tombs, their graves were to be kept level with the ground.

Regardless of such attempts to isolate and subordinate Christians, inevitably the divisions between the two religious groups were not always strictly maintained in the day-to-day business of life. For instance, a glance at some of the (Persian) Sufi hagiography of the tenth century suggests that at least some Moslems were unperturbed by, or perhaps resigned to the prospect of, the need to deal with—or even to rely upon—Christians, such as the Christian physicians whom they called in for treatment. (Mukaddasi, a tenth-century visitor to

Jerusalem, claimed that most of the physicians round the city were Christians; he also complained that the scribes of Syria and Egypt were all Christians. Christians and Jews, he grumbled, had gained the upper hand everywhere, a common popular complaint which sometimes forced Moslem leaders to tighten *dhimma* regulations.) In addition, the context of some conversion stories suggests that the religious barriers were not always particularly high. A Sufi, for instance, engaged in a contest of ascetic stoicism with a Christian monk, but so surpassed him that the monk became a Moslem. In another example, a Moslem was said to have taken a Christian youth with him on pilgrimage to Mecca. However, once within the holy Ka'ba, the young man was unable to find his way out again. Of course, it was perfectly permissible to convert Christians and Jews to the true faith, provided that Islam was in no way compromised in the process. In one tenth-century account, Christianity even earned a back-handed compliment: a Sufi, who witnessed certain curative miracles performed with the holy ashes of a Byzantine monk, wondered how a false faith could produce such marvels. In a vision Mohammad explained the miracles as a result of erroneous sincerity and self-discipline; they *could* have done much more, the Prophet concluded, if only they had followed the true faith.

During the eleventh century in the midst of the usual dynastic rivalries and Seljuk incursions, Christians still seem to have been relatively fairly treated. Even in Hakim's destruction of the Church of the Resurrection in Jerusalem, perhaps prompted by popular anti-Christian clamour rather than his 'madness', the paradox of Moslem-Christian co-existence is evident: his chief secretary, who drew up the document of destruction, was a Christian, like his vizier who signed it. Christians continued to depart for Jerusalem in small groups and on mass pilgrimages, for instance in the 1030s and during the 1060s. The difficulties this last venture (the so-called Great German Pilgrimage) encountered were probably only due to localized political disturbances, though Christian minorities in the Holy Land could always expect harassment as believers in a false religion.

Glaber described one such troublesome incident in the early eleventh century. One of the Christian Easter rites at Jerusalem centred on the sacred fire, when the extinguished lamps of the Holy Sepulchre were reputed to be miraculously relit on Holy Saturday, a prelude to the joyful resurrection services. On one of these occasions, Glaber reports, an impudent buffoon happened to be among the

Moslems who usually congregated near the Christians to witness the purported miracle. As the Christians stood about waiting to greet the magical fire with the words *Agios, Kyrie eleison*, in a schoolboyish attempt at mockery the Moslem suddenly shouted out this Greek formula, snatched a candle away from a startled Christian and made a dash for it, laughing and jeering as he went. Unfortunate, sacrilegious Saracen: he was immediately possessed by a devil (*arreptus a daemonio*), Glaber's informant claimed, and thrown into severe torment. Meanwhile the offended Christian ran after him and recovered his candle, whereupon the clownish Moslem died forthwith in the arms of his co-religionists. This threw them into a state of terror at which the Christians rejoiced, especially since immediately afterwards God rounded off the proceedings by causing fire to erupt from one of the seven lamps at the sepulchre, then to blaze along lighting up the others. Apart from Glaber's obvious motives for repeating this tale, it suggests something of the stresses that underlay Christian-Moslem relations in Jerusalem. And if it might seem that possession, torment and death were a rather harsh penalty for a bit of harmless showing-off in front of other Moslems, it must be recalled that belief in God-Christ's death and resurrection was a fundamental point of difference in the two religions, and this place was literally the nub of contention. For Moslems the so-called Sepulchre was worse than mere fraud and the Christian 'miracle' of the lamps patent nonsense. Whether or not an actual incident like this ever occurred, wildly transformed by Christians into miraculous retribution, the story as retold by Glaber neatly sums up doctrinal controversy.

Moslem antipathy towards this place is even more evident in their derogatory distortion of its name. The Arabic for the Christian Church of the Resurrection, (approximately) *al Kayâmah*, was altered by many Moslem writers to *al-Kumâmah*, dung-hill or shit-heap. Writing only a decade or two after Glaber narrated the incident mentioned above, Nasîr reckoned that 8,000 Christians could pack into the dung-hill, which was constructed in the Byzantine fashion; inside, Christian artists had portrayed a horrific version of hell and had depicted Jesus—peace be upon him—riding on an ass. Over a century later, Saladin's biographer Beha *ed*-Din wrote that Christian pilgrims held 'the shit' in great reverence, believing that it contained the Messiah's tomb. They also believed, he added, that a flame (or light) descended upon it every year at one of their feasts. Perhaps this linguistic desecration originated as a crude reply to the tradition (described in the last chapter) that the nearby Rock of Abraham and Mohammad was itself rescued from filth, dung and rubbish by al-Malik in the seventh century. In any event, word-play is a universal, natural way to express ideological hostility, as any graffitiologist knows. The Jews who ultimately rejected Mohammad referred to him not by the honorific title *rasul* but with the word *pasul*, 'corrupt', just as—a thousand years later—the Lollards of England derided the Virgin of Walsingham (a famous late-medieval Marian shrine) as the Witch of Falsingham. If in fact al-Malik *did* model his seventh-century Dome of the Rock upon the Church of the Sepulchre, there could be no better juxtaposition of Islamic attitudes; by the eleventh century al-Malik's presumed exemplar had become something of great repugnance to Moslems, for whom contact with excreta could engender ritual pollution.

The second period of confrontation, 1095-*c*. 1200, which saw the flood then ebb of Christian power in the Holy Land, was also not surprisingly a period of outspoken, often wild, verbal attack upon Moslems and their religion. The words put into Urban II's mouth by Robert of Rheims in the early twelfth century reflect this hysterical reaction: the conquerors of Jerusalem were in the habit of circumcising Christians and dribbling the blood into baptismal fonts, or hooking one end of Christian entrails to a stake and forcing them to wander around disembowelling themselves. As for acts of rape—evidently much worse than self-evisceration—'Urban' cannot bring himself to speak. The invective and misinformation were as common in the writings of crusaders as among armchair polemicists who overreacted to tales about these oriental devils. The brew of xenophobia, long fermenting and spiced for example with Spanish conflicts, exploded in and after the First Crusade: in the West Mohammad was now known as a magician, a sexual libertine, his religion an evil caricature of Christianity or a demonic inspiration of the Antichrist. During the twelfth century, a new sense of self- and especially group-consciousness stimulated both clergy and laity in the West, while Christological and Marian devotions enriched European Christendom, providing it with a heightened emotional content; from the twelfth century heretics and Jews suffered from popularly-led mob hatreds as well as from official persecutions mounted by both Church and lay rulers. A growing sense of identity required a separating from 'others': thus the Moslems, relegated to sub-human status, were known to Ambroise (Third Crusade) as 'base dogs', 'base cattle', 'pagan cattle', the 'unbelieving black-faced brood' and 'base folk and brown'. For many twelfth-century Christians, the Moslems as well as the Jews, Christ-denying dogs, richly deserved torment and death.

Though a few First Crusade-leaders believed in giving captives a chance to convert and save themselves from slavery or death, as twelfth-century conflicts wore on and earlier conquests evaporated, this policy declined. In the practical horrors of battle, stark religious hostility continued to manifest itself in many ways. An example of this, from the first three crusades, is the purported Moslem mistreatment of the cross. It is interesting to see how this theme was elaborated. During the First Crusade, says the priest Peter Tudebode, Jerusalem Moslems made a wooden cross, took it to the city walls and, in sight of the shocked Christians, beat it with sticks and then smashed it to pieces. William of Tyre, describing this event two generations later, adds that they even went so far as to spit upon the sacred object, while shouting sundry anti-Christian abuse. When the crusaders were attacking Lisbon en route to the Holy Land in the Second Crusade, the Moslems carried a cross to the city wall, spat on it, wiped their posteriors with it, urinated on it and finally flung it down to the outraged Christians, according to Osbern, who claims to have been there. Finally, during the Christian siege of Acre in the Third Crusade, Ambroise states that the enemy brought crosses from the city churches and abused them in full view, beating, defecating and urinating on them. For battlefield Christians such heinous behaviour—quite likely, for some Moslems had no scruples about desecrating Christian symbols centring on Christ's so-called death—epitomized the conflict, emphasized the perversity of all 'base folk and brown'.

On the other hand, several twelfth-century Christian writers were far more moderate in their judgments, even admitting that Moslems did not in fact worship Mohammad as their god, but practised a monotheism not unrelated to Judaism. William of Malmesbury, Petrus Alfonsi and Otto of Freising, though from divergent European backgrounds, recognized a certain community of belief between Christianity and Islam. The Abbot of Cluny (Peter the Venerable) was so interested in discovering ways to overcome their 'heresy' and entice them into the Christian fold that he had the Koran translated into Latin in the 1140s. As Southern remarks, however, the times were not yet ripe for this sort of approach. Military conflict and reverses do not provide an encouraging setting for sympathetic understanding of the enemy.

Though the crusades turned the mild castigation of earlier centuries into strident condemnation at least in some Christian circles, a similar shift in attitude is not so evident among the Moslems. The *dhimma* did not noticeably change, and Christians continued to survive and even to advance in Islamic society; for example, the twelfth-century Egyptian vizier Bahrām, called Saif al-Islām ('Sword of Islam'), was actually an Armenian Christian. By 1095 the Moslems had already experienced centuries of co-existence with cross-worshippers, had long formulated their denigratory opinions and were used to hearing the Church of the

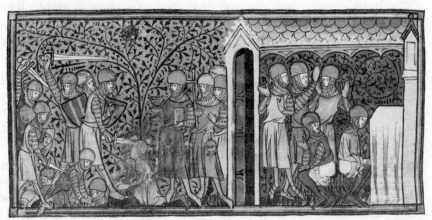

20 Each side accused the other of polluting holy places. Here two Saracens defecate before a Christian altar, while their colleagues carry off church implements and slaughter Christians.
(London, Brit. Library *MS Royal 16 G VI*, f. 185ᵛ.)

Sepulchre called the dung-heap. Christian invasions of their territories and cities naturally confirmed these opinions and, just as naturally, deepened pre-existing religious antipathies. When, for instance, the crusaders finally conquered Antioch during the First Crusade, they found evidence of this in the city's churches: the Moslems (at least according to William of Tyre) had gouged out the eyes of images of the saints, mutilated their noses and smeared them with dung and mud. For many twelfth-century Moslems the issues were seen in terms of religious confrontation, as they had been seen for centuries. When describing the course of warfare, the earliest Arab crusade historian (Ibn al-Qalanisi) interwove Koranic passages with his prose just as so many European writers habitually drew biblical imagery into their anti-Islamic tracts and sermons. For most Moslems, as for Christians, it was no ordinary war between peoples involving economic or political competition or geographical frontiers, but a war of belief against unbelief. At Tiberias—just before the crucial battle of Hattin in 1187—Imad ad-Din described the coming conflict in these terms: Islam faced unbelief, monotheism warred upon Trinitarianism, righteousness confronted error, (true) Faith opposed polytheism while the several circles of hell prepared to receive Christians and the several ranks of heaven joyously anticipated the Moslem dead. According to Beha *ed*-Din, one of Saladin's war-cries was 'For Islam, forward the monotheist army'. This clash of truth against error embittered the conflict and distorted common perceptions of the enemy, but the distortions had been evolving in Moslem minds for centuries. Even in twelfth-century Seville, where presumably Moslems had long experience of Christians, priests were blasted by Ibn 'Abdūn as evil-doing, fornicating Sodomites which, though undoubtedly true in some cases, can hardly be considered an unbiased view of the whole class. Christian women were supposed to be in the habit of carousing and fornicating with priests, while men of the cloth were said to keep at least two concubines each. As for the Holy Land, on the eve of Saladin's conquests, the traveller Ibn Jubayr viciously, but probably truthfully, described Acre as a den of unbelief and impiety, where pigs (Christians) and crosses abounded in a filthy, stinking city full of refuse and excrement.

Unless unusually provoked, Saladin seems to have looked upon his religious enemies with less rancour than most of his contemporaries, though he was extremely conscientious in his faith. As Bosworth notes, his own personal physician was a Jew, his brother Safadin's was a Christian. According to one of Gabrieli's sources (Abu Shama, d. 1267), this conqueror of Jerusalem once tried to shame his people into holy war by contrasting their negligent, demoralized laziness with the robust generosity of Christian crusaders, who zealously gave their all for Him whom they worshipped. When Christian preachers like St Bernard used the same cliché, however, they usually concentrated only on the debilitating vices and failings of Christians, disregarding any (hypothetical) contrary virtues among the Moslems. Even in victory Saladin's equanimity did not ordinarily desert him. Beha *ed*-Din says the charming, Arabic-speaking Reynald of Sidon came down from his castle to argue and reason with Saladin and his entourage not only about politics but also about religion. The Moslems pointed out to Reynald the errors of his faith—perhaps he could be coaxed into the True Belief? No; in the end, he and Saladin had a falling out and Reynald was sent disgraced to Damascus.

For Saladin the capture of Jerusalem was more than just another military triumph. As he wrote to King Richard I a few years later, 'Jerusalem belongs to us just as much as to you, and is more precious in our eyes than in yours.' After his troops secured the city in 1187 (with none of the carnage associated with the crusader takeover of 1099) and a thanksgiving sermon was preached, cries of *Allāh akbar* went up as the huge gilded cross atop the Dome of the Rock tumbled to the ground. Inside, the marble slabs placed over the Rock by the Christians to discourage relic-hunters were taken away. The building was purified and cleansed of filth left by the Christian dregs of humanity, as Imad ad-Din characterized them. The nearby mosque 'of Omar', part of which had been used as latrines by the Templars, was also rededicated to the One God. Whatever his inmost feelings about Christians may have been, some of Saladin's contemporaries emphasized the seamier side of the religious conflict. It was claimed in an Arabic source, for example, that the wily Conrad of Montferrat had a plan of Jerusalem drawn showing the 'dung hill', depicting a mounted Moslem warrior, whose horse was trampling and urinating on Christ's tomb. Conrad took this piece of propaganda to Europe and used it to incite mobs of potential crusaders—or so it was rumoured. The distortions that affected even educated minds in religious matters are illustrated by a passage from Imad ad-Din. In describing the battle of Hattin, when the crusaders lost the so-called True Cross, the rhetorician paints an interesting picture of imagined Christian attitudes towards that sacred emblem. The Cross, he writes, kept in a golden, bejewelled case, was the supreme object of Christian faith, a god which they were required to venerate. They made smaller copies of this god for their own houses, where they prostrated themselves before it. They bowed their foreheads down to the ground in the presence of the True Cross, some fainting away in passionate ecstasy at the very sight of it. Hence, its loss at Hattin was a mortal blow to the Christian cause, for their totem-god had been taken from them. Though we know that Imad ad-Din was partial to hyperbole and preciousness in his writing, nevertheless his impressions of Christian adulation of the cross may well have been shared, and believed to be true, by many less sophisticated Moslems.

The curious images reflected in the writings of twelfth-century Moslems and Christians such as Imad ad-Din or Ambroise continued to recur in propaganda pieces to the end of the Middle Ages. From the thirteenth century, however, other streams of thought, other attitudes began to surface in the west. Henceforth, by degrees the existence of a Moslem world was grudgingly accepted as a *fait accompli*, though attempts were made from time to time to alter this situation. The century opened with the sack of Christian Constantinople by crusaders, then witnessed two major attacks upon Egypt—both of which failed—and finally saw the fall of the last mainland Christian possession, Acre, in 1291. The only 'successful' important campaign of the century was led by the excommunicated Emperor Frederick II, who by astute, but over-ambitious, diplomacy peacefully regained most of Jerusalem and a few other cities in 1229 (lost again to the Moslems in 1244). Though popes and secular rulers (like England's King Edward I) continued to encourage or embark upon the adventure, the great days never returned. Disillusionment and condemnation of crusade ideologies are unmistakably clear from the thirteenth century. During the same century the commercial interests of European cities, especially Italian, expanded at an unparalleled rate after the capture of Constantinople. Italian trading colonies were scattered throughout the eastern Mediterranean and the Levant, in Egypt and north Africa; in Constantinople itself, along the Black Sea, even at the mouth of the Don on the Russian Sea of Azov. They navigated the deserts as well, for Marco Polo was not the only Italian to follow the silk route into China across the bleak Tarim Basin, where mysterious desert spirits filled the night air with musical sounds. Though Norman Daniel suggests that such economic links may not seriously have contributed to increased mutual understanding, at least commercial intercourse encouraged an atmosphere of mutual toleration, if only superficially and temporarily. In fact, Italian traders on occasion actually discouraged Christian military intervention when this would harm business with Moslem ports.

Another thirteenth-century development which helped to alter attitudes towards non-Christians was the rise of the Mongols. Westerners appreciated the potential value of these Asiatics, for if they could only be converted to Christianity, in theory the Moslems could be squeezed on two fronts. In the end, after the Mongols very nearly conquered their way to the Mediterranean, they accepted not Christianity but (at the end of the thirteenth century) Islam. While the options were still available, however, a number of remarkable political overtures were made by Christian leaders to the Mongols, and vice versa; the round-table discussion about religious issues between a Latin Christian, Nestorian Christians, Buddhists and Moslems held in the Khan's court in Mongolia (in 1254) is just one instance. A few far-sighted men recognized that oriental languages ought to be mastered if Christians were to bridge the east–west gap. For Roger Bacon this included Arabic, since he believed it was still possible to convince Moslems of their errors not through old-fashioned Bible-thumping and warfare but through the logical application of reasonable argument.

Bacon's somewhat naive faith in rationality was characteristic of many thirteenth-century intellectuals, for this has often been called the golden age of scholasticism—the rigorous application of Aristotelian logic and metaphysical constructs to problems of nature, man, society, God and the spirit. Not all who looked upon Islam with reason were scholastic philosophers, and not all scholastics approached that religion with calm detachment. Though Thomas Aquinas, *Doctor angelicus*, profited from Arabic commentaries upon Aristotle, nevertheless he categorized Mohammad's followers as bestial desert creatures and accused Mohammad himself of corrupting the Bible to 'prove' that it predicted his own advent. For him, war against such people was justified not because it might lead to their conversion, but because it would prevent them from interfering with the True Faith, Christianity. On the other hand, a fellow-Dominican, William of Tripoli, counselled moderation and even toleration in Christian-Islamic relations. Like Bacon, he believed that Moslems could be won over not by force but by reason, especially since their religion was so similar to Christianity. The Saracens, or at least the intelligent ones (*sapientes*), he wrote, were close to Christian belief, near the road to salvation; their Koran praised the Creator, extolled Jesus and honoured Mary above all women. Even William, however, could not ignore the Moslems' denial of Christ's death or their amazement at the Christian doctrine of the Trinity. And, like many other western commentators, he lingeringly condemned their heavenly garden of delights (*deliciarum*), where everyone had ninety-nine tender virgins to enjoy all day, though they always remained fresh and intact (*illibatas et integras*).

163

Though the pro-crusading enthusiasm of the eleventh and twelfth centuries was less marked in the thirteenth century (outbreaks of 'popular' movements occurred from time to time, however) and more moderate Christian voices were heard, it is evident, too, that the old animosity continued, in spite (or perhaps because) of growing commercial contacts, new interest in oriental politics and a greater appreciation of the possibilities of reasonable persuasion in religious matters. There are many examples of thirteenth-century ambiguities and animosities. Emperor Frederick II was supposed to have outraged Jerusalem Christians by defending the Moslems' right to perform their religious services in peace in the holy city. The Emperor even wanted to hear the Moslem call to prayer, and was disappointed when told that the *muezzin* had been silenced out of respect for Frederick. All of this would have been quite in keeping with the traditional image of the great ruler whom many Christians (from the pope down) did not trust. After all, like his grandfather, Roger, he was reputed to keep a multi-racial harem and to support Moslem scholars in his well-governed Sicilian realm. St Louis of France, on the other hand, had very little reason to admire Moslems because he was deeply convinced that they were his and God's enemies. After they had resoundingly defeated and captured the king, he rudely dismissed a 'Saracen' who had come to him and presented him with gifts, but who turned out to be a Frenchman from Provins (south-east of Paris), a convert to Islam, married to a Moslem woman, and the holder of important administrative posts in Egypt. After the failure of this inteview with the king, Joinville asked the renegade why he did not return to his own country. Fear of perpetual shame and poverty, should he ever return to Provins, kept him in Egypt; he also thought that he would be an object of daily insult among Frenchmen. He was probably right. In any event, the capture of King Louis aroused indignation and anti-Moslem sentiment in France, just as it threw jubilant crowds in Damascus into a frenzy of celebration. They stormed the Orthodox church of St Mary accompanied by singers and musicians, with the intention of destroying the place. At nearby Baalbek, Ibn al-Furāt continues, Christians hearing of Louis' defeat blackened the faces of the holy images in their churches, covering them with soot to indicate that even the saints were in mourning. The Baalbek Christians were fined by the local Moslem governor for this demonstration.

Throughout the thirteenth century the papacy continued to call for crusades and authorized financial collections, though these were often employed against European heretics or political enemies in the west. Popes also attempted to regulate Christian-Moslem relations through conciliar enactments, just as Moslem leaders had socially relegated Christians (as a protected minority) from the eighth century. The papacy, however, was less interested in the status of this minority than in its total separation from Christendom. For such purposes Moslems and Jews were usually considered one single group of god-killers. Until the First Crusade, Christian relationships with medieval Jews were not necessarily antipathetic. There were exceptions: Spanish Visigothic kings, accepting Christianity in the sixth century, began to persecute Jews. Jews were to accept baptism or suffer property confiscations, flogging, travel restrictions, scalping; Jewish men aiding in circumcisions were emasculated, Jewish women concerned in such rites had their noses cut off, a neat bit of symbolic transference that Freud (or Gogol for that matter) would have relished. P.D. King suggests that these restrictions expressed a new-found religious unity among Christians, the *societas fidelium Christi*, as one royal document put it. Gavin Langmuir, on the other hand, sees the Visigothic persecution in less simplistic terms. Early councils both in Spain and Gaul tried to keep Jews separate from Christians, a movement culminating in the Twelfth Council of Toledo (681), which may have influenced later Frankish laws. During the eleventh century such strictures were also applied to Moslems. Some of the canons of the Third Lateran Council (1179) dealt with this issue, but it was during the thirteenth-century pontificates of Innocent III and Gregory IX, two of medieval Europe's most powerful popes, that spiritual and social apartheid was most strongly expressed. The very fact that such legislation was enacted suggests a need to clarify Christian-Moslem relations; the simple martial ethos of the first three crusades was a thing of the past. Christians were not to serve Moslems either in menial positions or as merchants, nor to sail in their ships—sensible laws, from a military point of view, though usually ignored by enterprising Italian businessmen. Moslems (and Jews) were to wear distinctive clothing, were not to be seen in public on Christian holy days such as Good Friday and Easter, and were not to hold public office. These canons were repeated and expanded in the fourteenth century, when for example Clement V (d. 1314) tried to prevent the Moslems who lived among Christians from announcing prayers from their minarets, even from going on pilgrimage to Mecca.

Finally, an unambiguous statement of the older, aggressive approach is the work of Humbert of Romans, a Dominican crusade preacher who prepared a tract for the Second Council of Lyons (1274). This work is a useful guide to crusade ideology in later medieval Europe. In the present context, however, note the language used in Humbert's affective response to Moslems: they are 'wicked infidels', 'extremely wicked men and particular enemies of Christendom'; Saracens 'have an insatiable thirst for Christian blood' and fight in an 'unjust cause'. Since Moslems are very 'hostile to Christians', crusaders must 'eradicate these worst of men' and 'banish their filthy practices'. Their 'sins' and 'great crimes' are intolerable, as is their law, 'which forbids them ever to hear Christ spoken of'. Saracens are like Sodomites, committing filthy deeds and thinking they can wash them all away with water in the morning (a misunderstanding of pre-prayer ablutions, or perhaps about the ritual washing of the dying?). In their Koran, because they curse all believers in three gods in one, they 'persecute Christ' and therefore deserve death. Humbert concludes by referring yet again to 'the filthy practices of their damnable worship', their pride, malice and sins. In this tract the old attitudes are uppermost in the Dominican's thoughts, just as new attitudes are evident in the writings of that other Dominican, William of Tripoli.

Mohammad stumbled along in agony, 'from chin/ Down to the fart-hole split as by a cleaver' in Dorothy L. Sayers' translation of Dante's *Inferno*. The great Tuscan placed Mohammad in the eighth circle for fomenting schism among mankind; hence his appropriate punishment. Yet Dante consigned the chivalrous Saladin not to underworld torment but to neutral Limbo and the company of virtuous pagans, such as the ancient Greeks—though the poet makes Saladin stand 'aloof, alone' from the other shades. These cantos express much of the thirteenth-century ambiguity in Christian attitudes, which continued unabated into the fourteenth and later centuries. Europeans certainly had even less reason to rejoice at developments in the Near East; as the fourteenth century unrolled, it became clear that earlier losses, culminating at Acre in 1291, might never be made good, though plans for the recovery of the Holy Land continued to find their way into papal and royal archives. In the later thirteenth century, the Mamluks united Egypt and Syria under a forceful regime, but from the fourteenth century the Ottoman Turks presented a new threat, certainly to Byzantium and, in time, to Europe itself. Though there had been heroic attempts and even partial successes for Christians in the thirteenth century—with Louis IX and Frederick II for instance—there were no similar moments of relief during the next century. The only full-scale crusade organized in the traditional manner (by King Peter II de Lusignan of Cyprus) against the traditional objective (Egypt) ended in an orgy of pillage and destruction at Alexandria in 1365, after which the crusaders sailed home to enjoy their loot. In their wake they left enraged Mamluks and disconcerted Venetians, who condemned this threat to their rich Egyptian trade. Italian dealings with the Levant continued after the restoration of the Byzantine emperors to Constantinople in 1261, as did the old friction between northern Europeans thirsty for Moslem blood and southern Europeans hungry for Moslem commodities. Italian city-states and their merchants were also quite willing to make war on each other, or to conclude competing peace treaties with Ottoman or Mamluk factions, for the sake of commerce, which further complicated matters for would-be crusaders. At the end of the century Europe responded once again to the call, this time from King Sigismund of Hungary, who had good reason to fear Ottoman westward expansion. In this essentially defensive action, thousands of crusaders, eastern Europeans as well as many from Italy, France, Burgundy and Germany, were slaughtered in 1396 at Nicopolis on the modern Romanian–Bulgarian border.

Fourteenth-century crusades, then, ended in disaster just as the thirteenth century had closed with the fall of Acre. The response to that outrage of 1291 was understandably one of shock and dismay, echoing through subsequent decades. The writings of Ricoldo of Monte-Croce, a Dominican missionary in the Near East, illustrate this sense of anxiety. Around 1300 he composed 'letters' to the victims of Moslem aggression, attempting to console the dead as well as himself, for clearly he was disturbed by the notion that his God could have allowed such things. He claims, *inter alia*, that he saw Moslems tie a cross to a horse's tail and drag it through the town of Siwâs (in eastern Anatolia) after the fall of Tripoli (1289), and that there was generalized profanation of Christian churches throughout the Near East. But the worst moments occurred a few years later while he was engaged in Koranic studies as part of his missionary work at Baghdad. Reports were received about the capture of Acre and the slaughter of its Christian residents; Ricoldo says he then saw the booty being carried into Baghdad. Anxiously he looked for his fellow-Dominicans among the prisoners, but found only their writings and books, some of which (Gregory's *Moralia in Job*, for instance) he purchased. He knew then that they had all died, for Dominicans would never willingly part with such treasures. When a Moslem wench taunted him with a blood-stained tunic purportedly belonging to one of the Dominicans of Acre, Ricoldo's fears were confirmed. He breaks into eulogy in the midst of this narration, congratulating his fellow-friars for their heroic last stand. He admits that at first he had grieved but now was happy, for surely they were rewarded in heaven as martyrs. Immediately after this optimistic note, however, Ricoldo betrays his deeper distress—*Heu michi, quia natus sum videre contritionem populi mei!! . . . tantam deiectionem fidei Christiane!*—'Oh that I was born to see the oppression of my people. . . such abasement of the Christian faith!' Then, in anaphoric lament based on classical models, he asks the poignant question, *Ubi sunt . . .* 'Where is Tripoli, where is Acre, where are the churches of the Christians who were there; where are the relics of the saints, where the monks and nuns . . . Where is the multitude of Christians who used to be there?' Addressing the dead friars, he asks, Does it not seem that God is working wonders for Saracens and against Christians? Did God and the angels pray for Mohammad after all, as is written in the Koran? 'I am afraid that in a few years no Christians will be found in the whole world' (*in toto mundo*). In closing his letter Ricoldo requests his dead comrades to ask St Dominic to beg God for help, especially for the Holy Land, even though the Christians had offended heaven by their sins. Amidst the rhetoric and self-consciousness of Ricoldo's letters, the frustrated bewilderment that will mark fourteenth-century attitudes is plain enough.

Another manifestation of post-1291 anxiety broke out in the West about the same time that Ricoldo was writing his letters to the dead. As mentioned above, many Europeans looked upon the Mongols as potential allies against Islam, and entertained their embassies during the thirteenth century. In 1300, great excitement gripped the West when, in the course of the grand Jubilee in Rome, news began to spread from Italy into the rest of Europe that the Mongol leader Ghazan had defeated the Moslems, freed the prisoners of Tripoli and Acre, and turned the Holy Land over to the Christians. Pope Boniface VIII, writing to King Edward I of England to announce the wonderful victory of the Christian convert Ghazan, contrasted Mongol successes with Christian torpor and called for support for the newly-regained territories. Enthusiasm for another crusade began to rise. All of this faded when facts overtook rumours. Though it was true that Ghazan had gained military control in Syria for a few months in early 1300, that was the only foundation to the tale, since he had been a Moslem from 1295 and had no intention of handing over territory to the Christians. As Sylvia Schein suggests, these rumours, born of anxiety and hope, were greatly embroidered and disseminated by the masses of Christians present in Rome for the Jubilee; even the pope was misled by the euphoria. By 1301, the excitement about the so-called recovery of the Holy Land was at an end. The episode is an interesting indicator of the tensions and apprehensions that the West would never quite escape.

This undercurrent was manifested again in a more sinister way during 1321. Rumours began—particularly in southern France—that a great conspiracy had been hatched amongst the lepers and Jews of Europe, and the Moslem leaders of Spain: Moslems were supplying money and poisons to Jews and especially to lepers, who then infected wells so that Christians either died or became lepers (symbolically associated with heretics) like themselves. Jews naturally hated Christians, whereas the lepers hoped to escape the ignominy they suffered, in changing themselves from minority to majority— according to the rumours. The Moslems of course sought to recover territories from the debilitated Christians. Malcolm Barber has shown how the testimony elicited by inquisitors was used to ramify the plot. The disturbed imaginations of would-be victims and inquisitorial witnesses reflected a bizarre patchwork of images, derived from sources as varied as crusade propagandists and the infamous trials of the Templars. Leper 'commanders' were said to have met Moslem leaders and promised to renounce Christianity, sealing their pact by trampling and spitting upon a crucifix. In the hysterical outbreak of 1321, through what R.I. Moore calls a 'tangled nightmare of association', all of Christendom's enemies were lumped together to become, in effect, one enemy. Among the many reasons for this outburst must surely be counted frustration in the aftermath of decisive Moslem victories and uncertainty about the future of the Holy Land. As it happens, 1321 was also a year of mass violence in Egypt, where Moslems went on a rampage of church-destruction. Their complaint was the usual one, that *dhimmis*, Jews and especially Christians, were again accumulating too much ministerial power over True Believers. Christian churches were mobbed in Cairo, Alexandria and other cities of the Nile. Later in the same year when a fire broke out in Cairo, Christians were accused of arson. During this period, popular as well as official hostility was also directed against Christian missionaries from time to time, though in some cases it seems that the victims deliberately invited persecution. One of the often-cited examples is Raymond Lull, from Majorca, a layman who devoted himself to missionary work among the Moslems. He knew Arabic and, like Roger Bacon, encouraged its study. Dedicated to converting the infidel, he visited north Africa in pursuance of this dream but, like St Francis nearly a century earlier, he met only with disappointment. This did not deter him, nor did his zeal decline: he seems to have been expelled in 1308 for publicly denouncing Islam, and is said to have been martyred about 1315 on this third journey to north Africa, though the circumstances of his death are still debated. His life and writings have become increasingly interesting to medievalists in recent years.

In times of peace, Moslem authorities were usually (though perhaps grudgingly) tolerant of Christian clergy in their midst, but there were certain limits beyond which they were not allowed, as seen in the laws regulating Christian behaviour. Throughout Islam the *qadi* or judge continued to ferret out unorthodoxy or religious subversion through the inquisition (*mihna*). In such a climate Christian preachers would have been well advised to curtail their enthusiasm. What could happen when they did not is well illustrated by the fate of four Franciscans of Jerusalem. The four friars, residents of the Franciscan house on Mt Sion, had lived there for several years. By the early 1390s they had convinced themselves of their duty to set the followers of Mohammad on the right path, and prepared written statements to this effect. One November morning they marched up to the mosque 'of Omar' with their documents, but were not allowed to enter. When the Moslems discovered that they had a message for the *qadi*, they were taken to his house. There they read out the contents of their rolls of parchment, which can be summed up as follows : You [the *qadi* and every other Moslem in earshot] are in a state of eternal damnation since your law [the Koran] is not God's law, nor is it good but rather evil law, arising from neither Old nor New Testaments. In your law there are many lies, impossibilities, derisory things and contradictions, leading people not to good but to evil and to innumerable vices. After their blast against the Koran, with specific examples of its 'lies', the friars launched an attack upon Mohammad himself: he was no prophet of God, nor did any miracles confirm this (as among Old Testament

170

prophets). In fact, Mohammad was a murderer, a glutton and a pillager as well as a luster after wives, concubines and slave-girls. A sinner without virtues, his message was not to be believed.

After hearing this tirade, the *qadi* was, understandably, 'greatly angered' (*vehementer est iratus*). Outraged Moslems encircled the four men, while the warden of their house and the keeper of the hospice for Jerusalem pilgrims were called to the scene. The *qadi* asked the friars whether they had spoken as men of deliberation or as scatterbrained fools (*fatui et amentes et a ratione deviantes*), and whether the pope or some Christian king had put them up to this. The friars, elated in their zeal, replied that God had sent them, having selected them to announce the truth to the *qadi*: if he did not believe, and accept baptism, he would be condemned to the depths of hell. The reply from the *qadi*, that they were to withdraw all they had said and become Moslems or suffer death, met with a loud, clear refusal to retract what had been said. They were ready to die, for everything they had said was true, holy and orthodox. The *qadi* there and then pronounced sentence of death. As soon as the crowd heard this, they began shouting and beating the friars until at last the Franciscans fell half-dead to the ground. When they regained consciousness about an hour later, the *qadi* had them stripped, bound and tied to stakes, where they were whipped so cruelly that their bodies appeared to be completely flayed. He then put them into cells where they were kept in wooden stocks which prevented sleep or even rest. At last, on the third day, they were taken to the place where criminals were punished. There, in front of a crowd holding swords and knives, the *qadi* again asked them to retract their words and become Moslems. Again they refused, calling on him to become a Christian or suffer eternal torment. Hearing this the crowd, drunk with rage, fell upon them and cut them to pieces until nothing human-looking remained. The bloody gobbets were thrown onto a bonfire but—in the best of Christian hagiographical traditions—they would not burn at once, so the crowd remained to pile on wood until all was reduced to ashes; they hid the bones so that other Christians could not find and honour them. After a pious claim that God had caused this to happen for the comfort and consolation of all faithful Christians, the account closes with a list of the Jerusalem Christians and pilgrims who had witnessed the gruesome events, and had presumably been encouraged by them.

The imaginative literature of the fourteenth century also provides ample evidence of continuing ambivalence in Christian attitudes towards Islam. The famous book translated from French into English (probably during the 1370s), 'Mandeville's' *Travels*, presents on the whole a sympathetic view of Moslem society and belief. Almost nothing is known about the author, though some of his sources have been identified. He produced a curious mixture of fiction and fact based upon imaginative tales, the accepted natural history of his day and Holy Land itineraries, to mention only the most evident bases of the work. There is the usual Jerusalem-pilgrim chatter about wonderful sights: the Dome of the Rock where the young Virgin Mary sat when learning her psalter, where Christ was circumcised and where he once preached; Christ's fingerprints and footprints in stone, or the Virgin's tomb. But besides this familiar material, in the course of the narrative the author also discusses Moslem theology. He shows some familiarity with Koranic teachings, such as the honour shown to the Virgin and Christ, or the perfidy of the Jews who claim to have killed Jesus, who was not crucified but taken deathless to God. Because they accepted many Christian doctrines and came so near to Christianity (an echo of William of Tripoli), Saracens might be converted by preaching. Mandeville knows that there are important hurdles, such as their denial of the Trinity. The author claims that he once talked with 'the Sultan', who contrasted vile Christian habits such as tavern-haunting, whoring, fighting, cheating—even on Sundays— with the good, faithful way the Saracens worshipped their God. Mandeville admits that it is a 'great slander' to Christians that, in fact, they deserved such criticism. Christians, the sultan claims, will only regain the Holy Land if they mend their ways, a theme long familiar to earlier crusade writers. The *Travels* was a very popular work, translated into many languages and printed in several editions. As just one indication of its continuing influence, it turns up during a sixteenth-century hearing before the Roman Inquisition. Menocchio, who asserted among other blasphemous things that Jesus was but a prophet and not God, was put to death around 1600. This simple miller knew Mandeville and may even, Ginzburg suggests, have read a translation of the Koran.

Whereas 'Mandeville' claims to find worthy attitudes among the Moslems, another fourteenth-century English literary production positively revels in emphasizing the warlike animosity between Christian and Saracen. The poem *Richard Coer de Lion*, based on a thirteenth-century work, embodies much of the popular xenophobia and bloodthirstiness of the earliest crusading ages, emphasizing it to the point of parody. During the Third Crusade, Richard kills not 3,000 or 5,000 Moslems outside Acre, but 60,000, to the sweet accompaniment of angelic choirs who laud the deed. As he travels, Richard kills off Saracens like dogs, leaving a trail of blood to mark his progress. In the light of our earlier consideration of the significance of purported cannibalism in the First Crusade, it is interesting to read that King Richard himself robustly enjoyed a meal of young, fat, well-garnished Saracen. After feeding a similar repast to some of Saladin's unsuspecting ambassadors, Richard claimed that the most nourishing food for a Christian was Saracen flesh.

As the medieval centuries drew to a close, the Ottomans continued to increase the area under their control, finally capturing Constantinople in 1453. Henceforth the crusade would be a matter of self-preservation for central and eastern Europeans rather than an attempt by the Franks to regain Jerusalem. Though Pope Pius II called more than once for a crusade, though intellectuals like John of Segovia and Nicholas of Cusa involved themselves in Koranic studies and rational strategies to deal with Islam, the West did not respond in any significant fashion. Ambassadors and pilgrims continued to visit the Holy Land, with varying fortunes: Bertrandon de la Broquière even heard a Moslem leader tell his men that the same God who created Christians had also created Saracens; likewise friar Felix, on pilgrimage in Jerusalem, was insulted as well as treated kindly by the natives. In fact, he epitomizes the ambiguity that developed in and after the thirteenth century in the West. He recognized the Moslem proximity to Christianity, their piety (they all behaved like monks) and the way they cared for their mosques, in such contrast to Christians. Yet, in the last days of his pilgrimage as he prepared to return to Europe, Felix secretly went several times to a local Moslem shrine and scattered the stones of which it was built, a private, futile gesture against Islamic 'superstition'.

By the end of the Middle Ages, the vituperative condemnation of Islam so characteristic of the period 1095-*c.* 1200 had become a dull cliché. For many westerners Islam remained a puzzle, like Mohammad himself, the merchant who preached the Bible and served Antichrist. It cannot be said that western attitudes are any less ambivalent today.

8

Minorities at Risk: Women and Jews

'By God's bonnet'—that was his favourite oath—'we shall
talk of this day yet, you and I, sitting at home with our
ladies.'

(Joinville)

We have seen that the crusades grew out of far-reaching social and
psychological currents which deepened and broadened throughout the
eleventh century. Similarly, the consequences of the movement
involved much more than armed pilgrimage to the Holy Land,
impinged upon a variety of other aspects of contemporary European
society and affected many who fell outside the qualification of
Christian crusader or Moslem enemy. Though many others could
be considered from this point of view, here we briefly examine the
general effects of the crusades upon only two groups, women and
Jews.

Though generations of historians and popularizers have fixed the
archetype, the crusading knight, firmly in the public mind, it is less
easy to picture the women who went along on these ventures. Women
followed the pilgrimage routes of medieval Europe as avidly as men,
and the reports left by some of them, like Etheria of Aquitaine (who
went to Palestine in the fourth century) and Margery Kempe (an
English raving mystic-cum-tourist who accompanied and disrupted
many a fifteenth-century pilgrimage by her pious howling) contribute
a great deal to our knowledge of medieval pilgrimage in general. But
the crusades, though they are often called pilgrimage in the medieval
sources, were, as contemporaries knew, very special kinds of
pilgrimage. Women suffered while on ordinary pilgrimage to the Holy
Land, and they could hardly expect lighter treatment on the crusades.
And yet they went. It seems to have been common enough for the
nobility to bring their wives and, sometimes, families. The case of
Eleanor of Aquitaine, who accompanied her husband Louis VII of
France on the Second Crusade, is a well-known, even notorious
example. While in the Holy Land she and her uncle Raymond, the
Prince of Antioch, were rumoured to have become involved in an

affair. According to the twelfth-century historian William of Tyre, Raymond was determined to steal Louis' wife from him: 'The queen readily assented to this design, for she was a foolish woman.' Whatever may have been the facts of the case, and whatever else she may have been, the future wife of Henry II of England was no fool. In any event she ended her marriage to the French king shortly after returning from the Levant. Other well-known ladies accompanied their husbands on these dangerous journeys, for example the wives of Baldwin of Boulogne and Raymond of Toulouse, leaders in the First Crusade, and the wife of Richard the Lion-heart, who married him in the course of the Third Crusade. Another French king was more fortunate than his predecessor, when it came to marital fidelity. St Louis' wife Margaret accompanied him on his ill-omened crusade to Egypt in the mid-thirteenth century, pregnant though she was. She was so frightened of Saracens that she kept an old and respected knight near by to comfort her when nightmares about the brood of Allah happened to wake her up.

Most of the women who accompanied the crusaders were the wives of ordinary pilgrim-warriors, or independent but respectable females, or the usual crowd of whores and hangers-on to be found near any army camp, as well as the domestics who looked after the other needs of the crusaders. The late Maureen Purcell suggested that these women were not technically crusaders (*crucesignatae*) until the thirteenth century, but they certainly participated as such from the very start of the movement. Sometimes the proportion of women must have been relatively high, considering the dangerous nature of the expeditions. On the First Crusade the armies were held up at Antioch on their way to take Jerusalem when a pestilence struck: it was reported, incredibly, that 'nearly fifty thousand' women died within a few days. Even though medieval statistics are untrustworthy, in this case the writer is clearly saying that a great many women died; their overall numbers may well have been quite high. Whenever a fight was in the offing, women and other non-combatants (the clergy, the sick, the old and children) were usually herded together in some secure position while the infantry, knights and their leaders formed up for action. But there were bound to be fatalities. Some non-combatants, including women, were killed by enemy action while on the march or in camp, regardless of security measures taken by the crusaders. When security was faulty, the results were correspondingly more serious. As a prelude to the First Crusade, Peter the Hermit's band was wiped out just beyond

Constantinople, in the course of which the Turks invaded the base-camp of the Christians:

> And going within the tents, they destroyed with the sword whomever they found, the weak and the feeble, clerics, monks, old women, nursing children, persons of every age. But they led away young girls whose face and form was pleasing in their eyes, and beardless youths of comely countenance.

Moslem girls and boys were likewise often spared by the Christians, sometimes for baptism when this could be effected, but basically because they were a useful and valuable commodity. In one action against Caesarea in the early twelfth century, most of the adult population was put to death, but the crusaders spared the boys and girls: they 'bought and sold them, the comely and the ugly, among themselves...' There were other occasions, of course, when Christians massacred the enemy regardless of sex or age, as in the fall of Antioch in the First Crusade, when they 'spared neither sex nor condition and paid no respect to age . . . They killed the servants, . . . mothers of families and the children of nobles.'

Sexual abuse of prisoners—male as well as female, according to some historians—was common enough in these encounters. Among the rabble who accompanied the First Crusade, the Tafurs were supposedly habituated to raping women of whatever religious disposition. Rumours of such outrages may have prompted one chronicler to make the following statement about 'proper' knights on the First Crusade: 'In regard to the women found in the tents of the foe the Franks did them no evil but drove lances into their bellies.' In accordance with the received prejudices concerning the Moslems, their men were assumed by the Christians to be over-sexed, and consequently all female Christian captives almost certainly condemned to a fate worse than death. This accusation, usually levelled at minorities by majorities wherever and whenever found, was given more 'justification' in the minds of medieval Christians, since according to Islamic law a man could have four wives. Quite apart from stories told by Christians about outrages to their women, a wild version of what was supposed to have happened after Saladin captured Jerusalem in 1187 is more suggestive of the Moslem writer's erotic fancies, than the real fate of captive women:

> How many well-guarded women were profaned... and pretty things put to the test, and virgins dishonoured and proud women deflowered, and lovely women's red lips kissed, and dark women

prostrated, and untamed ones tamed, and happy ones made to weep.
How many noblemen took them as concubines . . . and celibates were
satisfied by them, and thirsty men sated by them, and turbulent men
able to give vent to their passion.

This particular writer, Imad ad-Din (encountered elsewhere in this
book) was given to fanciful and high-flown rhetoric, whether
describing the violence of sex or of battle. No doubt Christian women
were abused, though some outraged Christian chroniclers claimed that
not all of them seem to have minded.

The role of most non-combatant women was passive, but there are
clear indications that women sometimes took a more active part in the
fighting. This might be as elementary as bringing water to the fighting
men, as the women of Bohemond's camp did at a skirmish beyond
Nicaea and at the siege of Jerusalem, in addition to cheering and
encouraging the men as best they could. At Damietta during the
so-called Fifth Crusade in the early thirteenth century, they brought
water, wine and bread, as well as stones to use as projectiles, to the
warriors. Others assisted the fighters in more positive ways, like the
woman helping to fill a moat at Acre during the Third Crusade. After
depositing the load she had been carrying, she was shot with an arrow.
While she lay dying she asked her husband to use her own body to help
fill up the moat, which was done. 'No man', wrote a contemporary,
'ever should forget such [a] woman.' There are also reports of women
actually taking up arms and fighting alongside the men. As William of
Tyre claimed, women even fought at Jerusalem in the First Crusade
regardless of their 'natural weakness'. During the Third Crusade
actions at the city of Acre, three Frankish women 'fought from
horseback and were recognized as women only when captured and
stripped of their armour'; a Christian woman in a green mantle fired
arrows at Saladin's troops, wounding several. At last she was
overpowered and killed and her bow was taken to Saladin, 'who was
greatly astonished'. A Moslem who wandered across the battlefield
after the fighting was over noticed the bodies of two women: 'Someone
told me that he had seen four women engaged in the fight, two of
whom were taken prisoners.' Imad ad-Din claimed that among the
Franks 'there were indeed women who rode into battle with cuirasses
and helmets, dressed in men's clothes.' Women occasionally
participated in even more bloodthirsty activities: when a Turkish
galley was taken, Christian women went on board, according to a
contemporary, seized the captured Moslems by the hair, cut off their

heads and bore them back in triumph to the shore. Even allowing for the rhetorical exaggeration in the Moslem and Christian writers who reported these cases, it is clear that, although women played a minor role from the military point of view, in some instances their participation augmented the overall effort to defeat the Moslems and 'rescue' the Holy Land.

The intriguing story of Margaret of Beverley may well reflect some of the experiences of other women participants whose crusading careers went unrecorded. Margaret was born while her parents Sybil and Hulnon, from Beverley in northern England, were on pilgrimage in the Holy Land about the middle of the twelfth century. The pious Margaret later returned as a pilgrim to the Levant, underwent her many adventures, then came back to finish her life in a convent in France; there she told her story to her brother, a monk of Froimont (Beauvais), who put it into verse. The story begins with Margaret in Jerusalem while it was under attack by Saladin. She says she defended the city like a man, putting a cooking-pot on her head as a helmet and carrying water to the men on the walls; she was injured by fragments from a boulder big as a millstone fired by Saracen engines. After the fall of the city she paid her bezants and left with other ransomed Christians, heading towards nearby Lachis. Though they had bought their freedom at Jerusalem, the refugees were once again enslaved by Moslems, and Margaret remained in bondage for fifteen months. She was forced to carry out menial jobs such as gathering stones and wood for her masters and was beaten with switches for disobedience. Through summer heat and winter frosts she bore all with patience, always fatigued and undernourished: 'I bathed my chains in my tears.' Finally a pious man from Tyre, in thanks for the birth of a male heir, offered to pay the ransom of various Christian slaves, of whom Margaret was one.

Freed from captivity a second time, her troubles were far from over. In fact she was now completely on her own, wearing nothing but a tattered garment that scarcely covered her nakedness, travelling by desolate routes to avoid towns and possible recapture; she kept herself alive for five days with a single bread roll, then had to eat roots for another five days or so. She was torn between the fear of going into settlements, and the fear of ending up as a meal for wild beasts. Her only comfort was a psalter, but even this was nearly lost, when a Turk forced her to give it up. A few moments later, however, he ran back to her, threw himself at her feet in repentance, and returned the holy book to her. Margaret finally arrived in the region of Antioch, where once again she was arrested by the Moslems on suspicion of theft (of a knife). Condemned to death, in a cell surrounded by people speaking a language she could not understand (*parthica lingua*), she was praying when the Saracen commander heard her mention the name Mary, and ordered her release—much to the disgust of his fellow-Moslems. Finally Margaret returned to Europe during the truce between Richard I and Saladin; she visited Compostella and Rome, then made her way to France and to her brother's monastery. He could hardly recognize her (*inventus tandem quae sim vix credit*). She told him the name of their parents, that there were three children, a boy who died soon after baptism, Thomas—the monk standing before her—and a girl, now addressing Thomas. At last he believed her: 'We mingled our tears together.' He convinced her to enter a convent, which she did after telling him about her adventures. As she says—and we can well believe it—'my tale filled him with sighs'.

Women served the crusading armies and pilgrims in yet other ways, much to the regret of Holy Mother Church. The sexual needs of masses of men on the move, perhaps separated from their mates for years, have always presented a problem for the leaders of war. During the Middle Ages it was never easy to draw the line between pilgrims and ordinary camp-followers. Pilgrimage, as a general medieval custom, provided a means for satisfying sexual appetites through casual encounters and mercenary arrangements (and encouraged them, as some churchmen complained). On the extended pilgrimage of a crusade, where women were scattered indiscriminately among armies larger than one usually saw on the battlefields of Europe, the risk of sin was great indeed. It was acknowledged that sin could be a cause of defeat in battle: obviously, God frowned upon a band of sinners who had taken holy vows, and might punish them by giving victory to the Moslems, a chastisement for Christian souls as well as bodies. Fornication, therefore, was a matter of military concern. In the midst of their troubles at Antioch during the First Crusade, army leaders and prelates decided that the troops had displeased the Lord by their dissipation. They therefore expelled the women from the camp, presumably allowing the noble and obviously respectable ladies to remain. Having rid themselves of the source of their difficulties, the crusaders duly captured the city. It seems, however, that they had failed to learn their lesson, for as soon as they were inside the gates many of them 'sought out unlawful women without delay'. As a result,

Fulcher of Chartres suggested, God brought further punishment in the form of another band of Moslems, who now besieged the crusaders. For Vincent of Prague, the failure of the Second Crusade was attributed to noblemen who refused to leave off mingling with 'that sort of woman [*consortia muliercularum*]'. The third crusading army had the same problems. After Acre was captured in 1191, the troops settled down in the city to enjoy 'many damsels beautiful/ And with the wines and women they/ Caroused in vile and shameful way'. Consequently, to avoid God's wrath for such behaviour, when the army moved on it was decreed that the loose women should stay behind in Acre. Only certain females were allowed to continue on with the crusaders, 'Good old dames who toiled' and washed for the crusaders, who were 'good as apes for picking fleas', evidently a service much in demand. The army trudged south, to Jaffa, and while resting there the whores of Acre began reappearing among them: 'Back to the host the women came/ And plied the trade of lust and shame.' Ambroise adds that they even went into the ships and barges to do their plying.

The activities of these women of pleasure were described by Imad ad-Din. We have already quoted his frantic description of the fate of the captured women of Jerusalem. In the following passage, which his modern editor calls 'baroque pornography', Imad ad-Din outdoes himself. He is describing some 'lovely Frankish women' who have come to the Holy Land about the time of the Third Crusade to sell themselves even, he adds, to Moslem men. They are 'like tipsy adolescents, making love and selling themselves for gold, bold and ardent, loving and passionate, pink-faced and unblushing, black-eyed and bullying', with 'fleshy thighs, blue-eyed and grey-eyed, broken-down little fools'. They set up their tents, and groups of them, 'lovely young girls', supplied the men's needs in these enclosures:

> They dedicated as a holy offering what they kept between their thighs; they were openly licentious . . . brought their silver anklets up to touch their golden ear-rings, and were willingly spread out on the carpet of amorous sport . . . They were the places where tent-pegs were driven in, they invited swords to enter their sheaths . . . welcomed birds into the nest of their thighs, caught in their nets the horns of butting rams . . .

The presence of such women also caused problems for the Christians who attacked Constantinople in the Fourth Crusade. Indeed, it was such a problem that the bishops among the crusading host commanded that all the 'evil women' were to be rounded up, put on a ship and sent far away from the army. After Constantinople had been taken, however, there seems to have been some relaxation of the rules, for we find a 'certain harlot' singing ribald songs while seated on the august throne of the holy patriach. Not all such goings-on went unpunished in this life, let alone the next. In the mid-thirteenth century a knight found in a brothel was given the choice of being led through the crusader camp by the whore, or turning in his horse and arms and leaving the army. He chose the latter as the less degrading.

So far we have considered the women who accompanied the crusaders, but of course a great many women were left behind after those tearful farewells which the chroniclers and poets described so fondly. Although Herlihy has suggested that the crusades may have helped to raise the general condition of women in the later Middle Ages by throwing responsibility onto their shoulders in their husbands' absence, the opposite is just as evident. The fragile status of most women was made even more apparent when their men went off to battle the infidel. Perhaps we cannot blame some women for wanting to go along, or others for trying to prevent their men from going at all. The preaching-tour of Archbishop Baldwin in Wales provides ample illustrations of such reluctance. The wife of Rhys ap Gruffydd of south Wales changed his mind for him by 'exercising her womanly charms', as Gerald of Wales wrote, while another wife resorted to more direct means, seizing her husband's cloak and belt and so preventing him from going up to take the cross. Not all Welshmen were so docile, for a certain Arthenus took the cross without asking his wife's leave since, as he said, 'This is man's work. . . there is no point in asking the advice of a woman.' For those wives who remained behind, the Church guaranteed to protect them in their persons and property until their absent spouses should return. Even so, there are enough instances of litigation about parcels of land, for example, to suggest that this protection was not always effective. In the early thirteenth century John came back to his family and lands in Suffolk only to find that during his absence in Jerusalem a certain Thomas had helped himself to thirty acres by the simple expedient of taking it from John's wife, Matilda. Such possibilities must have disturbed the journeys of many ardent pilgrims as they set out on crusade. No wonder that Stephen of Blois wrote to his wife urging her to take care of lands, children and vassals. It was only natural that, when new groups of Christians arrived in the Holy Land, 'each of us', as one contemporary explains, 'anxiously inquired concerning his homeland and his loved ones. The new arrivals told us all that they knew. When we heard good news we rejoiced, when they told of misfortune we were saddened'. The encroachments perpetrated in King Richard's European domains in his absence (by the French king and his brother John) are a spectacular example of what went on in many smaller lordships bereft of their lords. When Joinville was asked to join King Louis' crusade of 1270 he demurred, remarking that his earlier absence in Egypt had brought ruin and impoverishment to the people of his French estates because of intrusions by outsiders.

Some crusaders must have been thrown into states of outrage or depression when they heard scandalous rumours about their distant wives. There is a certain irony in a statement made by Bernard of Clairvaux while preaching the Second Crusade. He was so proud of the effectiveness of his sermons that he claimed that the cities and castles of the West were deserted and seven women could scarcely find one man to keep them company. During this same crusade one party of Christians was taunted by Moslems shouting merrily from their city walls about 'the many children who were going to be born at home while we were gone' and that 'our wives would not be anxious about our deaths, since home was well supplied with little bastards'. Not all of the men who stayed at home, however, were as blatant as the French poet who praised the crusades for removing jealous husbands and leaving lovers in quiet possession of their ladies. The Church tried to reduce the risk of adultery by requiring that both husband and wife must agree, and give mutual consent, to the man's taking a crusading vow and departing for distant lands. By mutual consent they were in effect agreeing to remain chaste, and it was hoped that this would cut down on adultery; marriage vows should not be put at risk by crusading vows. So far so good. When Pope Innocent III took over, however, the rules were changed. This great lawyer, very interested in encouraging the crusading movement, decreed that husbands and wives could go off on crusade *without* seeking the permission of their partners. In this he seemed to slight marital fidelity. Thirteenth-century canon lawyers who succeeded Innocent found a way around the problem by agreeing that it might be legal for a husband to desert his wife for a crusade, but it was not moral since it created an invitation to sin. There were many practical as well as canonical issues involved. In a letter written by one prelate to another in the early twelfth century, it was suggested that crusaders who came home to discover their wives in the throes of an affair should either take them back forgiven or live with them but without sexual intercourse.

If the crusader died while on campaign, his wife was free to remarry. Joinville was shocked when the funeral of one of his knights was interrupted by the loud conversation of some other knights. He was even more shocked when they laughed at his rebuke and said that they were arranging the remarriage of the dead man's wife. In canon law, the woman whose husband had died on crusade could remarry after the lapse of a year. If he were merely a prisoner of war she had no right to remarry, no matter how long he remained in captivity. She had but two options, to wait it out or to join him. The difficulties began when there was uncertainty about the fate of a husband who was missing in action. At first canon lawyers suggested that in such circumstances a remarriage was illegal. After the mid-twelfth century or so, perhaps because more and more cases of this nature resulted from continuing crusading activity, the lawyers relented. They agreed that a woman should wait five years (an old Roman law) after her husband was missing. Meanwhile she ought to inquire from his commander about certification of his death or, if this were not possible, she should seek out information in the place where her husband was last seen alive. By the later thirteenth century, popes were following the suggestions of canonists, and allowing a reasonable presumption of death when the circumstances seemed to require it; the wife would then be free to remarry. The fact that the crusades caused complications in the lives of many canon lawyers (to say nothing of ordinary laymen) can be seen in the following curious legal principle from the thirteenth century, an example of the legal mind trying to cope with the peculiar conditions raised by the crusades. After a first husband was presumed to be dead and the wife remarried, she must allow her second husband to have intercourse whenever he wished, but she herself, of *her* own desire and will, was not to seek intercourse with him. Most lawyers were reasonable men, though, and few would have endorsed the above unenforceable principle. Nor would many have endorsed the suggestion of a leading canonist who claimed that a missing husband should not be presumed dead until 100 years had passed. The uncertainties which developed when a crusader was missing continued to plague women and their families at home. In Leicester two women were battling over some land: Alice said that her husband was still alive in the Holy Land, but her opponent claimed that he had died there. This uncertainty affected men as well. John tried to obtain some acreage in Oxfordshire in the early thirteenth century, but since the absent landholder was not yet proven to have died in the Holy Land, the case was put off indefinitely.

Finally, and paradoxically, sometimes the reappearance of a presumed-dead husband created more complications than it solved. Innocent III himself was advised of a case in Italy in the early thirteenth century: Palmerius, who was thought to have been killed, reappeared after several years' captivity. His wife Gilla had remarried, and Palmerius brought an action to recover both wife and lands. Gilla retorted that her first husband had died, and that the present claimant was an impostor since he could not play the harp like her Palmerius, or sing in French and Latin, or play draughts; besides this, he had a different appearance from her dead husband, too—his face was the wrong size, for example. On the claimant's behalf his family maintained that he had the same bent finger, the same scar on his face and the same two toes crossed in an unusual way, just as the original Palmerius had. Pope and cardinals pondered this case and then decided to let the second marriage stand. The resurrected Palmerius was to leave the couple alone.

Though women were put at risk both when on crusade and when remaining at home and trying to protect hearth and kin, at least the Church openly maintained a policy of protection for the weaker sex. The Christian attitude towards the Jews, on the other hand, was far from protective or consistent. Although crusaders were sometimes victims of nature or their fellow-Christians, they themselves were quite capable of inflicting the worst cruelties on others long before a single Saracen was anywhere to be seen. They were especially liable to indulge their passions for pillage and murder (without the inconvenience of leaving Europe) at the expense of the Jews. Crusader-gangs justified their atrocities by claiming to rid themselves of Christ-murderers in their midst before going off to slay Moslems. The worst, but by no means the only, massacres were carried out by the 'unofficial' peoples' movement in the First Crusade, led by the likes of Fulk, Gottschalk and Emicho of Leiningen. The Jews of Rhineland cities like Speyer, Mainz, Cologne and Worms suffered the most protracted attacks and those of Regensburg and Prague were victims of similar outbursts. Spain, France and England, too, had their own anti-Jewish riots associated with later crusades.

The city of Worms, for example, was the scene of a massacre led by Emicho in May 1096. Worms, home of the famous Jewish scholar Rashi in the 1050s and 1060s, proud of its beautiful Byzantine-style synagogue, contained one of the oldest Jewish communities of the Rhineland. The Jewish cemetery, just outside the line of the medieval city wall to the south-west, is one of the oldest in Europe, with monuments—now mere stumps of stone—going back to the twelfth century. Today, though little is left from the Middle Ages in the much-bombed and rebuilt city, one section of the old wall and gateway still stands to the north of the inner city. Outside the wall there is a children's playground; just inside, an alley whose name indicates that this was the Jewish quarter—Judengasse, 'Jews' Lane'. Here too is the synagogue, now an unpretentious building with a plaque stating simply that it was built in 1034 and often destroyed over the past 900 years, the last time in 1938.

In May 1096 when the Worms Jewry heard of some killings at Speyer, some of them rushed down the lanes to the bishop's palace across town. Others, believing in their Christian neighbours who had promised to protect them, and to whom they had entrusted their wealth for safe-keeping, stayed in their homes. It was an empty promise, a 'broken twig', and soon the little alleys and lanes were littered with men, women and children left dead and naked by the crusader mobs. The Jews' houses were pulled down and plundered, the Torah was trodden on, kicked about in the filth of the road and ripped apart. Many Jews were said to have committed suicide after killing their neighbours and kin—fiancé killed bride, 'women slew their darling children'. The rabble then attacked the remnant sheltering at the episcopal palace. The sheer numbers of crusaders made resistance impossible. To prevent defilement at the hands of Christians, the trapped Jews chose to kill each other rather than accept Christian baptism. Meschulam bar Isaac snatched up his son, whom God had given to his wife only in her old age, and cried out that he would offer him to the Eternal One. His wife begged him to kill her first so that she would not have to see the deed. He refused. Picking up his knife he said the blessing for an offering, the little boy said 'Amen' and was killed. Isaac, son of Daniel, was captured by crusaders and led to a church with a rope round his neck. There they said to him, 'You can still be saved; will you change your faith?' Since he could not speak he indicated with his finger that they should cut off his head, which they did. By 26 May, just over a week after they had arrived, the Christians swarmed off towards Mainz, leaving some 800 Jewish victims behind.

The most detailed descriptions, written by Jews, were substantiated by Christian writers as well. Even worse tales of atrocity resulted from the attack on Mainz. There the Jews had heard of the slayings at Worms and other places, and had put themselves under the archbishop's protection. Even so, their fate was inescapable. A feeling of helplessness, of resignation to God's will, was reinforced when two Jewish men heard ghosts at prayer inside the synagogue one night— a sure sign of impending doom, according to medieval Jewish folk-beliefs. The Christian mob camped outside the city in their tents. The Jews, hoping to strengthen the bonds with their protectors, handed over a quantity of silver to the archbishop and seven pounds of gold to the local count. It was a waste of money, for a party of Mainz citizens opened the city gates: an army 'like the sands of the seashore' attacked and drove the Jews, who fought back, into the archbishop's courtyard and palace. The prelate's men fled, while he himself took refuge in his church. The Jews, trapped in the palace, realized that they were finished. They sharpened their knives—a sacrifice made with a nicked blade was ritually invalid—and prepared to kill each other. As the Christians entered the courtyard and began killing, so, too, Jewish women began to slay their children, the men to slaughter their wives: 'Blood flowed to blood, and the blood of men was mixed with the blood of women, of fathers with children, brothers with sisters. . .' Some of the women threw gold coins from the windows to distract the crusaders while the mass suicide took place. One woman with two sons and two daughters begged a friend to kill them lest 'the Christians take them alive and baptize them in their faith'. The friend picked up the youngest son, Isaac, and cut his throat; the mother caught his blood in the folds of her cloak. When her other son Aaron saw this he cried 'Mother, don't kill me' and ran to hide under a chest. The two daughters were killed next. Then the mother called

> 'Aaron, where are you? I cannot spare you, you cannot move me to pity'; she dragged him by the foot from the chest under which he had been hiding, and offered him to the Sublime God. Then she lay her children in both her arms, two on one and two on the other side, while they were still twitching. She sat there and lamented as the enemy burst into the room.

They killed her, and when her husband learned of the tragedy he fell on his sword. Many others were said to have taken their own lives in the same way, like Mar Samuel bar Mordechai the Elder, who 'took his knife and thrust it into his belly so that his entrails gushed out onto the ground'.

Some Jews who were baptized by force or through fear returned to their old religion after the crusaders had gone, even, on occasion, with the approval of individual clergymen. In other cases, however, enforced baptism seems to have caused an attack of anxiety that can scarcely be distinguished from madness. Isaac the Righteous, for instance, decided to bring a 'sin-offering' to God for having allowed himself to be baptized:

> He took his two children, his son and daughter, at midnight and led
> them through the courtyard; he brought them before the Holy Ark,
> and slew them there for the sanctification of the Name of God. . .
> With their blood he sprinkled the pillars of the Holy Ark [saying]:
> 'This blood is my reconciliation for all my evil-doing.'

Then he set fire to his mother's house, burning her alive. Next Isaac went into the synagogue and, chanting in a louder and louder voice, ran about setting fire to it. Christians yelled through the windows that he should save himself, and held out a pole towards him, trying to rescue their recently-won convert. He refused their help, dying in the flames. In the end more than 900 Jews were said to have perished at Mainz. As a Saxon chronicler wrote, 'it was pitiful to see the great and many heaps of bodies that were carried out of the city of Mainz on carts'. Some Jews, refusing to accept a defeatist attitude, chose to die fighting for their faith, hoping to kill at least a few ungodly Christians before their own lives were lost. Others pretended to accept baptism only to be able to harangue the Christians and tell them what they really thought of their flimsy godling, a creature like any other creature, subject to death and putrefaction, a 'god of nothingness'; Jewish women taunted the Christian mobs, calling Christ the bastard son of a menstruating whore. Naturally, such actions only enraged the crowds and drove them to further acts of cruelty.

When Edessa fell, and then some forty years later Jerusalem, the Second and Third Crusades began like the First with attacks on European Jews. As an abbot of Cluny wrote during the Second Crusade,

> What is the good of going to the end of the world at great loss of men
> and money to fight the Saracens, when we permit among us other
> infidels who are a thousand times more guilty towards Christ than
> the Mohammedans?

In the Rhineland a zealous Cistercian monk urged recruits to the

Second Crusade to begin their holy march by killing Jews, with the result that 'in numerous cities of Gaul and Germany. . . a large number of Jews were killed in this stormy uprising'. The anti-judaic undercurrents in England stirred up by the fall of Jerusalem surfaced in riots at the coronation of King Richard I, who had already vowed to go to the Holy Land. Jews suffered at York, Norwich, Stamford, Bury St Edmunds; in London, too, they began 'to immolate the Jews to their father, the Devil. It took them so long . . . that the holocaust [*holocaustum*] was barely completed on the second day'. Throughout the kingdom, the chronicler Richard of Devizes rejoiced, 'they dispatched their bloodsuckers to hell'. He adds, with a note of disappointment perhaps, 'Winchester alone spared its worms.' Even in the fourteenth century during another spontaneous 'crusade' launched by peasants, Jews were attacked in southern France; once again they were said to have preferred death at their own hands rather than life with the uncircumcised. We have also seen their inculpation in the poisoning scare of 1321.

The slaughter of the First Crusade, however, remained the blackest memory for the Jews of Europe until overshadowed by the even greater slaughter of our own age. In the thirteenth century one Jewish commentator explained the mourning period between Passover and Pentecost as a commemoration of the atrocities of the First Crusade—even though the mourning motif actually went back at least to the eighth century AD in the West. Certainly the bitterness, hatred and aggression of the First Crusade are overwhelmingly clear in Christian writings. One chronicler praised the forcible baptism of 'those impious Jews', some of whom 'returned to Judaism even as dogs to their own vomit'. Many Christians of the First Crusade arrived in the Near East with their anti-judaism as rampant as ever, inflamed by occasional instances of Moslem-Jewish co-operation against the crusaders. In a vision, Christ himself appeared to one of the members of a southern French contingent during the First Crusade, as indicated in an earlier chapter. Asked for his opinion about Jews, Christ replied, 'I entertain hatred against them as unbelievers and rank them the lowest of all races.'

The First Crusade massacres profoundly influenced attitudes towards the Jews. Jews were forced into the role of money-lender during the twelfth century, useful to private individuals as well as to kings, and forced out of a feudal society which ran on Christian oaths and Christian rites. Being pushed to the social peripheries, Jews became an unassimilated category, the 'matter out of place' described by Mary Douglas, and therefore a threatening source of danger. From the eleventh century, too, we have seen that one can begin to speak of a Christendom, a unity of belief and practice in Europe which was only an ideal in earlier centuries. In this process of self-definition, outsiders, whether heretics, Jews or Saracens, were themselves more clearly marked out as the enemy. The legacy of this attitude—as far as Jews were concerned—would be tales of immorality, of evil rites done by night, of ritual killings of Christian children, of poisoned wells and other plots; as Christian society changed, so too did attitudes towards the Jews. The outrages of the crusaders were signs of things to come.

On the other hand, many kings and princes as well as Church leaders tried to protect the Jews, from both selfish and altruistic motives. A chronicler writing of the First Crusade massacres recognized the dangerous forces at work: even excommunication pronounced by the clergy and the 'menaces of punishment on the part of many of the princes' had little effect in restraining Christians. The historian William of Tyre condemned the 'mad excesses' of the mobs who 'cruelly massacred the Jewish people in the cities and towns through which they passed'. In the Second Crusade Bernard of Clairvaux reprimanded and silenced the Cistercian monk described above, who had stirred up anti-judaism in the Rhineland. Bernard also wrote to the English, urging them to join the crusade, but adding a caution against persecuting Jews. Sometimes Christian protection of Jews went beyond mere words. During the Second Crusade uprisings at Würzburg, according to a Jewish chronicler, a Jewish girl was dragged into a church and—after she spat on a crucifix—was beaten unconscious and left for dead. 'Then a Christian washer-woman came, who dragged her home and there concealed her. So she was saved.' Next day the bishop had the dead Jews collected in a cart, along with their chopped-off parts such as thumbs, hands, feet and limbs. He had them cleaned, anointed with oil and buried in his own garden. Later on, a wealthy Jewish couple bought the garden and established it as a Jewish burial-ground.

Regardless of attempts by some Christians to restrain the animus of their fellows, the massacres continued, the hatreds deepened. Christian anti-judaism, spurred on by the outrages of the First Crusade, itself a result of the Christianization of Europe in the eleventh century, evolved into that now-familiar form, anti-semitism; the stereotypes collected around and were projected against Abraham's people. At the end of the Middle Ages, Franciscan pilgrims were warned by the warden of the convent of Mt Sion in Jerusalem that Jews were not to be trusted, for 'their whole object in life is to cheat us and rob us of our money'. Like Moslems, they were fit only for Christian scorn, an attitude which the crusades helped to define and transmit to our own times.

9

Decline of an Ideal

I see Christianity routed. I do not believe there has ever been
such a loss. It gives good reason to stop believing in God and
to adore Mohammad.

(The troubadour Austorc d'Aurillac)

By the end of the Middle Ages the Europe which had created the idea
of crusade had undergone profound changes. Christendom had
dissolved into a collection of mutually hostile kingdoms and
principalities; the damaging Hundred Years' War between France and
England, which ended only in the mid-fifteenth century, was for
England a prelude to dynastic battles in the Wars of the Roses; the
Holy Roman Empire was a loose collection of ecclesiastical and secular
states. Spain, however, had achieved the unification which made it one
of the leading powers of sixteenth-century Europe. Spain would battle
France for the rich pickings of Italy, a country divided by rivalries
between kingdoms, city-states and the papacy, an institution which
itself lost European influence as it withdrew into the maze of Italian
politics. The old enemy of Christendom, too, had changed. Successors
to the once-powerful Mamluks, the Ottoman Turks during the late
fifteenth and early sixteenth century created an empire that
lasted—amazingly—until the twentieth century. After Anatolia (with
Constantinople), the Balkans and eastern Europe, the Ottomans
moved against Persia, Syria and Egypt; Salim 'the grim' took Cairo in
1517. The Moslems, a once-divided enemy that had invited Christian
interference by fighting amongst themselves, and by positive
collaboration with Christians, were now united, well-ruled and
strong.

In addition to these external forces of change directly affecting the
crusades both as ideal and as reality, even from the beginning the great
adventure carried within it erosive elements that contributed to its
weakness and ultimate decline. An obvious source of weakness was the
incessant rivalry among crusade leaders and between these leaders and
Byzantium, as noted in earlier chapters. Even before 1095, the Norman
Robert Guiscard took pleasure in blinding and removing the noses of
Venetian allies of Emperor Alexius Comnenus, while Alexius sought

191

to enlist the pope in his conflict with Guiscard. The stormy relations between Alexius and the first crusaders en route to the Holy Land, and the jealousies between leading factions which threatened their continuing progress to Jerusalem, are a commonplace of crusade historiography. Tancred attacked Baldwin, killing some of his men and horses near Mamistra; Bohemond and the Count of Toulouse stubbornly quarrelled over possession of Maarat and Antioch. These are but a few examples of a serious dilemma that faced all crusaders. The internecine combat continued even after the fall of Jerusalem, for instance in Bohemond's continuing battle with Byzantium. In such circumstances, it is not surprising that, according to Ibn al-Qalanisi, Emperor Alexius sent ambassadors to Baghdad inviting the Moslems to help him force the crusaders out of Syria. Competition between crusader states sometimes had extremely serious repercussions, such as the capture of Edessa and the subsequent calamitous Second Crusade: Raymond of Antioch, reports William of Tyre, 'rejoiced in the count's misfortunes' when the city fell in 1144. The next prince of Antioch, Raymond of Châtillon, turned against his own co-religionists in the horrendous pillage and murder of the peaceful Christian inhabitants of Cyprus (in 1156). Later in the century, Saladin's successes were followed by the Third Crusade, and once again internal Christian rivalries seriously weakened the crusader front. When, after being ransomed, Guy of Lusignan, King of Jerusalem, attempted to enter the 'safe' Christian city of Tyre, he was turned away by his rival, Conrad of Montferrat. Disgruntled, Guy went off on his own to besiege Acre. When Richard of England arrived in the Levant, he too was turned away from Tyre by Conrad, then joined the assault on Acre, which fell in 1191. Although, in taking the city, the Lion-heart quarrelled with the Duke of Austria, his worst enemy was King Philip II of France. Considering his crusading vow discharged, Philip sailed back to Europe and continued to undermine Richard's power in the West. Meanwhile, Richard embroiled himself in the feud between Guy, whom he and the Pisans supported, and Conrad, who was backed by the French and Genoese. By early 1192 many of the French troops left behind by Philip II began deserting Richard and heading for Acre, where they threw themselves into the Guy-versus-Conrad rivalry with such relish that, as Ambroise says,

> Shouting and confusion filled
> The town, and men were slain and killed.

Shortly afterwards, some of the French began pulling out of the campaign altogether in spite of Richard's tearful objections. In April 1192, in the midst of the continuing dispute between Guy and Conrad, the latter was stabbed to death by Assassins. Naturally Richard was blamed by his Christian enemies. Finally, after realizing the tactical problems facing him in Palestine and the dangers to his authority in Europe, Richard made a treaty with Saladin in which Christians were granted freedom of pilgrimage to Jerusalem. Even here, the old animosities stirred again, for Richard tried but failed to keep the duplicitous French from enjoying this newly-won right to pray at the Holy Sepulchre. Upon leaving the Levant in October 1192, the English king was captured by the Duke of Austria and imprisoned by Austria's overlord, Emperor Henry VI. No matter how honourable his captivity, it was an ignominious but fitting end to a crusade permeated by rivalry and hostility between Christian camps.

Of all the instances of inter-Christian rivalry, however, the Fourth Crusade is the most striking. The expedition began to go wrong when the Venetians diverted it to the recapture of the city of Zara, across the Adriatic. In spite of the objections of the Cistercian Abbot of Vaux who reminded the crusade leaders that they wore the sign of the cross and that the people of Zara were Christians, the city was taken and sacked. Venetians and French, Villehardouin reports, then fell out over division of the spoils, killing and wounding each other in a grim confrontation. After patching together a truce the Venetians next set their sights on Constantinople. When this became known, however, to their credit some of the leaders abandoned the expedition and either returned home or went to the Holy Land on their own. Once again the Abbot of Vaux stood before the assembled noblemen and declared that he and others of like mind had not come this far to make war on Christians. Nevertheless, greed and the old enmity between Latin and Greek prevailed in the end. The fact that not all prelates condemned the attack is clear from the eye-witness account of Robert de Clari, who says that the crusaders were harangued by certain bishops who claimed that their cause was righteous and the treacherous Greeks were worse than Jews. It is ironic that during the first assault, when the French raised their scaling ladders, they were met not by Greeks but by a contingent of English and Scandinavian mercenaries (*d'Englois et de Danois*, Villehardouin says), wielding their terrifying battle-axes. Eventually the attackers forced an entry and the richest city was theirs. As noted in an earlier chapter, holy relics attracted clerical attention, whereas most of the other jubilant victors sought more mundane treasures. They trampled on holy images, smashed reliquaries for their gems and precious metals and threw the relics into the gutter. Hagia Sophia's altar itself was dismantled and shared out while horses and mules were tethered in the sanctuary. Outside, as a contemporary Greek writer (Nicetas Choniates) laments, nothing was heard but weeping and tumult, the groans of wounded and dying men in the streets, the screams of women and girls being raped in alleys. When the

21 Acre, taken by the crusaders in 1103, was recaptured by Saladin in 1187. Outside Acre King Richard I of England massacred thousands of helpless captives after he reconquered the city in 1191. Its Christian inhabitants died in a bloodbath when it fell to the Moslems in 1291.
(*The Holy Land*, vol. 2, London 1843. Oxford, Bodley Mason EE 68)

pillage was over, the Venetians reaped their reward—the virtual domination of eastern Mediterranean trade—and the Latin Empire of Constantinople was established. Shocked by the depravity of this conquest, Pope Innocent III condemned those Christians, whose swords dripped with Christian blood, and lamented the rape of innocent girls and matrons and the sacrilegious theft and destruction of holy objects. The shrewd pope also feared that these actions would ruin the crusade cause in the eyes of other western Christians.

Frederick II's crusade, also condemned by a powerful pope (Gregory IX) but for different reasons, inevitably embroiled the controversial ruler in conflict with other Christians, among whom

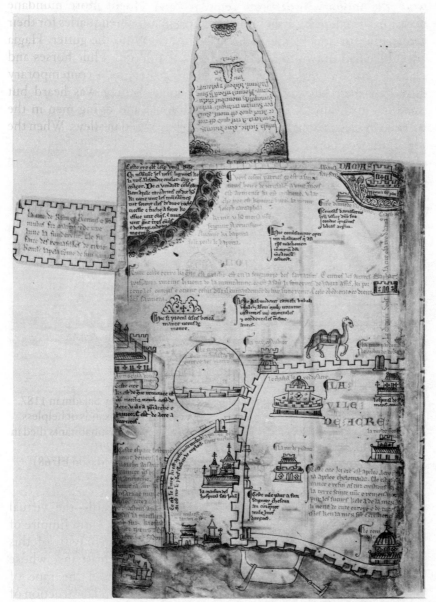

22 Schematic layout of Damascus, Antioch and, at bottom, 'La Ville de Acre',
showing (bottom left) the fortified Christian suburb which, like the rest of the
city, was taken in 1291.
(London, Brit. Library *MS Royal 14 CVII*, f.4ᵛ.)

were the military orders of Templars and Hospitallers. On one occasion Frederick even found himself attacking, or at least threatening to attack, the Templars of Acre. When his near-eastern adventure had drawn to a close and he went down to the harbour to embark one May morning in 1229, some of the good people of Acre displayed their hatred by showering him with animal innards and dung. As for Louis IX's first venture, the Venetians opposed it at first, worried as usual about their trade with Egypt. Competition of another sort hindered many English barons from joining the French king. King Henry III, who did not want to lose their services to the crown, persuaded them to commute their crusader vows. In any case, after Louis' failure in Egypt he sailed to the Holy Land, where he was able to restrain the hostilities among Venetian, Genoese and Pisan colonies and between Templars and Hospitallers. After the king left for France, the rivalries began again. Within a decade the Genoese were helping the Byzantine emperor regain control of (Latin) Constantinople, whose trade had been dominated by their old rivals, the Venetians. This sort of chaos carried on right up to the final loss of Acre, whose streets had seen many a clash involving Christian factions, and amongst native groups protected by rival Christian patrons. It was a massacre of peaceful Moslems in Acre in August 1290 that roused the Mamluk sultan, whose son finally stormed the city and slaughtered most of the inhabitants in May 1291. The military orders and the Italian factions put aside their hostilities and tried to defend Acre together, but it was far too late.

Just as the crusaders often failed because they were unable to mount a unified offensive free from internal bickering, in the same way Moslem defences suffered from lack of harmony among Islamic factions and between political leaders. To cite but a few examples, Ibn al-Athir says of Christian successes in the First Crusade:

> While the Franks—God damn them!—were conquering and settling in a part of the territories of Islam, the rulers and armies of Islam were fighting among themselves.

As for the Third Crusade, the Christian, Ambroise, claimed that

> The Lord God made a quarrel rise
> Among them, with most bitter words
> Between the mamelukes and kurds.

Even Saladin himself, his biographer notes, was the target of an attempted murder by Assassins. The old story continued into the

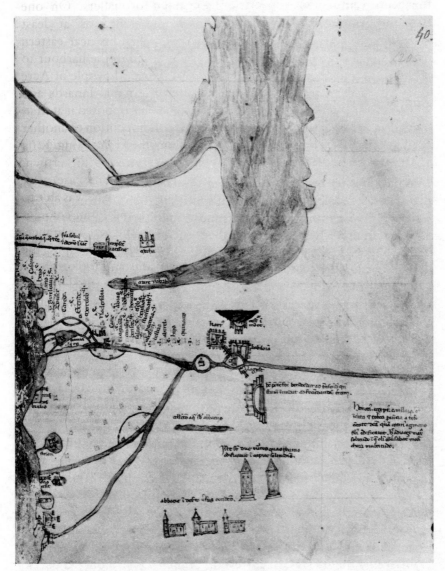

23 Egypt, especially after 1200, became an important theatre of crusader operations. This contemporary map (east at top) shows not only the various tributaries of the delta, with Damietta, but Cairo and 'Babylon' (centre), and (top) the Arabian peninsula with Mecca ('Mecha'), the Red Sea, Persian Gulf and Arabian Sea.

(Oxford, Bodley *MS Tanner 190*, f. 205^R.)

thirteenth century, on Frederick II's crusade for instance, when, as Roger of Wendover says

> the sultan of Babylon was so severely harassed by internal war in all directions. . . he was compelled to make a truce of ten years with the Emperor.

And, as a final example, Joinville observed that the

> Sultan of Cairo, who was expecting our King [Louis IX] to arrive in Egypt in the spring, thought that in the meantime he would go and overthrow his mortal enemy, the Sultan of Homs. . .

Internal division not only weakened the Islamic cause, but also, on many occasions, led to alliances with the Christians. During the First Crusade the Egyptian (Sh'ite) Fatimids established friendly relations with incoming crusaders against their enemies, the (Sunnite) Seljuk Turks and Caliph of Baghdad. According to William of Tyre, 'for many years, a deep and inveterate enmity had existed between the Orientals [the Seljuks] and the Egyptians', which led the latter to welcome crusader successes. This is the background to that passage in the anonymous *Gesta* when the crusaders at Antioch presented 100 Turkish heads to Fatimid ambassadors from Cairo, camped nearby. As crusader successes increased, however, Fatimid enthusiasm for the alliance declined.

Christian-Moslem co-operation had one of two consequences: either Christians allied with Moslems to make war on other Moslems, or Christians fought other Christians with Moslem assistance. As for the first relationship, in addition to the examples already given from the First Crusade, another famous incident involved Prince Raymond of Antioch, who allied with the Assassins against Nur ed-Din, son of Zengi the conqueror of Edessa. After Raymond and his men were defeated, his skull was sent as a trophy to Baghdad. A few years afterwards when Nur ed-Din threatened Damascus, the Franks agreed to help defend the city, a fact which disgusted even some of the Damascenes themselves. In any event, Nur ed-Din conquered the city (having been allowed in through the Jewish quarter) in 1154. A flagrant case of collaboration and double-dealing occurred in the 1160s when the new King of Jerusalem, Amalric I (Amaury), went fishing in troubled Egyptian waters. After being repulsed in 1163, he was invited back, this time as an ally, to get Nur ed-Din's men (Shirkuh and Saladin) out of the country. After a truce in 1167 Amalric was once again called in by the Egyptian leader Shawar. By 1168, when it was clear that Shawar would not be able to pay Amalric his agreed fees for services rendered, the King of Jerusalem again invaded the land of the Nile. He called upon the Hospitallers for help, since the Templars, who had already established a separate treaty with Egypt, refused to join in. Finally, the Egyptian leader switched sides again and joined Shirkuh. The Franks were out of Egypt by 1169 and, in 1171, the Fatimids of Egypt were defeated; Saladin was in charge, with many conquests still before him.

Even King Louis IX was quite willing to enter into Moslem alliances to further the Christian cause. He sought out the Assassins for this purpose and sent emissaries to the Mongols. Joinville describes how a needed Moslem ally was fêted at Acre, whose streets were carpeted with cloth of gold and silk for the sultan's progress through the city. Though they might be subject to misinterpretation back home, these arrangements between Moslems and Christians, given the lack of crusader manpower and the confusing, shifting conditions of Levantine politics, were usually justified. On the other hand, aggressive alliances with Moslems against other Christians could not be so easily accepted. The rivalries between crusade leaders described at the beginning of this chapter were sometimes greatly exacerbated by the employment of 'infidel' forces. One instance was the entangled situation of 1108 detailed by Runciman, in which Baldwin and Joscelin, with their Moslem allies, were defeated by the army of Tancred and *his* Moslem allies; the issue was control of Edessa. During Saladin's successful reign, he attracted the interest of competing crusader factions (as well as the Byzantine emperor). In the course of Raymond of St Gilles' battle with Guy of Lusignan over control of Jerusalem, the former entered into negotiations with Saladin; other ensuing intrigues led to discord, disunity and the fall of the holy city. An even more flagrant example involved Conrad of Montferrat, who agreed to disrupt the Frankish cause and attack Christian Acre, if Saladin would give him Sidon and Beirut. In the end, however, Conrad backed out, but it was clear to Saladin that he could easily play the Franks off against each other. J. J. Saunders drew attention to a letter of 1183 in which Saladin told the Abbasid caliph that the Franks were even supplying him with arms with which to kill other Franks.

The crusading cause was weakened, then, by the tendency for western noble leaders to take their natural sense of rivalry and competition with them from Europe into the Near East. Another source of inter-Christian rivalry was the old antipathy between

Oriental and Latin Christianity. This hostility explains the actions of the native Christians at Tripoli, for instance, who in 1137 secretly guided a Moslem force to a successful engagement with the local Frankish contingent. By far the greatest enmity, however, was generated by the Frankish-Byzantine relationship. Even before Clermont, as noted above, Alexius Comnenus had asked the Seljuk sultan for military help against the Normans of southern Italy. After the first waves of official crusaders had passed through Constantinople, he kept up diplomatic correspondence with the Fatimid Egyptians and, a few years later, as William of Tyre claims, he encouraged the Seljuks to withstand the rapacious westerners. The *Damascus Chronicle* records further instances of help requested, and aid sent, from the Seljuks to the Byzantines ruled by Alexius. Similarly, the eve of the Third Crusade found Saladin and the Byzantine emperor allied against their common enemy, the crusaders. After Saladin took Jerusalem, he maintained friendly relations with Emperor Isaac II Angelus, who sent the Moslem leader his ambassadors with treaties in Greek and Arabic, sealed with a golden seal, as well as 4,000 iron lances and 5,000 swords, among other gifts. It was rumoured that Saladin provided Isaac with poisoned wine and flour to distribute to crusaders en route through Byzantium. Whatever the truth of that accusation, there is no doubt that Saladin sent a *minbar* (ornate pulpit used in mosques) to Constantinople for the encouragement of Moslem residents of the city. With the emperor's permission Saladin also sent a band of religious leaders along with the *minbar*. Isaac treated western crusaders, and their ambassadors, with great contempt. According to Ibn-al-Athir, he also promised Saladin he would hinder Frederick Barbarossa, who was leading his German army to the Holy Land. By 1190, however, Saladin realized that the Byzantine alliance was a liability, because the military value of Isaac's empire was negligible. Though the Byzantine-Moslem accord had little practical effect, it undoubtedly contributed to that simmering cauldron of hostility between Greek and Latin, which boiled over in the Fourth Crusade.

Alongside the grand but temporary political alliances between Moslems and Christians, and the lesser economic ones condemned by Pope Innocent III in 1215 (for example, when he prohibited Christians selling arms and ships to the Saracens), there were many instances of collaboration on a more personal level. Saladin and the Franks were battling for Acre for such a long time that, during lulls in the combat, sometimes a Moslem and a Christian relieved the monotony by joining in peaceful conversation; sometimes, Beha ed-Din claims, the two parties even sang and danced together, 'and afterwards they would begin fighting again'. At Acre, during the First Crusade, crusaders broke off, even before the city was taken, to feast, count up their spoils and enjoy the delights of 'pagan dancing girls', as they are euphemistically called, about whom the Lord God made his displeasure known (with the help of a visionary priest). Fraternization of another sort occurred at Tyre after it fell to the crusaders in 1124. The conquered Tyrians came out to the Christians and, as William of Tyre put it,

> It gave them great delight to examine the form of the machines, to gaze at the height of the movable towers and the variety of weapons; they admired the position of the camp and even desired to know the names of the leaders.

When the tables were turned in Egypt in 1221, the defeated Christians were visited by their enemies, who brought them food to save them from starvation. Such stories of Christian-Moslem co-operation, no matter how transient, humane or justified the relationship, were usually received with incomprehension in Europe. Westerners were also disturbed by stories of desertion that eventually filtered back to indignant (but non-crusading) Christians. As in the case of collaboration, however, there were degrees of culpability not always acknowledged in the west. In some cases, in fact, 'desertion' was actually more honourable than perseverance. As noted, some noblemen—like Simon de Montfort, who would lead the Albigensian crusade in southern France—refused to go along with the Zara attack, but this was true of the lower ranks as well. Villehardouin claimed that about 500 such men were drowned when their ship foundered as they left Zara. In the earlier Third Crusade, after King Richard decided that it was strategically impossible to move against Jerusalem, Ambroise remarked that many 'deserted' the enterprise. In such cases, desertion was not a matter of cowardice but of principle, a protestation that the proper object of military operations was neglected by those in command.

Less militarily justifiable, but quite understandable in human terms, were the desertions inspired by the crushing lack of food and other supplies, a catastrophe frequently suffered by crusaders. Two famous examples were the sieges at Antioch and Acre in the First and Third Crusades. In the first case, Fulcher noted that the poor, having so little with which to support themselves, were the first to desert;

William of Tyre felt that camp conditions—starvation, dampness and rain, pestilence—brought on this failure of nerve. Peter the Hermit was among the deserters, though he later returned (or was brought back) to the fray. After taking the city and then being besieged by the Moslems, many crusaders of both high rank and low, unable to endure the hunger and other hardships, let themselves down over the walls with ropes and baskets, by night. They then headed towards the coast and safer climes or joined the enemy, thereby denying Christ as well as revealing military secrets. Nearly a century later at Acre, famine was so rampant among the Christian besiegers that many joined Saladin's army where, Ambroise complained, they repudiated the efficacy of baptism and denied that God could be born of a virgin or be crucified. Crusade commentators usually looked upon such acts as cowardice, though often their censure was tempered with regard for the inhuman conditions involved. In other cases, however, conditions hardly seemed to justify desertions. Even before reaching the Holy Land, the resolution and dedication began draining away from some would-be infidel-slayers. En route through Italy on the First Crusade, Fulcher's group stopped in Rome to offer up their prayers. Unfortunately the city was split, as usual, into rival factions, in this instance those favouring Pope Urban II and the followers of the antipope Clement III. When the crusaders were caught in the cross-fire—stoned by the antipope's supporters as they prayed in St Peter's, for instance—many of them, weakened by cowardice, returned to the safety of their homes. Fulcher condemns them for this and it must be admitted that, if this was their reaction to a touch of urban disorder, they would have been of little value as soldiers of Christ in a distant, harsh land facing an enemy intent upon killing them. When the remainder left Rome and were awaiting passage, many had second thoughts, sold their bows and turned their backs on the whole venture. Finally, after witnessing the drowning of some 400 men and women and their animals off Brindisi, yet another cowardly contingent set out homeward rather than risk the perils of the sea. Altogether, Fulcher's group (he travelled with Baldwin of Boulogne from mid-1097) seems to have been especially prone to the weaknesses most abhorred by a warrior-nobility. Yet, ironically, the man with whom Fulcher originally began his crusading venture was not only a member of the most elevated of noble ranks, but also was, or became, a classic example of crusader cowardice. Stephen, Count of Blois and Chartres, had been one of those who fled the walls of Antioch in the First Crusade. As Orderic Vitalis reports, after

Stephen (father of King Stephen of England) returned home, he was 'continually reproached because he had fled disgracefully' from the siege. Many people chided him, especially his wife Adela, who, as the daughter of a man who had pulled off one of the boldest and most successful military gambles of that or any other age—the conquest of England in 1066—very likely was acutely humiliated by her husband's disgrace. Orderic says she used a combination of conjugal caresses and scolding to such effect that Stephen agreed to go back to the Holy Land in 1101 on what came to be known (to some) as the 'crusade of the faint-hearted', consisting as it did of many who had lost their nerve on the first expedition. Stephen, and presumably Adela, finally were able to wipe out the disgrace, when the good Count of Blois was killed in action.

Even before the First Crusade, contemporaries were recording examples of desertion and open collaboration with the enemy, such as the imperial overlord of Antioch, who, in the 1080s, gave up his city to the Turks and became a Moslem. (During the twelfth century, a nephew of the Byzantine emperor himself switched to Islam and married a Seljuk princess.) By the time the Third Crusade was under way, westerners had become inured to stories of turncoat crusaders, such as the French deserters who attacked, killed or enslaved fellow-Christians on Cyprus, or the crusaders who joined Saladin. Once, after some deserters were given a ship, they captured a vessel heading for the crusader camp at Acre and brought Saladin the booty and captives. No wonder, as Beha ed-Din wrote, that the Moslems rejoiced to see how God defeated the enemy with their own men, thereby saving Moslems the trouble. Such behaviour continued through the thirteenth century: at Damietta during the Fifth Crusade, a Frenchman among the sultan's men was heard yelling abuse at the crusaders; we have seen that King Louis brusquely rejected the overtures of an apostate Frenchman in Egypt, but he had no choice about agreeing to a document of capitulation drawn up by a renegade priest, as Joinville calls him, who had joined the Saracens. Certainly there are parallel instances of Moslems allying with Christian armies, or stealing quietly away from besieged cities, but these would have been received in the West as quite acceptable examples of Moslem perfidy and cowardice; in addition, it was assumed that they would have recognized the superiority of Christianity and, therefore, would have abandoned their infidel beliefs. What was *not* understandable and therefore acceptable was the opposite movement: what right-thinking

Christian would ever join an inferior race of men who worshipped the idolator Mohammad? Instances of apostasy or merely of living like Moslems continued to be reported in Europe, causing doubts about Christians in the Holy Land who seemed to be weakened by the evil influence of the aliens amongst whom they lived.

It must be said, however, that even in the later thirteenth century there were still some who professed to believe in traditional crusade ideals. When Pope Gregory X was laying the groundwork for the Second Council of Lyons (1274), he issued a request for guidance on crusading policy. One of those who turned in a thesis was Humbert of Romans, who had retired as head of the Dominicans in 1263. Humbert, though he had often preached the crusade and recruited soldiers for Christ, does not seem to have been particularly well-informed about Moslem ways; to him they were infidels sunk in lustful inebriation, fit only for killing. Yet—he complains—in his day, hardly anyone among the nobility encouraged his peers to become crusaders, though once upon a time even a simple hermit, Peter, had roused all Christendom to Holy War. Humbert's writings reveal much about contemporary attitudes. Not all who complained about Christian indifference were ecclesiastics. The troubadour Rutebeuf blamed the avaricious Church for the fact that *Li feux de charitei est frois/ En chacun cuer de crestiien*: The glow of charity is chill in every Christian heart, and neither young nor old now fought for God. In spite of the fact that pro-crusade sentiments continued to be heard in the thirteenth and later centuries, Throop suggests that by the time of the Council of Lyons in the 1270s, 'bitterly hostile public opinion' about further crusade expeditions was a more typical attitude. Though modern historians have made it clear that after the fall of Acre in 1291 the West by no means turned its back on the Levant (it could not afford to, for many reasons), nevertheless it would seem that thirteenth-century criticism did in fact reflect growing antagonism and disillusion with the near-eastern adventure. This attitude, as Luttrell points out, continued to develop, even to become increasingly bitter, during the fourteenth century.

Various themes can be identified in the literature of thirteenth-century crusade criticism—themes that had often appeared in less vitriolic forms in the twelfth century. One of these called attention to the unsuitability of would-be crusaders. Though many who mentioned these faults did so hoping to stimulate improvement and consequent successful prosecution of the crusade, by the thirteenth century they could also be taken as examples of why the crusades had become hopeless enterprises. The tradition that pilgrimage (and by extension crusade) was in fact open to abuse and, therefore, required regulation if not prohibition, goes back at least to the eighth and ninth centuries. By the eleventh century, stress was being placed on pilgrimage with the heart, not the feet, on altered inner attitudes, not exterior locations. But this had always been a minority opinion (which outlived the Middle Ages); people *would* go on pilgrimage and, after 1095, on crusade for many reasons, not all worthy. In the aftermath of the Second Crusade the complaint was heard that some men became crusaders merely to see new lands, others to escape poverty or the harsh rule of their lords, even to avoid punishment for wrong-doing. For William of Tyre, the people arriving in the Holy Land during the Second Crusade only made matters worse for those they claimed to help. Usamah recognized in the later twelfth century that it was always the newcomers who were more inhumane towards the Moslems, exasperating local Franks who had fitted themselves into near-eastern ways. In the thirteenth century, the theme of false crusaders aroused Jacques de Vitry (Bishop of Acre), who lamented that so many came out only to escape boredom or punishment; he protested that the Holy Land was turning into a penal colony, a dumping-ground for the undesirables and have-nots of Europe. Even heretics were sent east to expiate their errors by battling infidels, an irony to which Throop rightly draws attention. As the thirteenth century progressed it became clearer in the West that the enthusiastic, self-sacrificing motives which had drawn at least a sizeable proportion of crusaders to the Holy Land in an earlier age were no longer operative; growing recognition of this can only have weakened interest in supporting the enterprise itself.

This is equally true of a second theme in thirteenth-century anti-crusade propaganda—the quarrelsome and dissolute life led by crusaders who had settled in the Holy Land, as well as their collaboration with the 'enemy'. Battles between crusade leaders were openly recognized in the West in the twelfth and particularly thirteenth centuries as serious problems. By the early thirteenth century, Jacques de Vitry was complaining of this and of the internecine quarrels among Italian merchants of Genoa, Pisa and Venice, who 'more often join battle against one another than against the treacherous infidels' and are more interested in trade than battling for Christ. One of the theses submitted to Pope Gregory X in the 1270s was the biting *Collectio de Scandalis Ecclesiae*, in which the author made it clear that the crusades were failing because of quarrels among the Christian Levantine princes. Another criticism drew attention to their penchant for idleness, women and wine. This last criticism seems to have been more commonly aimed at the lower ranks. Ever since the First Crusade, military setbacks had been blamed on drinking, swearing, gambling and whoring; note the allure of sin-ridden Acre during the Third Crusade, for instance, when troops deserted King Richard for more pleasant occupations. A century ago Hans Prutz conveniently collected together numerous examples of medieval criticism of such activities: to cite a few from the twelfth century, Christians in the Holy Land were accused of harbouring the old spirit of corruption; of being less virtuous than the Turks; of being experts in drunkenness, fornication, adultery, rape and sodomy; of giving themselves up to such lubricious pleasures as the bath. Thirteenth-century critics continued the invective, even remarking that the crusades had an *adverse* effect on participants, taking good men away and returning them physically and morally wounded to Europe. Jacques de Vitry was especially critical of crusaders who had accommodated themselves to the Near East: they adopted all the evil habits of the Moslems, sending their wives more often to the baths than to church, or pampering their children with luxuries, bringing them up unfit for battle, like women, ornamented and dressed in soft robes. These descendants of manly warriors now openly abused pilgrims and crusaders who came to the Holy Land, calling them foolish idiots. Jacques de Vitry's censure seems to have had little effect, for the feasting, drinking and whoring continued. The same objections were raised about the Fifth and Sixth Crusades, for instance, and though such behaviour was an inevitable consequence of contemporary warfare, it was increasingly seen to be one of the causes of declining success; moral corruption went hand in hand with military failure. By the fourteenth century, in Marino Sanudo's words, it was the rare crusader who was not infected with the sickness of greed or lust.

A third theme especially common to thirteenth-century commentaries and poems on the crusades is closely associated with changing patterns of community and authority in medieval Europe as a whole. By now even the clergy were rejecting papal leadership in some instances. In some kingdoms they—and the laity—often found themselves objecting to taxation which apparently went to support non-existent crusades. Misuse of crusade funds became a standard complaint in the thirteenth century, generating a concomitant unwillingness to contribute. When Gregory X divided Christendom into twenty-six tax districts, he stirred up a hornet's nest of resentment, for the familiar triple-locked money-box had become a symbol of papal greed present in every parish church. Charges of papal embezzlement were raised by both clerical and lay writers: the crusade languished, it seemed, while popes spent the money fighting their own enemies closer to home. 'Rome, you do little harm to the Saracens, but you massacre Greeks and Latins,' claimed a thirteenth-century Provençal poet. Secular governments came under fire, too. The crusade taxes raised in England and France before the Third Crusade brought outcries on both sides of the channel, while in the thirteenth century Matthew Paris claimed that King Henry III only took the cross in order to provide an excuse for further taxation of his subjects. Equal, or perhaps even greater, indignation was expressed about another abuse of spiritual powers, allowing or even forcing crusaders to buy their way out of their vows. By the thirteenth century this had undeniably become a way to raise money for the papacy. 'Rome... for money you take away the cross from those who took it for God,' one contemporary asserted, while a Templar in Arsuf lamented, in terms that Luther would have appreciated, that the pope 'permits the redemption of our cross for money... They sell God and indulgences for silver.' Often Dominican and Franciscan crusade-preachers were accused of complicity (for example by Matthew Paris) in the plot, though some of them accepted the job of papal taxman with the greatest reluctance. The troubadour Rutebeuf asked what became of the money collected by Franciscans and Dominicans, answering, 'They spend it on themselves...' Whether personally culpable or not, there is no doubt that thirteenth-century crusade preachers 'selling the cross' sometimes received short shrift from their audiences. Their seeming debasement of a spiritual ideal lessened commitment to the ideal itself.

Another element contributing to the lessening of enthusiasm was the growing realization that, in fact, the crusades were no longer succeeding. Ever since the failure of the Second Crusade, in spite of St Bernard's justifications of it, the attitude that God himself may not have blessed the enterprise began to gain ground. The argument that failure was due to the sinfulness of the crusaders was, however, relatively plausible and served to stifle doubts about the essentially holy aspect of the crusades. But with the defeat of King Louis IX in Egypt in the mid-thirteenth century, this situation changed. Though one could understand God thwarting unworthy sinners, how or why should he have put such an ignominious end to Louis' crusade? After all, he was one of Europe's heroes, the archetypal pious king, who became a canonized saint (in 1297). The educated might claim to see a hidden design behind it all, or resign themselves to ignorance of God's ways, but for ordinary folk the paradox was not so easily glossed over.

Finally, by the thirteenth century certain Christian writers had begun openly to question some of the assumptions fundamental to the holy war, as seen above. For a summary of some of these criticisms one returns to Humbert of Romans, who tried to answer them point by point. For instance, in his brief presented to Gregory X for the Lyons council (1274), he said it was claimed that Christians should not shed blood; it was also argued by anti-crusaders that Christian leaders should not expose fellow-Christians to death at infidel hands. Furthermore, it was claimed that the crusades were pointless since Christians were outnumbered in the Holy Land and disadvantaged in a strange country, and that Christians did not really want to stay there anyway. Humbert also offered rebuttal to the proposition that Christians should not attack the Moslems when the latter were at peace. Finally, he noted that some had pointed out that Christian treatment of Jews, Saracens and barbarians (like the pagan Prussians) was quite ambivalent; if one tolerated—however badly—Jews, then why not Saracens too? Humbert's catalogue of complaints concludes with the objection that apparently God was no longer on the crusaders' side, having given Saladin a victory and brought death to Frederick I and to Louis IX as well as to countless innocent crusaders. Elsewhere (giving advice about how to preach the cross), when Humbert addressed the reasons why men ignored the call to crusade, he brought things down to a more personal level. People were too busy enjoying themselves, getting drunk and fornicating, to give it up for the Holy Land, and they also feared physical illness, wounds and death. Some were too devoted to their own territories to leave them unguarded, others were too mean to spend the necessary money for the journey. Bad advice often deterred would-be crusaders, and finally, Humbert complained, many were kept at home out of devotion to friends and family, especially to their lady-loves. Hence, many pretended to be unable to answer the call, or claimed to disbelieve in the indulgences offered for such services.

It is true that many of the above excuses were raised and debated in the twelfth century. Ralph Niger, for example, asked why anyone should go east, when so many problems, such as heretics (in particular the Cathars), faced society and the Church in the west. Next, he suggested that the exotic, treacherous, perfumed eastern Christians were being justly punished by God for their manifold sins, dealings with the Moslems and doctrinal errors, and in any case, those crusaders who *had* gone to the Levant and later asked for help were little better than criminals and vagabonds. The harrowing of the Near East was part of God's plan, and should not be tampered with. Niger even went so far as to suggest that Saracens were human just like Christians and should be treated as such. He also asserted that it was sinful to expose oneself to dangers of a spiritual and physical nature, which the crusader must inevitably do, and furthermore it was especially wrong for certain people such as the clergy, women and the poor to go in the first place. All of his arguments were repeated and augmented in the thirteenth century, which marked the turning-point in western attitudes towards the holy adventure. By then the critics among both clergy and laity were far more vocal as, in the late Maureen Purcell's words, mystical and military aims began to pull apart the movement. By the thirteenth century the great, enthusiastic adventure had become an institution, burdened with all the dross and abuses of many other medieval institutions. The eschatological, non-rational, visionary and popular ideals of the First (and even Second) Crusade had by the mid-thirteenth century become proprietary concerns for the nobility, or papal and political ideologies. An anonymous thirteenth-century song advised men to beware crusade sermons, which would turn them into prisoners of the cross; but by the thirteenth century, such advice was becoming unnecessary.

Conclusion

Though it is difficult to summarize and draw conclusions about such a varied and long-lasting movement as the crusades, certain generalizations are unavoidable. For instance, it is apparent that the expression 'the crusades' must be qualified, for the First Crusade differed in many ways from those which followed. Thousands of Europeans, affected by the emotional and social upheavals of the eleventh century, undertook a long, dangerous trek towards a mystical goal which was, for them, both a place and a state of salvation. During the next two centuries, crusades became increasingly structured, moving from general to specific aims and means; the idealism of the First Crusade was superseded by sometimes incompatible ideologies imposed from above by the papacy, by the noble and royal leaders of later expeditions, and by the secular rulers of *Outremer*.

Concurrently, Christendom itself was changing: the crusades exemplified these changes, revealing much about the dynamics of religious, economic and political realignments and alterations in western Europe. To take the religious aspect as an example, the crusades encouraged a growing concern about gaining indulgences, first by service abroad, then eventually by purchase of exemption from such service; the papacy attracted more and more criticism—from thirteenth-century poets who castigated Roman greed, for instance—because of what appeared to be diversions from the crusading impulse. By the sixteenth century, such matters would become important issues in the breakdown of European religious unity. Certainly this is not to suggest that the crusades led to the Reformation, but merely that the later crusades disclosed ominous stresses within a Europe that would ultimately undergo a Reformation. In the same way, conflict between French and English crusaders during the Third Crusade was a harbinger of that later confrontation known as the Hundred Years'

War. Crusader activities and interrelationships in the Holy Land, then, as well as European responses to calls for crusades, provide models of wider, more deeply rooted attitudes, ambiguities and animosities within western Europe; in this sense, each crusade was a microcosm, a diminished image of Christendom.

Another inevitable conclusion to any general study of the crusades is the fact that many questions remain unanswered, perhaps unanswerable. The sorting out of motivations, for instance, still engages the interest of scholars, as does the very composition of the groups called 'crusaders': for each knightly or noble participant, for each foot-soldier or archer, how many unarmed pilgrims, women, clergymen, went along as 'crusaders'? Did the lower classes, as Kedar suggested, continue to participate as avidly in the thirteenth century as they did in the twelfth century? How many women were actively, and how many passively, 'crusaders'? Such problems, considered individually, may seem to be mere froth that floats on the surface, puzzles propounded for the delectation of scholars. Yet every clue that can be found is meaningful, every attempt to answer such questions is worth considering because, as suggested above, each crusader band that detached itself from Europe reveals to the historian varying aspects of contemporary society.

Another conclusion to be drawn from a study of the crusades is that Moslem reactions to and interactions with the crusaders, who were intrusive elements, is a topic that is usually relegated to secondary status by western historians. Yet the Islamic viewpoint is as deserving of study as the Christian; fortunately, some western scholars (who are not primarily Orientalists) are forcefully and convincingly presenting the crusades in an Islamic context, pushing us away from the Christian-centred world into a wider universe, instigating a long-overdue Copernican revolution in Christian-Moslem studies. There is a practical side to this as well: the need to understand Islam and the various peoples who call themselves Moslems is as pressing today as it ever was; and yet modern western European Christians seem in general to be as ignorant of the fundamentals of Islam as their twelfth-century predecessors. The words of a thirteenth-century Jew, Ibn Kammūna of Baghdad, concerning the lack of comprehension between Jews and Moslems of his day, apply equally well to modern Christians and Moslems:

(D)espite numerous contacts of the bulk of the Jews with the Muslims, many Jews still do not know the basic Islamic tenets known by the rank and file Muslims, let alone the elite. It is even more natural that a similar situation should obtain on the Muslim side. . .

The question of Christian-Moslem interaction naturally includes the problem of the Christian attitude towards war. An examination of the course of the crusades has led some historians to suggest that Church doctrine was deliberately manipulated to suit specific ends: though committed to condemning bloodshed, the Church itself promoted it. Keith Haines even goes so far as to remark that in Europe

> It is impossible to discern a totally pacifist ideology amongst virtually any of the leading moral, theological or political philosophers of the twelfth and thirteenth centuries. . .

Another leading crusade historian has also recently emphasized how the fundamental message of Christian charity was reinterpreted to suit crusade exigencies. Crusade preachers, for instance, must have deliberately presented Christian *caritas* to their audiences in such a way as to play upon the xenophobia of the masses.

One final conclusion to be drawn from the crusading experience is the futility—in practical terms—of the Christian attempt to co-exist with Moslems peacefully in the Holy Land, while trying to maintain political control of the area. Permanent peace between Moslems and Christians, in Moslem territory, was not feasible: caught between an Islam newly dedicated to *jihad* (from Saladin's time) on the one side, and mistrusting, uncomprehending westerners on the other, the Christian Europeans of *Outremer* were, as Riley-Smith points out, in an untenable position. Christian residents in the Holy Land, then, were surrounded by hostile forces, harassed by problems of logistics and military support and by divisions of opinion in Europe about crusader policy; difficulties of a similar nature would confront many modern European states in their own colonial enterprises. Eventually expelled from positions of political and military power in the Levant, Christians were allowed to return to the Holy City only as pilgrims and suppliants at the Tomb of Christ, as they had been for centuries before that fateful sermon preached by Urban II in 1095.

Notes *and* Sources

Abbreviations

AB	Analecta Bollandiana
AHR	American Historical Review
CPR	Calendar of Patent Rolls
CR	Close Rolls
C&Y	Canterbury and York Society
EHR	English Historical Review
JEH	Journal of Ecclesiastical History
LCL	Loeb Classical Library
LRS	Lincoln Record Society
MGH	Monumenta Germaniae Historia
PL	Patrologia Latina (Migne)
P&P	Past and Present
PPTS	Palestine Pilgrims' Text Society
RHC	Recueil des Historiens des Croisades
RS	Rolls Series
SS	Surtees Society
TRHS	Transactions of the Royal Historical Society

Introduction

PAGE

1   Quote from al-Abidwardi: Francesco Gabrieli, *Arab Historians of the Crusades*, tr. E. J. Costello fr. Ital. ed. 1957 (London, 1969), p. 12. Hereafter, *Arab Hist.*

     Acre, 1286: Hans Eberhard Mayer, *The Crusades*, tr. John Gillingham fr. Germ. ed. of 1965 (Oxford, 1972), 273. Hereafter Mayer, *Crusades*. Acre, 1291: *Arab Hist.*, 343 ff.

Chapter 1

7   'He who fights . . . .': Bernard Lewis, ed., tr. *Islam: from the prophet*

Muhammad to the Capture of Constantinople (2 vol., London, 1974), I. 210. Hereafter Lewis, *Islam*.

9–10   *Annals* and Franks: *Carolingian Chronicles: Royal Frankish Annals and Nithard's Histories*, tr. B. W. Scholz with Barbara Rogers (U. Michigan, 1970), 78, 82, 86, 91–2, 96.

11   *Ammianus Marcellinus*, tr. J. C. Rolfe, LCL (Cambs. Mass. 1971), Vol. I, 26–29.

       King Harald's Saga, tr., intro. M. Magnusson and Hermann Pálsson (Harmondsworth, 1966), 51.

13   Holy war: James A. Brundage, *Medieval Canon Law and the Crusader* (London, 1969), 25–27. Hereafter Brundage, *Canon Law*. Carl Erdmann, *The Origin of the Idea of Crusade*, tr. of Germ. ed. of 1935, notes by M. W. Baldwin and W. Goffart (1977), esp. Ch. II. The English ed. calls attention to developments in scholarship since the original publication of *Die Entstehung des Kreuzzugsgedankens*.

       Feudalism: after the Second Crusade 'almost the entire West became so still that not only the waging of war but even the carrying of arms in public was considered wrong.' Otto of Freising, *The Deeds of Frederick Barbarossa*, tr., C. Mierow and R. Emery (U. Columbia, Records Civ. No. 49, 1953), 78.

14   Lucian, *The Passing of Peregrinus*, tr. A. M. Harmon, LCL, Vol. v (1936/72), 13.

15   Predispositions: E. O. Blake, 'The Formation of the "Crusade Idea" ', *JEH*, XXI (1970), 11–31, esp. 17–30.

16   Angers monks: Georges Duby, *Rural Economy and Country Life in the Medieval West*, tr. C. Postan fr. Fr. ed. 1962 (Columbia So. Carolina, 1968), 410.

17   Crusading aspirations: Colin Morris, *The Discovery of the Individual, 1050–1200* (London, 1972), 150–51.

18   Norman Cohn, *The Pursuit of the Millennium*, (London, 1970) esp. Ch. 3, 'The Messianism of the Disoriented Poor'. Hereafter Cohn, *Pursuit*. R. W. Southern, *The Making of the M. A.* (1953, ed. of London, 1968), 50. *The Poem of the Cid*, tr. L. B. Simpson (U. Calif. Press, 1957), 67.

19   *The Alexiad of Anna Comnena*, tr. E. R. A. Sewter (Harmondsworth, 1969), 422–23. Hereafter *Alexiad*. For a jaundiced view of Alexius'

motives, and reference to crusader suspicions about him, see Peter Charanis, 'A Greek Source on the Origin of the First Crusade', *Speculum*, XXIV (1949), 93–4.

20   Indulgences: H. E. J. Cowdrey, 'Pope Urban II's preaching of the First Crusade', *History*, 55 (1970), 177–88; Mayer, *Crusades*, 26; Brundage, *Canon Law*, 148–9.

21   Moved to enthusiasm: an assumption questioned long ago by F. Duncalf in 'The Peasants' Crusade', *AHR*, XXVI (1920–21), 440–53.

25   Fronto: N. Lewis and M. Reinhold, ed., *Roman Civilization, Sourcebook II: The Empire* (N.Y., 1966), 511–12.

26   Fourth Crusade: a competent, recent study is Donald E. Queller, *The Fourth Crusade* (Leicester, 1978).

27   'Children's crusade': the best contemporary evidence suggests a mass movement of the rural poor protesting the failure of the Church to exalt apostolic poverty. The French movement seems to have been unknown to contemporaries south of the Loire, and the imputation of 'crusade' to the French and possibly to the German bands is a later medieval embellishment. The participants may have included children, but the words used by contemporary chroniclers do not emphasize this at all. Here the oppression '*puer*' quite often refers to social station rather than age [rather like the derogatory use of 'boy' by white American southerners when referring to Negroes]; in any case the chroniclers also indicated 'adults', 'men and women', 'the poor', 'adolescents and old people'. Later medieval commentators invented the stress upon 'children' and over-stated the case in claiming that this was a 'crusade'. For the French processions, there is no contemporary suggestion that the goal was the Holy Land, though some among the German bands that reached Italy may have been imbued with crusading zeal. See Peter Raedts, 'The Children's Crusade of 1212', *Jour. of Medieval Hist.*, III (1977), 279–323, with full biblio. on 320–323. As Raedts notes, some seventy years ago Munro threw doubts on the participation or leadership of children, though Munro did not look into the question of fundamental motivations prompting the mass movements: D. C. Munro, 'The Children's Crusade', *AHR*, 19 (1914), 516–24.

29   Fall of Acre: discussion of this ill-fated city in D. Jacoby, 'Crusader Acre in the Thirteenth Century: Urban Layout and Topography', *Studi Medievali*, 3rd ser., XX (1979), 1–46.

Pius II: *Memoirs of a Renaissance Pope: The Commentaries of Pius II*, tr. F. A. Gragg, ed./intro. L. C. Gabel (N.Y., 1959), 119.

Chapter 2

30   Jacques de Vitry and Odo of Châteauroux in Joannes Baptista Cardinalis Pitra, *Analecta Novissima Spicilegii Solesmensis* altera continuatio, Tom II, Tusculana (1888), 427, 314. Hereafter Pitra, *Analecta*.

31   Bernard's miracles: Helmhold, *The Chronicle of the Slavs*, tr. E. J. Tschau (Columbia, Records. Civ. No. 21, 1935), 170–71. Dom Jean Leclercq, 'Pour l'histoire de l'encyclique de saint Bernard sur la croisade', *Etudes de civilisation médiévale (IXe–XIIe siècles): Mélanges offerts à Edmond-René Labande* (Poitiers, 1974), 479–90. Hereafter *Mélanges . . . Labande*. And Leclercq's 'L'encyclique de saint Bernard en faveur de la croisade', *Revue Bénédictine*, 81 (1971), 282–308.

Gerald of Wales, *The Journey through Wales and The Description of Wales*, tr. L. Thorpe (Harmondsworth, 1978), 75–6, 185–6, 200–202, 204–205. Hereafter, Gerald of Wales. For a recent study of Gerald, see Robert Bartlett, *Giraldus Cambrensis* (OUP, 1982).

The Franciscan: G. G. Coulton, *Medieval Village, Manor and Monastery* (N.Y., 1960 ed. of *The Medieval Village*, 1925), 102.

32   Bishop of Lincoln: *The Rolls and Register of Bishop Oliver Sutton*, Vol. III, ed. R. Hill, LRS, Vol. 48 (1954), 195. Hereafter *Reg. Sutton*.

Preaching and wonders: Geoffroy de Villehardouin, *The Conquest of Constantinople*, tr. M. Shaw in *Joinville and Villehardouin: Chronicles of the Crusades* (Harmondsworth, 1963), 29, hereafter cited Villehardouin. Oliver of Paderborn in Louise and Jonathan Riley-Smith, *The Crusades: Idea and Reality, 1095–1274* (London, 1981), 135–6. Hereafter Riley-Smith, *Crusades*; Gerald of Wales, 172.

33–35   Jacques de Vitry and Odo in Pitra, *Analecta*, 405–30, 331–33; for the fox and raven motif, see number 2177 in F. C. Tubach's extremely useful guide, *Index Exemplorum: A Handbook of Medieval Religious Tales*, Folklore Fellows Communications No. 204, Helsinki, 1969.

36   Villehardouin, 29; on indulgences see Robert Somerville, 'The Council of Clermont and the First Crusade', *Studia Gratiana XX*

(1976) 329; Giles Constable, 'The Second Crusade as seen by Contemporaries', *Traditio*, IX (1953), 249; Brundage, *Canon Law*, 148; Pitra, *Analecta*, 442 (Jacques de Vitry).

Josephus, *Jewish Wars*, in the transl. by the 18th c. divine and scientist, Wm. Whiston (Bk. VI, Chap. 1, section 5); for a more recent trans. see G. A. Williamson, *The Jewish War* (Harmondsworth, 1959), 306.

37 St. Bernard in James A. Brundage, *The Crusades: A Documentary Survey* (Madison, Wisc:, 1962), 91–2. Hereafter Brundage, *Crusades*. Exempla collection: Number 324 in *Le Speculum Laicorum*, ed. J. Th. Welter, Paris, 1914; man leaping into crowd in Pitra, *Analecta*, 428–9 (J. de Vitry).

Griffith: *CPR*, Henry III (1232–47), 17; Clement III in P. Jaffé, *Regesta pontificum romanorum* (Leipzig, 1888), entry 16, 670 in II. 576 (17 Feb. 1191); *sub protectione Dei* in *Acta Stephani Langton*, ed. K. Major, *C & Y*, Vol. 50 (1950), 61.

38 Attorneys: *CPR* Henry III (1266–72), 441–443. See Brundage, *Canon Law*, 161–87 for a succinct discussion of privileges and abuses.

John Cleymund: *Reg. Sutton*, 159–60 (Ref. 32).

39 *Registrum Hamonis Hethe*, Vol. I, ed. C. Johnson, *C & Y*, Vol. 48 (1948), 387–89.

Wicked crusaders: Jacques de Vitry, quoted in P. A. Throop, *Criticism of the Crusade* (Amsterdam, 1940), 98, hereafter Throop, *Criticism*; Otto of Freising, *Deeds*, 75–6 (Ref. 13); Gerald of Wales, 114; Stephen of Blois in A. C. Krey, *The First Crusade: The Accounts of Eye-Witnesses and Participants* (Princeton, 1921), 129–32, 160–61. Hereafter Krey, *First Crusade*.

(Anon.) *Gesta Francorum et Aliorum Hierosolimitanorum*, ed. R. Hill (Oxford, 1962), 19–20. Hereafter *Gesta*. Here Brundage's translation (in *Crusades*, 50) is preferred.

40 *Alexiad*, 311, and cf. 319. (Ref. 19); Moslem historian is Ibn al-Athir in Gabrieli, *Arab Historians*, 183. (Ref. 1)

Patriarch of Jesu. & Abp. Rheims in Edward Peters, ed. *The First Crusade. The Chronicle of Fulcher of Chartres and Other Source Materials*; (Phil., 1971), 229, 219. Hereafter Peters, *First Crusade*. For the tearful Welsh prince, see Gerald of Wales, 182–3.

41–42 James A. Brundage, ' "Cruce Signari": The Rite for taking the

Cross in England', *Traditio*, Vol. 22 (1966), 289–310, esp. Appendix III, and K. Pennington, 'Rite for taking the cross in the twelfth century', *Traditio*, Vol. 30 (1974), 429–35.

Crosses in skin: D. C. Munro, 'A Crusader', *Speculum* vol. VII (1932), 329; drowned crusaders in Fulcher of Chartres, *A History of the Expedition to Jerusalem, 1095–1127*, tr. F. Ryan, ed. H. Fink (U. Tennessee Press, 1969), 76–7. Hereafter *Fulcher*.

Drunken vows: Throop, *Criticism*, 102 (Ref. 39); see Brundage, *Canon Law*, 125–35, for redemption of vows.

43   Piacenza loans: Don Gaëtano Tononi, 'Actes Constatant la Participation des Plaisançais à la Ire Croisade' in *Archives de l'Orient Latin* (2 Vol., Paris 1881, 1884), I. 395–401; confraternities, Jean Richard, 'La confrérie de la croisade: à propos d'un épisode de la première croisade' in *Mélanges . . . Labande*, 617–22 (Ref. 31); Fourth Crusade, Jean Longnon, 'Sur les croisés de la quatrième croisade' *Jour. des Savants*, Apr.-June 1977, 124; Italian's will on Fifth Crusade, W. S. Morris, 'A Crusader's Testament', *Speculum*, Vol. 27 (1952), 197–8. Eugenius III's decree in Brundage, *Canon Law*, 176.

43–44   For taxation generally, Wm. E. Lunt, *Financial Relations of the Papacy with England to 1327* (Cambridge, Mass., 1939), and Riley-Smith, *Crusades*, 143–53 (Ref. 32). 'Saladin Tithe' in Wm. Stubbs, *Select Charters*, 9th ed. (1913), 189. Archbishop Baldwin 'selling' indulgences, Gerald of Wales, 132–3; cf. Brundage, *Canon Law*, 154.

45   Richard's judicial visitation in Stubbs, *Select Charters*, 254.

See *Historical Manuscripts Commission, Var. Coll.*, I (1901), 235–6, from muniments of the Dean and Chapter of Canterbury Cathedral, No. 227, for the Lincolnshire visitation.

40,000 names: Roger of Wendover, in Edward Peters, ed., *Christian Society and the Crusades, 1198–1229* (Phila., 1971), 146. Hereafter Peters, *Christian Society*.

46   Lord of Rome: Ibn al-Athir in Gabrieli, *Arab Historians*, 255–56. Riley-Smith, *Crusaders*, 145–48, on *Graves orientalis terrae*. Gregory X: Lunt, *Financial Rel.*, 448.

For political ramifications, see B. Beebe, 'The English Baronage and the Crusade of 1270', *Bull. of Inst. of Histor. Research*, Vol. 48 (1975), 127–48.

47   Papal taxes in England: *Register of Walter Giffard, lord archbishop of York, 1266–1279*, ed. Wm. Brown, *SS*, Vol. 109 (1904), 234, 161; 274–77; commutations as 'penances', 277–86.

47–48   Leasing manors: for the 1230s, see *CPR*, Hen. III (1232–47), 74, 93, 101; for 1270s, *CPR*, Hen. III (1266–72), 425, 441. On the crusade of Edward I, see M. Powicke, *The Thirteenth Century, 1216–1307* (Oxford, 2nd ed. 1962), 219–24, 264–67, 499–500.

        Nineteen-point interrogatories in *Reg. Sutton*, 156–59 (Ref. 32); commutations at lower rate, Brundage, *Canon Law*, 136–7.

Chapter 3

49   Ambroise: *The Crusade of Richard Lion-Heart by Ambroise*, tr. M. J. Hubert with notes by J. L. La Monte (Columbia U. Press, 1941 repr. 1976), 182. Hereafter, Ambroise.

        Ekkehard in Krey, *First Crusade*, 42–3 (Ref. 39).

        'wives urged husbands': *Itinerarium peregrinorum et Gesta Regis Ricardi*, tr. K. Fenwick (Lond., 1958), 29, hereafter *Itinerarium*; the lingering kiss of Fulcher, 74 (Ref. 41–42).

50   Tours: see Ambroise, 42; the tearful-farewell motif in Tubach, *Index Exemplorum*, No. 1392 (Ref. 33–35).

        'If my body', Richard L. Crocker, 'Early Crusade Songs' in T. P. Murphy, ed., *The Holy War* (Ohio U. Press, 1976), 85, 91 (based upon the standard collection by J. Bedier and P. Aubry, *Les Chansons de Croisade* Paris, 1909). 'A hundred times', Riley-Smith, *Crusades*, 158 (Ref. 32); 'O, when they cry', Crocker, 'Early Crusade Songs', 93; Villehardouin, 40 (Ref. 32).

51   Jean de Joinville, *The Life of St. Louis* (in *Joinville and Villehardouin*, 195 (Ref. 32), hereafter Joinville; Gerald of Wales, 80 (Ref. 31).

53   Fulcher, 77–78 describes the journey completed on 14 May, 1097. For marching-rates see J. W. Nesbitt, 'The Rate of March of Crusading Armies in Europe; a Study and Computation', *Traditio*, Vol. 19 (1963), 167–82.

        Sea traffic: *Ludolph von Suchem's Description of the Holy Land, Written 1350*, tr. A. Stewart, *PPTS*, Vol. XII (London 1895), 12, hereafter Ludolph; Denys Hay, *Europe in the Fourteenth and Fifteenth Centuries* (Lond, 1966), 364; Richard's voyage in Ambroise, 75; *Chronicle of Richard of Devizes of the Time of King Richard The First*, tr. J. T. Appleby (Lond., 1963), 15–16, 28. Hereafter, Richard of Devizes.

54   Villehardouin, 58.

55   Ludolph, 15–16, describes the curious fish, while Humbert of
       Romans is noted by Throop, *Criticism* (Ref. 39). For the intrepid
       English seamen, *Raymond of Aguilers, Historia Francorum qui
       ceperunt Jerusalem*, tr. J. H. and L. L. Hill (Phila., 1968), 113,
       hereafter Raymond of Aguilers.

       400 drown: Fulcher, 76–7. Saladin's attitude towards the sea in
       Beha ed-Din, *Life of Saladin*, tr. C. W. Wilson, *PPTS* (Lond.,
       1897), 26. Hereafter, Beha ed-Din. For the discussion between the
       Egyptian and St. Louis, see *Ayyubids, Mamlukes and Crusaders:
       Selections from the Tarikh al-Duwal wa'l-Mulūk of Ibn al-Furat*, tr. U.
       and M. C. Lyons with notes and intro. by J. Riley-Smith, 2 vols.
       (1971), II. 42. For Arabic attitudes towards the sea, cf. André
       Miguel, 'Origine et carte des mers dans la géographie arabe aux
       approches de l'an mil', *Annales: Économies, Sociétés, Civilisations*, 35,
       No. 3–4 (May–Aug. 1980), 452–461. (This is a special number
       devoted to 'Recherches sur l'Islam: Histoire et Anthropologie',
       pp. 415–867.) Miguel emphasizes the extent to which the Arabs
       feared the mysterious sea: 'Satan n'est par loin: même enfermé dans
       une île du bout de la mer, c'est peut-être lui, finalement, qui regne
       sous les eaux.' (p. 461).

       Nausea: *Itinerarium*, 41 (Ref. 49).

56   *Felix Fabri*, tr. A. Stewart, Vol. I of *PPTS* (London, 1892), Vol. 7
       p. 145; see also the enjoyable version of H. F. M. Prescott, *Friar
       Felix at Large* (New Haven, 1950), 51, 53–54. Riley-Smith,
       Crusades, 161.

57   'Wonderful Jerusalem': Crocker, 'Early Crusade Songs', 83.

       Yorkshire bridge: *CR*, Hen. III (1227–31), 35 (A.D. 1228), cf.
       Ambroise 46–7 for a wooden bridge collapsing into the Rhine,
       killing some en route to the Holy Land during the Final Crusade.
       The Bishop of Norwich as robbery victim in Richard of Devizes,
       10–11 (Ref. 53).

58   Cemeteries: Peters, *First Crusade*, 43, from Fulcher (Ref. 40).

       William of Tyre: A History of the Deeds done beyond the sea, tr. E.
       Babcock and A. C. Krey, 2 vol. (Columbia 1941, repr. 1971), I.
       101–102, 115. Hereafter, William of Tyre. *Gesta*, 8 (Ref. 39).
       Peters, *First Crusade*, 118–119, from Raymond of Aguilers.

59   Beha ed-Din, 198–201 (Ref. 55) mentions Moslem-Byzantine

deals. The unflattering criticism of Constantinople and Greeks generally in Brundage, *Crusades*, 107–110, from Odo of Deuil.

61   'debonair': Ambroise, 49–50, 53–59.

On guides to the Holy Land, see *Gesta* 14, Raymond of Aguilers, 108 (Ref. 55), William of Tyre, I. 330, II. 178.

62   *Gesta*, 3–4, provides gruesome details for Peter the Hermits' group. For the 500 victims of heat and thirst, Wm. of Tyre, I. 174; see Fulcher in Peters, *First Crusade*, 48. The poor state of crusaders at Jerusalem in Peters, *First Crusade*, 203–4, from Ray. of Aguilers; Wm. of Tyre, I. 352–3. 'Many are cut off . . .': *Saewulf*, tr. the Bp. of Clifton, Vol. IV of *PPTS* (London, 1896), 9. Wm. of Tyre, I. 125.

63   Fulcher, 131 and Ambroise, 299, 304 for effects of winter and rains. The worried knights sell their armour: *Gesta*, 27. Beha ed-Din, 183, 191–2, describes the plight of Barbarossa's army.

Disease: *The Damascus Chronicle of the Crusades*, tr. H. A. R. Gibb (London, 1932), 295. Hereafter, *Damascus Chron.* Joinville, 241, Wm. of Tyre I. 309–20.

64   Scurvy: Ambroise, 183; Joinville, 293; *Gesta*, 17 deals with famine at Nicaea, whereas the pitiful situation at Antioch is described in Fulcher, 96. For contemporary prices of food and livestock 'back home', see Leopold Delisle, *Etudes sur la condition de la Classe Agricole et l'Etat de l'Agriculture en Normandie au Moyen Age* (Evreux, 1851), 611. Further notices of starvation and its results (including cannibalism) in Krey, *First Crusade*, 173 (Ref. 39); *Peter Tudebode, Historia Hierosolymitano Itinere*, tr. J. H. & L. L. Hill (Phil. 1974), 80; *Gesta*, 62; Wm. of Tyre I. 271; Gabrieli, *Arab Hist.*, 7 and Peters, *First Crusade*, 234–5, crusade leaders to the pope (1099).

65   Fulcher, 112, for meals of Saracen buttock; the disgust experienced by such behaviour in Raymond of Aguilers, 81 (Ref. 55); Wm. of Tyre I. 314.

Ambroise, 182–3, 185, 247–8 deals with starvation on the Third Crusade, Villehardouin, 68–9 describes such problems for the Fourth Crusade, while the Fifth Crusade is treated in Peters, *Christian Soc.* 130 (Oliver of Paderborn) (Ref. 45); Joinville, 197, for the stockpiling prior to the Sixth Crusade.

66   C. R. Cheney, *Medieval Texts and Studies* (Oxford, 1973), prints an English trans. of the papal letter on pp. 18–19; Ambroise, 242–3,

358, 366, 244–5 for miscellaneous causes of death including ravenous crocodiles.

Chapter 4

67   Chapter-heading: al-Abiwardi in Gabrieli, *Arab Hist.*, 12.

'Perceval, or the Story of the Grail' in *Medieval Romances*, ed. R. S. and L. H. Loomis (N.Y., 1957), 10.

Painful display: Beha ed-Din, 189.

68   Kamal ad-Din in Gabrieli, *Arab Hist.*, 38; Beha ed-Din, 260 (stones and arrows).

Horses: Fulcher, ii, Beha ed-Din, 380; for cavalry charge, *Alexiad*, 171, 202, 349; R. C. Smail, *Crusading Warfare (1097–1193)*, (CUP, 1956), Chap. 5. Charge at Arsuf: *Damascus Chron.*, 292; cf. 284 (Ref. 63); Beha ed-Din, 290.

69   Crossbow: *Alexiad*, 316–17.

God's names: *Ambroise*, 161.

mercenaries: Jean Richard, 'An Account of the Battle of Hattin, referring to the Frankish Mercenaries in Oriental Moslem States', *Speculum*, Vol. XXVII (1952), 168–77, esp. 174–5.

Pilgrims drafted: Wm. of Tyre, II. 221–2.

70   Jonathan Riley-Smith, 'Peace never established: The case of the Kingdom of Jerusalem', *Trans. Roy. Hist. Soc.*, 5th Ser., Vol. 28 (1978), 87–90, discusses the crusader/resident distinction.

B. Z. Kedar, 'The Passenger List of a Crusade Ship, 1250: towards the History of the Popular Element on the Seventh Crusade', *Studi Medievali*, 3rd Ser. (1972), 267–279; cf. Walter Porges, 'The Clergy, the Poor, and The Non-Combatants on the First Crusade,' *Speculum*, Vol. XXI (1946), 1–23, and Wm. of Tyre, I. 170, 247; II. 175.

71   L. A. M. Sumberg, 'The *Tafurs* and the First Crusade', *Medieval Studies* (U. Toronto), Vol. XXI (1959), 224–46; Cohn, *Pursuit*, 65–67 (Ref. 18).

Peters, *Christian Soc.*, 115, 129 (Oliver of Paderborn); Joinville, 233.

Aquinas: *Summa Theol*. Pt II of 2nd pt., Q. 41; 'The Latin customs' in *Alexiad*, 317–8; the bellicose priest, Joinville, 230, 245.

72   the nun: Porges, 'Non-Combatants', 18.

      Alexiad, 421 for the stench of army camps.

      See Appendix II in Runciman, *Crusades*, Vol. I, 'The numerical
      strength of the crusaders', for discussion of statistics. Wm. of Tyre,
      I. 349 on the 1099 Jerusalem siege.

73   Ratios among crusaders: Wm. of Tyre, I. 315; Peters, *First Crusade*,
      212–3 (Ray. of Aguilers); Runciman, *Crusades*, I. 337;
      Villehardouin, 33; Peters, *Christian Society*, 142.

74   See J. Partington, *History of Greek Fire and Gunpowder*, 1960.

75   Pope's standard: Peters, *First Crusade*, 63 (Fulcher).

      Banners and drums: Joinville, 222; *Itinerarium*, 59–60 (Ref. 49).

      War cries: Peters, *First Crusade* 120–21 (Ray. of Ag.).

76   War cries: *Gesta*, 7; B. Lacroix, 'Deus le volt! la théologie d'un cri'
      in *Mélanges . . . Labande*, 461–70, esp. 463 (Ref. 31).

      Military songs: Krey, *First Crusade*, 141.

      Brundage, *Crusades*, 87 (Otto of Freising) for 'loose-living'
      noblemen, and Beha ed-Din, 241.

77   Count of Jaffa: Joinville, 203–4.

      Wedding, 1183: Beha ed-Din, 43; Runciman, *Crusades*, II.
      440–41.

      Disgraced knights: *An Arab-Syrian Gentleman and Warrior: Memoirs
      of Usāmah ibn Munqidh*, tr. P. K. Hitti (Columbia U. Press, 1929),
      93. Hereafter, Usāmah.

78   Peters, *Christian Soc.*, 81 (Oliver of Paderborn) for internal
      class-rivalries among crusaders, and Joinville, 222, 224.

79   Nobles assist the poor: Ambroise, 176, 187–90.

      'pauperes nostri': Raymond of Aguilers, 86 (Ref. 55); the Latin
      from *Le 'Liber' de Raymond d'Aguilers publié par John Hugh et Laurita
      L. Hill*, intro., P. Wolff. Documents Relatifs a l'Histoire des
      Croisades publiés par l'Académe des Inscr. et Belles-Lettres, IX,
      (Paris, 1969), 106. For the sudden enrichment of the poor, see
      Krey, *First Crusade*, 149; Raymond of Aguilers, 43; *pauperes* in the
      Latin version, 61.

      Dividing the plunder: Villehardouin, 94; Fulcher 99; Wm. of
      Tyre, II. 19.

80   Wm. of Tyre, I. 269, for Moslem derision of faulty crusader
       weapons.

       Raymond of Aguilers (Hill tr.), 64 on survival quotient and horses;
       see also Fulcher, 161; Baldwin's battered rescuer in Ambroise,
       374.

       Wm. of Tyre, I. 173; Krey, *First Crusade*, 156; Ambroise, 240–41,
       167, for survival-rates of different classes.

       Peters, *First Crusade*, 49 (Fulcher).

81   Germans v. French: Brundage, *Crusades*, 109 (Odo of Deuil), and
       French v. English, Ambroise, 393; for English v. Cologne/Flemish
       crusaders, see *De expugnatione Lyxbonensi*, tr. C. W. David (N.Y.,
       1936), 133–35.

       Raymond of Aguilers (Hill tr.), 116.

       Rival breaches: *De expug. Lyxbonensi*, 147, cf. 177 ff., Runciman,
       Crusades, II. 339.

82   *Alexiad*, 333.

       Joshua Prawer, *The Latin Kingdom of Jerusalem* (Lond., 1972), 69;
       Tancred v. Baldwin in Wm. of Tyre, I. 180–84. The Moslem note
       of 1111: *Damascus Chron.*, 118 (Ref. 63).

83   Gautier: Joinville, 208–9; discipline of 1147 in Wm. of Tyre, II.
       155–56; in 1183, Beha ed-Din, 90–91.

84   Painted pole: *Itinerarium*, 80 (Ref. 49); Beha ed-Din, 226–7.

85   Self control: Beha ed-Din, 282–3.

       Dead propped up: Wm. of Tyre, II. 153.

       Ambroise, 381–87 for the bedouin spies. Resident spies in
       Christian camps undoubtedly welcome heralds' orders, just as the
       demented ravings of a *mulier lunatica* loudly predicting doom in a
       crusader camp in the early twelfth century could only have worsened
       morale – *RHC Occ.*, V. 104.

86   Disguise: Fulcher, 161; *Damascus Chron.*, 323; See Usāmah, 71
       (Ref. 77); *Gesta*, 84.

87   Joinville, 225–6. Burning of grass: Wm. of Tyre, I. 292, cf. II.
       154; the 300 kidnappers, Beha ed-Din, 255, 306.

       Beha ed-Din, 167–70, 219–20, 222 for Moslem leaders' problems
       with their men. Use of Christian mercenaries in W. H. C. Frend,

'Nomads and Christianity in the Middle Ages', *JEH*, Vol. 26 (1975), 209–21, and Richard article (Ref. 69).

88   W. M. Watt, 'Islamic Conceptions of the Holy War' in Murphy, *Holy War*, 141–56 (Ref. 50), on conflict between Islamic practice and theory. The vociferous preachers at Baghdad in 1110, Gabrieli, *Arab Hist.*, 29.

Joinville, 201, 204, 214, cf. *Gesta*, 95 for communications methods used by Moslem armies; also Beha ed-Din, 193, 251, 259, 292; Ambroise, 197; Wm. of Tyre, I. 302; Raymond of Aguilers (Hill tr.), 114; Fulcher, 284.

89   *Gesta*, 18 for gabbling Turks; Agincourt foreshadowed in Beha ed-Din, 23; fearsome, colourful Turks in Ambroise, 153–4.

Chapter 5

90   Ibn al-Athir: Gabrieli, *Arab Hist.*, 125

First World War: Ronald Blythe, *Akenfield* (1969), 44.

91–92   Fulcher, 179.

Ambroise, 86–8 on Richard at Cyprus; for Constantinople, see Villehardouin, 66. Battle at Jaffa, Ambroise, 417–19; at Acre, Ambroise, 161–2.

93   See Brundage, *Crusades*, 33–5 (Ref. 37) for carnage by Kilij Arslan; Runciman, II. 146; Smail (Ref. 68), esp. 189–97.

94   Imad ad-Din in Gabrieli, *Arab Hist.*, 128.

95   Battle frenzy: Wm. of Tyre, I. 234; Ambroise, 342–7; 'Libellus de Expugnatione Terrae Sanctae per Saladinum', ed. J. Stevenson (RS) in Brundage, *Crusades*, 160; Joinville, 221; Beha ed-Din, 173; *Itinerarium* (Ref. 49), 132.

Hitti, *Usāmah* (Ref. 77), 68–9.

96   Ambroise, 166 on the clever Welsh archer; Richard's Messina boulder, *Itinerarium*, 63.

97   Sorties: Wm. of Tyre, I. 211; Ambroise, 206–7.

Sieges: *Gesta*, 41; Wm. of Tyre, I. 163, 241, 311.

Bohemond's roasted spies, Wm. of Tyre, I. 221–22.

Beha ed-Din, 205–6 describes the underwater messenger.

98 cf. J. Brundage, *Richard Lion Heart* (1974), 135–6 and J.
Gillingham, *Richard the Lionheart* (1976), 182–3 on Richard's
motives. Ambroise, 228; Beha ed-Din, 273.

99 'God permitted': Gabrieli, *Arab Hist.*, 349.

Ray. of Aguilers, 105; cf. *Ibid.* (Hill), 48 for delight in carnage.

100 *Gesta*, 91; Hill and Hill, 127–8 (Ray. of Aguilers); Wm. of Tyre, I.
371–2; Ray. of Aguilers, Peters, *First Crusade*, 214 ('just and
splendid judgement').

Alexiad, 311, 437 for Anna on atrocities; tortured Armenians in
Wm. of Tyre, I. 544.

101 Ambroise, 164 for incinerated genitals; the 'barnacle' in Joinville,
249.

102 Head-hunting and scalping: Wm. of Tyre, I. 227–28; Peters, *First
Crusade*, 223, 227; Fulcher, 94; Wm. of Tyre, I. 157; *Alexiad*, 443;
Joinville, 209; cf. Otto of Freising – a siege in Italy – *Deeds*, 304
(Ref. 13).

102–103 Disembowelling for gold: Josephus, *Jewish War*, tr. G. A.
Williamson (1959), 301; Peters, *First Crusade*, 15; *Gesta*, 80;
Fulcher, 122, 154–5; cf. Norman Daniel, *Arabs and Medieval Europe*
(2nd ed., 1979), 135.

103 Beha ed-Din, 167–8, 195–6; Fulcher, 280.

104 Fulcher, 132, on the horrors of fields of dead; see also Gabrieli, *Arab
Historians*, 59, 135–6, 190 and Oliver of Paderborn in Peters,
Christian Society, 94. The unburied: Fulcher in Peters, *First Crusade*,
42; *Alexiad*, 312–313; *Saewulf*, 9 (Ref. 62).

105 J. France, 'An unknown account of the capture of Jerusalem', *EHR*
(1972), 771–83 (crusaders remove corpses as penance); Louis IX in
Joinville, 237.

Recovery of dead: Ambroise, 148; Wm. of Tyre in Brundage,
Crusades, 133–4; Beha ed-Din, 228; *Expug. Lyx.*, 141–43 (Ref.
81).

Inhuman treatment: e.g., 3 men and a girl captured after Hattin
were each punished following second attempted escape by having
two teeth removed (*duos dentem molares cuilibet eorum excusserunt*),

Materials for the History of Thomas Becket, Vol. II, 271 (RS. 67) 7 vols., 1875–85. Torture: Ray. of Aguilers (Hill), 79.

106   Brundage, *Crusades*, 6, on Gunther of Bamberg; the living target in Albert of Aix (Runciman, I. 308–9).

Living projectiles: Peter Tudebode, *Historia de Hierosolymitano itinere*, ed. J. H. & L. L. Hill (Paris, 1977), 117; Frank Barlow, *Feudal Kingdom of England* (2nd ed., 1962), 257.

107   Beha ed-Din, 203, 231, 278–81, 289, 293, 295 on Saladin's treatment of prisoners.

107–108   Joinville, 243–47, 249–60.

109   B. Lewis, *Islam*, II. 243–4 (Ref. 7) on 'scraggy girl' etc.

110   On slaves: B. Lewis, *Islam*, II. 238–45.

Prisoners: Beha ed-Din, 239; Joinville, 245; Gabrieli, *Arab Hist.*, 68 (*Damascus Chron.*, 337); Beha ed-Din, 81, 114; Richard of Devizes, *Chronicle*, tr. J. T. Appleby (1963), 84; Ray. of Aguilers, 124 (Hill); Ibn Jubayr, *The Travels of Ibn Jubrayr*, tr. R. Broadhurst (Lond., 1952), 322.

111   See E. Ashtor, 'An essay on the diet of the various classes in the medieval Levant', *Biology of Man in History*, sel. from *Annales*, ed./tr. R. and E. Forster and O. and P. Ranum (Lond., 1975), 141, 144 (for Egyptian incomes).

Ransom: Gabrieli, *Arab Hist.*, 143; Ambroise, 402; Gabrieli, *Arab Hist.*, 143, 158–9, 162.

111–112   The Nablus prisoners and ransom: B. Lewis, *Islam*, II, 260; Claude Cahen, 'Une lettre d'un prisonnier musulman des Francs de Syrie', in *Melanges Edmond-René Labande* (1974), 83–7.

Chapter 6

115   Chapter-heading: Sura XIX.

Pauperes: see R. I. Moore, 'Family, Community and Cult on the Eve of the Gregorian Reform', *TRHS*, 5th ser, 30 (1980), 49–69. For this behaviour, R. Glaber, *Historium Libri Quinti*, Lib. IV Cap. 5–6 in *PL* 142, col. 678–681.

117   H. E. J. Cowdrey, 'The Peace and the Truce of God in the Eleventh Century', *P&P*, Vol. 46 (1970), 42–67.

Animals join: Albert of Aix in Peters, *First Crusade*, 104 (Ref. 40). Portents: Ekkehard of Aura in Krey, 46–7 (Ref. 39).

118   Paul Rousset, *Les origines et les caractères de la première croisade* (Neuchâtel, 1945) 90–92, 141; see also ch. IV, V, VII *passim*, and Paul Alphandery, *La chrétienté et l'idée de croisade*, 2 vol. (Paris, 1954–59) esp. Vol. I, pt. 1 Chap. 2, 'Emotion et mouvements précurseurs de la croisade'.

      Fulcher, 102 for visions at Antioch.

118–123 General refs. for the lance of Antioch include the following: Raymond of Aguilers in *RHC Occ.*, Vol. III, 282 ff.; cf. Hill tr./ed. of R. Aguilers, e.g. 66, 120–24, 128–9; *Gesta*, 57–69; Wm. of Tyre, I. 281, 286, 290, 325; S. Runciman, 'The Holy Lance', *AB*, Vol. 68 (1950), 197–209.

124   Ordeal: Peter Brown, 'Society and the Supernatural: A Medieval Change', *Daedalus*, 104 No. 2 (Spring 1975) 133–51; Alphandery, *La chrétienté*, I. 117.

      'Miror satis' etc: Ray. of Aguilers, *RHC Occ.*, III, 285; cf. the Latin of the Hill edition of Raymond of Aguilers, 123–24.

125   Visions/prayers before capturing Jerusalem: Ray. of Aguilers, *RHC Occ.*, III, 287; Brundage, *Crusades*, 63; Peters, *First Crusade*, 207–208; Wm. of Tyre, I. 366, cf. 367.

126   Visions after taking Jerusalem: Wm. of Tyre, I. 375.

      Hagenmeyer in Rousset, *Les origines*, 140.

127–128 True Cross: Peters, *First Crusade*, 217–18.

      Tafurs: N. Cohn, *Pursuit of Millennium*, 65–67. Interesting suggestions in Michel Rouche, 'Cannibalisme sacré chez les croisés populaire' in Yves-Marie Hilaire, ed., *La Religion Populaire* (Lille, 1981), 29–41. Mary Douglas, *Purity and Danger* (1966, ed. 1980), 178. Rouche, 'Cannibalisme', 36.

129   Wm. of Tyre, I. 470; a comet, triple sun, etc., and for 1217, 1218, Peters, *Christian Society* (Ref. 45), 48–9, 62.

      Exhumed Scot: J. Herbert, *Catalogue of Romances in the Dept. of MSS* (BM., Lond., 1910, repr. 1962), Vol. III, p. 27. Godric vision in *Libellus de vita et miraculis S. Godrici, Heremitae de Finchale*, ed. J. Stevenson, *SS*, 20 (1847), 384–8. Ambroise, 242, 376–77.

      Beha ed-Din, 162 for Acre procession, 1189; at Damietta in 1249, Joinville, 209.

130   Ambroise, 173, 187, 191 for canonical observances; making wills at Constantinople, Villehardouin, 65.

Abbot Martin in Peters, *Christian Society*, 19; the True Cross at Damietta, Peters, 66. The True Cross lost at Hattin: 'L'Estoire de Eracles Empereur' in *RHC Occ.*, Vol. II, 65–66; cf. *Chronique d'Ernoul*, ed. M. L. de Mas Latrie, Soc. de l'Hist. de France (1871), 170–71. Captor's prayers mentioned in D. Rock, *Church of Our Fathers* (1849), II. 367.

131   See Janet Nelson's remarks in 'Religion in Histoire Totale', *Religion*, Vol. 10 (1980), 79, on the spectrum of 'religious' behaviour.

132   Mecca: Toufic Fahd, 'La Mekke' in M. Philonenko and M. Simon, *Les Pèlerinages* (1973), 75–6. This essay (pp. 65–94) is an excellent, succinct account of pilgrimage to Mecca and subsidiary rites and shrines.

Apocrypha: See exx. in M. R. James, *The Apocryphal N.T.* (OUP, 1953); Peters, *Christian Society*, 113.

Assassins: Joinville, 277–79.

Oliver of Paderborn in Peters, *Christian Society*, 77.

133   Scriptural canonicity: Lewis, *Islam*, II, 1–2 (Al-Bukhari) (Ref. 7).

134   Beha ed-Din, 210, Moslems praying at Acre; for mosques, see Sibt ibn al-Jauzi in Gabrieli, *Arab Hist.*, 62 (Damascus); Lewis, *Islam*, II. 16–18 (Tlemcen); II. 19–20 (Ibn al-Athir on Baghdad mosque); II. 13–15 (Al-Maqrizi, on Cairo mosque).

135   Michael Rogers, *The Spread of Islam* (1976), 82–84; Saladin's reputation, Gabrieli, *Arab Hist.*, 167, and for mourning at Damascus, see 272 (Ibn Wasil). Urban II in Wm. of Tyre, I. 90.

A. J. Arberry, tr., *Muslim Saints and Mystics* (from *Memorials* by Farid al-Din Attar) (Lond., 1966), 210–211, for Jonaid the mystic.

136   Richard W. Bulliet, *Conversion to Islam in the Medieval Period: An Essay in Quantitative History* (Harvard, 1979).

Mecca raid: Lewis, *Islam*, II. 67; W. Montgomery Watt, *The Majesty that was Islam* (Lond., 1974), 157.

Damascus Chron., 191, cf. p. 180.

137   Watt, *Majesty*, 116, 119, 130, on heresy and Inquisition among Moslems.

137–38   Mystics: Arberry, *Muslim Saints*, 226, 269–71, 281. Joinville, 274
(old woman in Damascus), al-Ghazali's defence of mystics, Lewis,
Islam, II. 20–21. For Saladin's crucifixion of a 'heretic' see Beha
ed-Din, 11.

139   Victor and E. Turner, *Image and Pilgrimage in Christian Culture*:
Anthropological Perspectives (Oxford, 1978), Chap. One, on
definitions of pilgrimage. T. Fahd, 'La Mekke, 87 (Ref. 132). For
the Mecca pilgrimage, see also Romain Roussel, *Les Pèlerinages a
travers les siècles* (Paris, 1954), 202–262.

Pilgrims crushed at 'Adams' shrine in Lewis, *Islam*, II. 30.

140   cf. Ibn-Taymia in Lewis, *Islam*, II. 35–39 on reverence for the dead.

A. Guillaume, *Islam*, 2nd ed. (1956), 108–110. R. W. Southern,
Western Views of Islam in the MA (1962), in 'additions to notes' at end
of 3rd (1980) printing, ref. to p. 55, n. 17.

R. Graves & R. Patai, *Hebrew Myths: The Book of Genesis* (N.Y.,
1964), 207–208.

141   John Wilkinson, *Jerusalem Pilgrims before the Crusades* (1977), 173;
Jerry M. Landay, *Dome of the Rock* (Lond., 1972), *passim*; Ibn Batriq
(d. 939) in Le R. P. A.-S. Marmardji (O.P.), *Textes géographiques
arabes sur la palestine* (Paris, 1951), 213; al-Tabari in Lewis, *Islam*,
II. 3, for rediscovery of the Rock.

Wilkinson, *Jeru. Pilgrims*, 95 on the 'temporary' mosque. El-Malik:
Ya qubi, 'History' (A.D. 874) in Marmardji, *Textes*, 210;
Wilkinson, *Jeru. Pilgrims*, ed. note p. 10.

142   Nâsir-i-Khusrau, *Diary of a Journey through Syria and Palestine in
1047*, tr. G. le Strange, *PPTS* (London, 1893), Vol. IV, 47.

Fulcher, 117, where the Dome is called *Templum domini*, the Lord's
Temple, re-interpreting along Christian lines; *Saewulf*, 16 (Ref.
62). Saladin's removal of Christian vandalism, Imad ad-Din in
Gabrieli, *Arab Hist.*, 168–71.

Al-Harawi (d. 1215), *Guide des lieux de pèlerinage* (Kitāb az-Ziyārāt),
tr. J. Sourdel–Thomine (Damascus, 1957), var. exx. pp. 12–80 of
holy sites; for Mary among Moslems, see J-M. Abd-el-Jalil, *Marie et
l'Islam* (Paris, 1950) *passim*.

143   T. Fahd, 'La Mekke', 85 on Moslem art.

Virgin's fingers: Nâsir, *Diary*, 34; Noah's tomb in Al-Harawi,
Guide, 23; Abraham's tomb, *Dam. Chron.*, 161; heads of John the
Baptist, Rogers, *Spread of Islam*, 120; for Christian claims, see

Mandeville's Travels, ed. M. Seymour (OUP, 1968), 82–3; Ibn Jubayr, *Travels* (Ref. 110), 318–19 on Adam's cattle. Anna and Joachim in Ludolph, 100–101 (Ref. 53).

144   Thomas W. Arnold, *The Old and New Testaments in Muslim Religious Art* (London, 1932), *passim*.

Rogers, *Spread of Islam*, 134, for burial near 'saints'. On 'proper' pilgrimages, T. Fahd, 'La Mekke', 93, and Lewis, *Islam*, II. 22–27, 47. For 'improper' motivation for pilgrimages, Nâsir, *Diary*, 48; Rogers, *Spread of Islam*, 127.

145   Curative columns: Al-Harawi, *Guide*, 37; Bryce Lyon, *High Middle Ages* (N.Y., 1964), 82. Other 'popular beliefs' in Beha ed-Din, 265, 110, 133, 157 and Wm. of Tyre, I. 365–6; cf. Ray. of Aguilers (Hill), 126.

Death, last rites: Joinville, 275; T. Fahd, 'La Mekke', 86; A. J. Wensinck, *A Handbook of Early Muhammadan Tradition* (Leiden, 1927), 51–53, 249, with topics alphabetically listed, a useful guide; al-Bukhari (d. 870) *Les traditions islamiques*, tr. O. Houdas and W. Marcais, Vol. I (Paris, 1903), Title 23, chap. 8 ff.; Lewis, *Islam*, II. 67.

146   Gabrieli, *Arab Hist.*, 65 (crusaders as polytheists).

B. Lewis, *Islam*, II. xvii–xxiii; cf. R. Bulliet, esp. chap. 11 (Ref. 136).

Chapter 7

147   Chapter-heading: Joinville, 243.

R. W. Southern, *Western Views of Islam in the Middle Ages* (Lond., 1962), *passim*. J. Moorhead, 'The Earliest Christian Theological Response to Islam', *Religion*, Vol. II (1981), 265–274.

148–49   Southern, *Western Views*, 16–18, 22.

149–50   J. M. Wallace–Hadrill, 'Bede's Europe' in *Early Medieval History* (Oxford, 1975), 60–75. *Annals*, Einhard and Notker: *Annales regni Francorum*, ed. F. Kurze, *MGH Scriptores* in usum scholarum, Vol. VI (1895), 124, 133; *Einhardi Vita Karoli Magni* ed. O. Holder-Egger, *MGH Scriptores*, Vol. XXV (1911), 19; G. Meyer von Knonau, *Monachus Sangallensis* [Notker], *Mitteilungen zur Vaterländischen Geschichte*, XXXVI, Vierte Folge VI (1920), 42.

151   Wallace-Hadrill, 'Bede's Europe', 65

153   J. Landay, *Dome of the Rock* (London, 1972) on Malik's Dome. Shift to universalism in W. M. Watt, *Islam and the Integration of Society* (Lond., 1961), 259; scriptures, Watt, 262–3, 266.

Lewis, *Islam*, II. 217–35 for pre-crusade rules.

154   Moslem rules for Christian dress in public: Lewis, *Islam*, II. 224–25; Walter L. Wakefield, *Heresy, Crusade and Inquisition in Southern France 1100–1250* (Lond., 1974), 255, for similar Inquisition rules in Europe.

155   Mukaddasi (c. 985 AD), *Description of Syria including Palestine*, tr. G. le Strange, *PPTS* (Lond., 1892), Vol. V, iii, p. 37, 77.

Sufi mystics: Ebrahim al-Khauwas in Arberry, *Muslim Saints*, 274–5, 283–84, 260 (Ref. 135).

Hakim's secretary: C. E. Bosworth, 'The "Protected Peoples" (Christians and Jews) in Medieval Egypt and Syria', *Bull of the John Rylands, Univ. Library of Manchester*, Vol. 62 (1979–80), 22, 24–25.

155–56   Glaber in *PL* 142, col. 681 for the so-called Easter miracle; and see an interesting discussion of this 'miracle' in Benedicta Ward's *Miracles and the Medieval Mind* (1982), 120–22.

156   Dung-heap: Beha ed-Din, 207–8 (ed. note); Gabrieli, *Arab, Hist.*, (note) p. 148; Nâsir, *Diary*, 59–61 (Ref. 142).

157   'Rasul': Watt, *Islam and Integration*, 260 (Ref. 153); for Walsingham, see R. Finucane, *Miracles and Pilgrims* (London, 1977), 200.

Urban II: Peters, *First Crusade*, 2–3 (Ref. 40); Mohammad as Antichrist: cf. N. Daniel, *The Arabs and Medieval Europe*, 2nd ed. (Lond., 1979), 238.

158   Ambroise, *passim*, e.g. 248, 301.

Cross outraged: Peter Tudebode (Hill), 115 (Ref. 64); Wm. of Tyre, I. 310, 359; Osbern in Brundage, *Crusades*, 101 (Ref. 37); Ambroise, 165. Southern, *Western Views*, 39–44.

159   Bahrãm: Bosworth, 'Protected Peoples', 23 (Ref. 155).

Wm. of Tyre, I. 298. Earliest Arab historian of crusades in Gabrieli, *Arab Hist.*, 39 (Ibn al-Qalanisi died in 1160).

160   Imad ad-Din in Gabrieli, *Arab Hist.*, 131; Beha ed-Din, Gabrieli,

192; Ibn 'Abdūn in Lewis, *Islam*, II. 162–3; Ibu Jubayr, *Travels*, 318 (Ref. 110).

Bosworth, 'Protected Peoples', 26–27; Gabrieli, *Arab Hist.*, 214–15.

161   Raynald: Beha ed-Din, 142–3, 155; letter to Richard I, Beha ed-Din, 307–309; Saladin's rededication of the Dome of the Rock in Beha ed-Din, 120; Imad ad-Din in Gabrieli, *Arab Hist.*, 147, cf. 144–146; the picture commissioned by Conrad of Montferrat in Beha ed-Din, 207–208.

Gabrieli, *Arab Hist.*, 136–7 (Imad ad-Din on the True Cross).

163   Roundtable: Southern, *Western Views*, 47–48.

Aquinas: W. M. Watt, Islamic Surveys No. 9: *The Influence of Islam on Medieval Europe* (Edinburgh, 1972), 74; Wm. of Tripoli: Hans Prutz, *Kulturgeschichte der Kreuzzüge* (Berlin, 1883), 590–97.

164   Frederick II at Jerusalem: Ibn Wasil in Gabrieli, *Arab Hist.*, 271–2, and Sibt ibn al-Jauzi, 274; the turncoat Christian from Provins in Joinville, 262. For Ibn al-Furāt, see U. and M. C. Lyons, tr. *Ayyubids, Mamlukes and Crusaders: Selections from the Tarikh al-Duwal wa'l-Mulūk of Ibn al-Furat*, 2 vols. (1971), II. 31.

165   P. D. King, *Law and Society in the Visigothic Kingdom* (CUP. 1972) 132 ff. on treatment of Jews. Twelfth Council of Toledo, in W. Ullmann, 'Public Welfare and Social Legislation in the Early Medieval Councils', *Studies in Church History*, Vol. 7 ed. G. J. Cuming and Derek Baker, *Councils and Assemblies* (Cambridge, 1971), 24.

Third Lateran: cf. Hefele-Leclercq (H. Leclercq, *Histoire des Conciles*), Tome V, 2° part (Paris 1913), p. 1104–1106 (canon 24, 26).

Visigoths and Jews: G. Langmuir, 'From Ambrose of Milan to Emicho of Leiningen: The Transformation of Hostility against Jews in Northern Christendom', *Settimane di studio del Centro itiliano di studi sull' alto medioevo* (Mar.–Apr., 1978), Vol. XXVI (1980), p. 341 ff.

N. Daniel, *Arabs & Med. Euro.*, 259–64 for Christian 'regulations' concerning Moslems.

166   Humbert: see *Opus Tripartitum* in J. Riley-Smith, *The Crusades* (1981), 103–117.

Dante: Penguin ed. 1949, p. 246; Saladin, p. 94.

167   Italians dealing with Moslems: cf. A. Luttrell, 'The Crusade in the Fourteenth Century' in *Europe in the Late Middle Ages*, ed. J. A. Hale *et al.* (1965), 122–54.

167–68   Ricoldo: see Letters in *Archives de l'Orient Latin*, II (Documents), 258 ff., 291

169   Silvia Schein, 'Gesta Dei per Mongolos, 1300', *EHR*, 94 (1979), 805–19.

         1321 conspiracy: Malcolm Barber, 'Lepers, Jews and Moslems: The Plot to Overthrow Christendom in 1321', *History*, 66 (1980), 1–17; R. I. Moore, *The Origins of European Dissent'* (1977), 249.

         Violence in Egypt: Bosworth, 'Protected Peoples', 34 (Ref. 155).

170   Raymond Lull: See art. in Cross, *Oxford Dictionary of the Christian Ch.*, 2nd ed. (1974), p. 845 for refs.

170–71   Franciscan 'martyrs': Paul Durrieu, 'Procès-verbal du martyre de quatre frères mineurs' in *Archives de l'Orient Latin*, Vol. I (1881), 539–46.

172   *Mandeville's Travels*, 50–88, 101–110; Carlo Ginzburg, *The Cheese and the Worms*, tr. J. and A. Tedeschi (Lond., 1980), 43 ff, 176.

         Animosity: see the Inquisitor's Manual of Eymeric (1376 AD), which condemns anyone invoking or building an altar to Mohammad in E. Peters, *The Magician, The Witch and the Law* (1978), 200.

         Coer de Lion: B. White, 'Saracens and Crusaders: from Fact to Allegory' in D. Pearsall & R. Waldron, *Medieval Literature and Civilization: Studies in Memory of G. N. Garmondsway* (Lond., 1969), 186–190.

173   Jerusalem pilgrims: Lucie Polak, 'Un récit de pèlerinage de 1488–1489', *Le Moyen âge*, LXXXVII (1981), 71–88; C. Schefer, ed. *Le Voyage d'Outremer de Bertrandon de la Broquière* (Paris, 1892), 72; Prescott, *Friar Felix at Large*, 200. Felix also believed that Mohammad began the custom of wearing a turban as a means to cure a hangover. *Felix Fabri*, PPTS, Vol. 7, p. 252.

Chapter 8

174   Chapter-heading: Joinville, 225.

175   Wm. of Tyre, II. 179–81; Margaret of France in Joinville, 262.

'Women Crusaders: A Temporary Canonical Aberration?',
Principalities, Powers and Estates, ed. L. O. Frappell (1979), 57–64,
'fifty thousand women' dead, Wm. of Tyre, I, 299; for combat
casualties, see *Gesta*, 29: women in Bohemond's army (in First
Crusade) killed by arrow shot into camp.

176   'going within tents': Albert of Aix in Peters, *First Crusade*, 111
(Ref. 40).

Fulcher, 154; Wm. of Tyre, I. 437 (selling of children by
crusaders); massacre at Antioch, Wm. of Tyre, I. 258.

'proper knights': Fulcher, 106. Fate of women captured in fall of
Jerusalem during 1187 is described by Imad ad-Din in Gabrieli,
Arab Hist., 163.

177   *Gesta*, 19; Wm. of Tyre, I. 367 (women at Nicaea and Jerusalem);
at Damietta, see Oliver of Paderborn in Peters, *Christian Society*, 78
(Ref. 45).

Ambroise, 163 (woman in moat); 'natural weakness', Wm. of Tyre,
I. 362. The three stripped women, Ibn al-Athir in Gabrieli, *Arab
Hist.*, 189; Christian woman in green mantle, Beha ed-Din, 261;
Moslem women fought crusaders, too. Four women: Beha ed-Din,
195; women in men's armour and clothing, Gabrieli, *Arab Hist.*,
207; the bloody actions of women on a Turkish galley, Ambroise,
152.

178–179 Margaret: F. M. Michaud, *Bibliothèque des Croisades*, III (Paris,
1829) 369–75 for the foll. on Margaret, which Michaud took from
A. Manrique, *Cisterciensium* III (Lyons, 1649), 198–9, 226–7,
262–3. The story was written by Margaret's brother Thomas, a
monk of Froimont, who died in the early 13th cent. He also wrote a
life of St. Thomas of Canterbury.

179   Wm. of Tyre, I. 220, for problems with whores on First Crusade;
the impatient crusaders seeking sex, cf. Fulcher, 101, in Peters'
translation (*First Crusade*, 60).

180–81   Vincent: *Annals* (A.D. 1148) in *MGH, SS*, 17, 663; Ambroise,
233–34, 277–78 on women at Acre. 'Baroque pornography': Imad
ad-Din in Gabrieli, *Arab Hist.* 204–206; there are several other
arabesque metaphors in this energetic passage.

Constantinople: Robt. de Clari in Peters, *Christian Society*, 15; the harlot on the patriarchal seat, Nicetas Choniates in Peters, 17. The crusader caught in a brothel, Joinville, 292.

181   David Herlihy, 'Land, Family and Women in Continental Europe, 701–1200', *Traditio* XVIII (1962), 89–120. Gerald, 76, 172 on Welsh women; see also Throop, 109 (Ref. 39)

John (Suffolk): *CPR*. II (1201–1203) p. 134, a case arising in A.D. 1202; Stephen of Blois' letter of 1098 in Krey, *First Crusade*, 157. Stephen added, 'You will surely see me as soon as I can possibly come.' True to his words, Stephen was one of the deserters at Antioch.

Fulcher, 149 on bearers of good and bad news.

182   Joinville, 346.

Brundage, *Crusades*, 91 for Bernard's boast; Moslem taunts about little bastards back home, *De expugnatione Lyxbonensi*, 131–3 (Ref. 81). French poet, Throop, *Criticism*, 35.

Wives and canon law: see J. Brundage, 'The Crusader's Wife' and 'The Crusader's Wife Revisited' in *Studia Gratiana*, 12 (1967), 2; 425–41, and 14 (1967) 4: 241–52, with full refs. and discussion of canon law on these points. Twelfth-century prelate's letter, Ivo of Chartres, a famous canonist, to Daimbert, Abp. of Sens. *PL* 162, col. 136–8 (*sine ulla carnis commistione*).

183   Joinville, 238.

Impossible laws about sex: Brundage, 'Crusader's Wife Revisited', 249 n. 19; the hundred-year rule, p. 250 (a suggestion by Hostiensis).

John (Oxon.): *CPR*, II, 1201–3, p. 275–6; *CPR*, III, 1203–5, p. 205.

184   Returned husband: C. Cheney and M. Cheney, 'A draft decretal of Pope Innocent III on a case of identity', *Quellen und Forschungen aus italienischen archiven und bibliotheken*, 41 (1961), 29–47.

185   A. Neubauer and M. Stern, *Hebräische Berichte über die Judenverfolgungen während der Kreuzzüge* (Berlin, 1892), 156, 173–75. Shloms Eidelberg's Engl. transl., *The Jews and the Crusaders* (U. of Wisc. Press, 1977), is said to be a more accurate reflection of the Hebrew original than the German of Neubauer and Stern (cf. *EHR*, Jan. 1980).

186   Praying ghosts in J. Trachtenberg, *Jewish Magic and Superstition* (1939), 62, 255.

186–87 Neubauer and Stern, 97–8, 100–103, 105–107, 181.

187   Mainz Jews: L. Poliakov, *The History of Antisemitism*, Vol. I (N.Y., 1965), 52, citing *Annales Sax.*, *MGH, SS*, IV, 729.

        Neubauer and Stern, 103, 156, 175 – Jews kill Christians and revile Christ, 101, 104.

        Cluny abbot: Poliakov, *Antisemitism*, 48.

188   'numerous cities': Otto of Freising, *Deeds*, 74 (Ref. 13). For Richard I, see R. B. Dobson, *The Jews of Medieval York and The Massacre of 1190* (York, 1974), *passim*. Richard of Devizes, *Chronicle*, 3–4. The 14th-century risings in Poliakov, *Antisemitism*, 103–4.

        mourning period: Trachtenberg, *Jewish Magic*, 255; dogs and vomit, Poliakov, *Antisemitism*, 51. For Christ as Jew-hater, see Raymond of Aguilers (Hill tr.), 95 (Ref. 55).

189   For an excellent analysis see Gavin Langmuir, 'From Ambrose of Milan to Emicho of Leiningen', *Settimane* etc. (Ref. 165).

        Christian leaders try to curtail anti-Jewish activities: J. Parkes, *The Jew in the Medieval Community* (Lond., 1938), 81; Wm. of Tyre, I. 112–13; on Bernard, Brundage, *Crusades*, 93; the Wurzburg uprising, Neubauer and Stern, 193–94. Jews not to be trusted: Felix Fabri (PPTS), 253 (Ref. 56).

Chapter 9

191   Chapter-heading: Throop, *Criticism*, 176 (Ref. 39).

192   *Alexiad*, 190, 126–28 (Guiscard v. Alexius); Tancred v. Baldwin and Bohemond v. Raymond of Toulouse, Wm. of Tyre, I. 185–6, 212–13.

        Alexius sends ambassadors to Baghdad, *Dam. Chron.* in Gabrieli, *Arab Hist.*, 29–30.

        Wm. of Tyre, II, 140–43.

192–93 Further examples of internal rivalry in Ambroise, 132, 315, 319–21, 328–38, 432–33.

193–94 Fourth-Crusade rivalry, Villehard. 47–51, 70, 74; and cf. Robert de Clari in Peters, *Christian Society*, 15, 16–18, 24.

194   Frederick II: Philip of Novara in Peters, *Christian Society*, 158–60; on Henry III, see Runciman III. 257, citing Mt. Paris.

196   For a survey of conflicting Islamic factions in Syria alone, see Gibb's Intro. to *Dam. Chron.*, where six rival groups are discussed.

      'While the Franks': Gabrieli *Arab Hist.* 18, cf. 11, 16; 'The Lord God', Ambroise, 416; Saladin and Assassins, Beha ed-Din, 74; 'the sultan of Babylon', Roger of Wendover in Peters, *Christian Society*, 152; Joinville, 200.

      Wm. of Tyre, I. 223; *Gesta* 37, 42; Wm of Tyre, I. 234–35, 326.

198   Christian-Moslem co-operation, cf. *Dam. Chron.* 299, where one Mos. leader threatens another: 'A company of the Franks is even now on the way to aid us to repel thee.'

      Dam. Chron, 304, for Franks 'helping' Damascus.

      Brundage, *Crusades* 138–40, for double-dealing in Egypt; Templars refuse to join, Beha ed-Din, 49–51.

      Joinville, 298.

199   Cf. Wm. of Tyre, I. 474 (conflict about Edessa); Ibn al-Athir in Gabrieli, *Arab Hist.*, 115 (fall of Jerusalem); Conrad of Montferrat in Beha ed-Din, 302–3; J. J. Saunders, *Aspects of the Crusades* (Christchurch [N.Z.], 1962), 34.

      Runciman, II. 202–3 (secret guides at Tripoli); Alexius Comnenus against the Normans, *Alexiad*, 137, 167; Wm. of Tyre, I. 432; *Dam. Chron.*, 80, 112.

      Ibn al-Athir, in Gabrieli, *Arab Hist.* 209 (Saladin and emperor); for friendly relations after the fall of Jerusalem, see C. M. Brand, 'The Byzantines and Saladin, 1185–1192: Opponents of the Third Crusade', *Speculum*, 37 (1962), 167–81; Beha ed-Din, 198–200.

200   Ibn al-Athir in Gabrieli, *Arab Hist.*, 209.

      Innocent III: Peters, *Christian Soc.* 45–46, and cf. Throop, 246. Ironically, in 1220, just five years after Innocent's condemnation , the Venetians concluded a political-commercial agreement with the Anatolian Turks, sealed with a golden seal. M. E. Martin, 'The Venetian-Seljuk treaty of 1220', *EHR*, XCV (1980), 321–30.

      Fraternization: Beha ed-Din, 161–62; Peters *First Crusade*, 174, 176; Wm. of Tyre, II. 20; Peters, *Christian Soc.*, 139.

201   Villehard, 52, 54 on the Zara attack; Ambroise, 305.

      Peters, *First Crusade*, 56 (Fulcher); Wm. of Tyre, I. 214–15, 267;

Gesta, 33, 56–57, 63; Ambroise, 185; inhuman conditions see Brundage, *Crusades*, 157; Beha ed-Din, 223; Peters, *First Crusade*, 38–39.

202   Brindisi drownings in Peters, *First Crusade*, 40 (Fulcher).

Stephen: Orderic Vitalis, *Ecclesiastical Hist.*, ed./tr. M. Chibnall, vol. V (Oxford, 1975), 325; Wm. of Tyre, I. 430–31, 444.

Alexiad, 198–99 on overlord of Antioch.
Beha ed-Din, 241, 313, 320 on Christian collaborators.

203   Beha ed-Din, 235–36; the Frenchman at Damietta, Oliver of Paderborn in Peters, *Christian Society*, 74; Joinville, 262, 254; for reluctant Moslem warriors, Beha ed-Din, 262–63.

In some cases, at least, crusaders tried to bridge the cultural abyss: there was the Moslem who was encouraged to read Arabic to Reynald of Sidon (Beha ed-Din, 142–43), the 'native manner' of eating employed by Joinville's knights (Joinv. 291), Wm. of Tyre's complaint that eastern crusade leaders scorned western medicine for 'oriental' ways (II. 292), and the famous passage from Fulcher, 'We who were Occidentals now have been made Orientals', etc. (Peters, *First Crusade*, 220–21). See also medical treatment and bathing practices discussed by Usāmah (in Gabrieli, *Arab Hist.*, 76–78).

Humbert: Alexander Murray, 'Religion among the poor in thirteenth-century France: the testimony of Humbert de Romans', *Traditio*, xxx (1974), 304; Throop, 191.

J. Bastin and E. Faral, ed., *Onze poèmes de Rutebeuf* (Documents Relatifs à l'Histoire des Croisades, Acad. Inscr. et. B.-L.), Vol. I (1946), 63.

204   Throop, 25 ('bitterly hostile').

Anthony Luttrell, 'The Crusade in the Fourteenth Century', in *Europe in the Late Middle Ages*, ed. J. R. Hale *et al.*, (Evanston [Ill.], 1965), 122–154.

Giles Constable, 'Opposition to Pilgrimage', *Studia Gratiana*, XIX (Rome, 1976), 123–46, for spiritual pilgrimages; on improper motives for crusading, see Brundage, *Crusades*, 121–22; Wm. of Tyre, II. 165.

Newcomers: Usāmah, 176 (Ref. 77). On false crusaders, Jacques de Vitry, *History of Jerusalem*, tr. A. Stewart, *PPTS*, Vol. XI (1896), 89–90.

205   de Vitry, *Hist. of Jerusalem*, 66–67 for Italian co-operation with

Moslems; Throop, 71 on the *Collectio*; criticisms of lower ranks in, e.g. Ambroise, 278; Peters, *Christian Soc.*, 106, 126; Joinville, 207.

H. Prutz, *Kulturgeschichte der Kreuzzüge* (Berlin, 1883), 527–29; Jacques de Vitry, *Hist. of Jerusalem*, 64–66.

206   Prutz, *Kulturgeschichte*, 527.

Changing patterns: see 'Indulgences Octroyées par Galerand, Évêque de Béryte', in *Archives de l'Orient Latin*, I, 405–406 (Ref. 43), where King Henry III prohibits preaching the crusade in England for political and financial reasons.

Guillem Figueira in Throop, 31; cf. 29 ('Rome, you do little,' etc.) in Crocker, 'Early Crusade Songs', 88 (Ref. 50); Mt. Paris, *Chron. Maj.* (*RS* 57: IV 102) in Throop, 72; Crocker, 'Early Crusade Songs' 94; Throop, 94, on buying one's way out of crusade; 'Rome . . . for money' etc.) – Huon de Saint Quentin in Throop, 93; the Arsuf Templar, Throop, 93.

207   Rutebeuf: Throop, 188.

Brundage, *Crusades*, 124 (crusades no longer succeeding); see Louis' crusade discussed by Runciman, III, 281.

Humbert: English tr. in Louise & Jonathan Riley-Smith, *The Crusades: Idea and Reality, 1095–1274* (Lond., 1981), 103 ff.

208   Humbert: *De praedicatione crucis*, discussed in Throop, 151–59.

Ralph Niger: See George B. Flahiff, 'Deus non vult: A Critic of the Third Crusade', *Medieval Studies*, 9 (1947), 162–88.

Maureen Purcell, *Papal Crusading Policy, 1244–1291* (Leiden, 1975), 183.

209   H. Pflaum, 'A Strange Crusaders' Song', *Speculum*, Vol. 10 (1935), 337–39, 13th-cent. anonymous song.

Conclusion

211   Motivations: see, for instance, E. R. Labande, 'Pellegrini o crociati? Mentalità e comportamenti a Gerusalemme nel secolo XII', *Aevum: Rassegna di scienze storiche linguistiche e filologiche*, 54.2 (1980), 217–30.

Over forty years ago Beatrice Siedschlag, a student of the crusade historian A. C. Krey, wrote a doctoral thesis on the identity of English crusaders between 1150 and 1220, distinguished from those who merely vowed to go to the Holy land; she listed some 366 individuals for this period. B. N. Siedschlag *English participation in the Crusades, 1150–1220*. Doctoral thesis, Bryn Mawr (Randolph, Wisc.) 1939; the lists on pp. 107–144.

B. Z. Kedar 'Passenger List' (Ref. 70). The question of women in the movement is addressed by M. Purcell in 'Women Crusaders', (Ref. 175).

Crusades in Islamic context: Professor Sidney Griffith, at Catholic Univ. of America in Washington, D.C., for instance.

212   'Despite numerous contacts' etc.: M. Perlman, tr., *Ibn Kammūnas' Examination of the Three Faiths* (U. Calif. Press, 1971), 77.

Keith Haines, 'Attitudes and Impediments to Pacifism in Medieval Europe', *Journ. of Medieval History*, Vol. 7, No. 4 (Dec. 1981), 385.

Caritas: J. Riley-Smith, 'Crusading as an Act of Love', *History*, 65 (1980), 190.

Riley-Smith, 'Peace never established', 87, 101 (Ref. 70).

Bibliographical Note

Historians continue to show strong interest in the Crusades, as indicated by the numerous articles which are scattered through dozens of specialized journals; these can be located through the standard bibliographical tools such as *International Guide to Medieval Studies* and *International Medieval Bibliography*. For medieval journals in general, see Richard H. Rouse, *Serial Bibliographies for Medieval Studies* (Univ. Calif. Press, 1969). Interesting papers will no doubt be discussed at the first conference of the Society for the Study of the Crusades and the Latin East, to be held in 1983.

Still the best overall guide to publications is Hans Eberhard Mayer, *Bibliographie zur Geschichte der Kreuzzüge* (Hanover, 1960), which lists articles up to 1958 in nearly 300 pages of material (the 1965 edition is actually a reprint of 1960). For publications from 1958 to 1967, see Mayer, 'Literaturbericht' über die Geschichte der Kreuzzüge' in *Historische Zeitschrift*, Shft. 3 (1969), 641–736. Bibliographies in Steven Runciman, *A History of the Crusades*, 3 vols. (Cambridge, 1951–54) are very useful, and Runciman also provides short analyses of sources and medieval writers. See also Kenneth M. Setton, *A History of the Crusades*, 4 vols. (London, 1969–77); volumes 1 and 2 have now reached 2nd edition. The best single-volume history in English trans. is Hans Eberhard Mayer, *The Crusades*, trans. from *Geschichte des Kreuzzüge* of 1965 by J. Gillingham (OUP, 1972).

For English translations from contemporary sources, see Mary Anne Ferguson, *Bibliography of English translations from Medieval Sources 1944–68* (Columbia, 1973), which updates the standard C. P. Farrar and A. P. Evans, *Bibliography of Translations* (1964). The following selected translations are of particular interest or importance: Anna Comnena, *The Alexiad* (Penguin, 1969); Beha ed-Din, *Life of Saladin* (PPTS, 1897); Brundage, James A., *The Crusades: A Documentary Survey* (Madison, 1962); Fulcher of Chartres, *A History of the Expedition to Jerusalem, 1095–1127* (U. Tennessee Press, 1969); Gabrieli, Francesco, *Arab Historians of the Crusades* (London, 1969); Gerald of Wales, *The Journey through Wales* and *The Description of Wales* (Penguin, 1978); *Gesta Francorum* (London, 1962); Ambroise, *The Crusade of Richard Lion-Heart*, tr. M. Hubert (Columbia U. Press, 1941 repr. 1976); *Joinville and Villehardouin: Chronicles of the Crusades* (Penguin, 1963); Lewis, Bernard, *Islam, from the*

Prophet Muhammad to the Capture of Constantinople, 2 vol. (London, 1974); Peters, Edward, *Christian Society and the Crusaders, 1198–1229* (U. Penn. Press, 1971); Peters, Edward, *The First Crusade. The Chronicle of Fulcher of Chartres and Other Source Materials* (U. Penn. Press, 1971); Riley-Smith, Louise and Jonathan, *The Crusades: Idea and Reality, 1095–1274* (London, 1981); Hitti, Philip K., *Memoirs of an Arab-Syrian Gentleman and Warrior: Usāmah ibn Munqidh* (Columbia, 1929); William of Tyre, *A History of the Deeds done beyond the sea*, 2 vols. (Columbia, 1941 repr. 1971).

Index